Critique, Social Media and the Information Society

In times of global capitalist crisis we are witnessing a return of critique in the form of a surging interest in critical theories (such as the critical political economy of Karl Marx) and social rebellions as a reaction to the commodification and instrumentalization of everything. On one hand, there are overdrawn claims that social media (Twitter, Facebook, YouTube, etc.) have caused uproars in countries like Tunisia and Egypt. On the other hand, the question arises as to what actual role social media play in contemporary capitalism, crisis, rebellions, the strengthening of the commons, and the potential creation of participatory democracy. The commodification of everything has resulted also in a commodification of the communication commons, including Internet communication that is today largely commercial in character.

This book deals with the questions of what kind of society and what kind of Internet are desirable, how capitalism, power structures and social media are connected, how political struggles are connected to social media, what current developments of the Internet and society tell us about potential futures, how an alternative Internet can look like, and how a participatory, commons-based Internet and a co-operative, participatory, sustainable information society can be achieved.

Christian Fuchs is Professor of Social Media Research at the University of Westminster's Communication and Media Research Institute.

Marisol Sandoval is a Lecturer in Culture, Policy and Management at City University, London.

Routledge Studies in Science, Technology and Society

Critique, Social Media and the Information Society

Edited by Christian Fuchs and
Marisol Sandoval

Routledge
Taylor & Francis Group

NEW YORK   LONDON

First published 2014
by Routledge
711 Third Avenue, New York, NY 10017

Simultaneously published in the UK
by Routledge
2 Park Square, Milton Park, Abingdon, Oxon OX14 4RN

*Routledge is an imprint of the Taylor & Francis Group,
an informa business*

Library of Congress Cataloging-in-Publication Data
Critique, social media and the information society / edited by Christian
 Fuchs and Marisol Sandoval.
  pages cm. — (Routledge studies in science, technology and society)
  Includes bibliographical references and index.
 1. Information society. 2. Social media. 3. Capitalism. 4. Power
(Social sciences) 5. Cooperation. I. Fuchs, Christian, 1976–
II. Sandoval, Marisol.
 HM851.C743 2013
 302.23'1—dc23
 2013021541

ISBN13: 978-0-415-84185-6 (hbk)
ISBN13: 978-0-415-72108-0 (pbk)
ISBN13: 978-0-203-76407-7 (ebk)

Typeset in Sabon
by IBT Global.

Contents

PART III
Critical Studies of Communication Labour

Figures

Tables

1 Introduction

Critique, Social Media and the Information Society in the Age of Capitalist Crisis

Christian Fuchs and Marisol Sandoval

1.1. INFORMATION SOCIETY?

This book presents contributions that analyse the societal dimension of the media critically. Although the contributions do not necessarily share the assumption that we live in an information society, they all express an interest in analysing media and information in their societal context, i.e. in relationship to the interaction of economy, politics and culture, and the power structures and patterns of stratification and inequalities that shape contemporary capitalist societies. There are many labels that one can use to describe contemporary society and many of them, such as capitalism, describe today's society in a more critical manner than the notions of the information or knowledge society that have all too often been captured by dominant interests in order to advance neoliberal policies. Nonetheless it is true that media, knowledge work and information technologies play a certain role in many contemporary societies and that the notion of the information society should therefore not simply be rejected, but critically assessed. Information is one of several relevant dimensions of contemporary society. Just like we can say that we live in informational capitalism, we can also say that we live in finance capitalism, hyperindustrial capitalism, crisis capitalism, etc (Fuchs 2012a). Informational capitalism signifies the extent to which the contemporary global economy and society are information- and media-based. This degree varies and can be measured in various ways. To speak of this tendency as informational capitalism means to neither reject nor glorify the information society discourse and to acknowledge that the contemporary information economy is shaped by a contradiction between productive forces and relations of production: It is capitalist at the level of the relations of production and to a certain degree informational on the level of the productive forces (Fuchs 2012a).

In 1968, six years before the publication of Daniel Bell's (1974) book *The coming of post-industrial society* that was path-breaking for the information society discourse (i.e. in a time before the high rise of the information society hypothesis), Theodor W. Adorno (1968/2003) gave an introductory keynote talk on the topic of "Late capitalism or industrial society?" at the annual meeting of the German Sociological Association. He said that the "fundamental question of the present structure of society" is "about the alternatives: late capitalism or industrial society". It is about

> whether the capitalist system still predominates according to its model, however modified, or whether the development of industry has rendered the concept of capitalism obsolete, together with the distinction between capitalist and noncapitalist states and even the critique of capitalism. In other words, the question is whether it is true that Marx is out of date. (1968/2003, 111)

Adorno pointed out dichotomous answers to this question (either/or) "are themselves predicaments modelled on dilemmas taken from an unfree society" (1968/2003, 113).

Adorno gave an answer to the question that took into account the importance and relation of the productive forces and the relations of production in the capitalist mode of production:

> In terms of critical, dialectical theory, I would like to propose as an initial, necessarily abstract answer that contemporary society undoubtedly is an industrial society according to the state of its *forces* of production. Industrial labor has everywhere become the model of society as such, regardless of the frontiers separating differing political systems. It has developed into a totality because methods modeled on those of industry are necessarily extended by the laws of economics to other realms of material production, administration, the sphere of distribution, and those that call themselves culture. In contrast, however, society is capitalist in its *relations* of production. People are still what they were in Marx's analysis in the middle of the nineteenth century [. . .] Production takes place today, as then, for the sake of profit. (1968/2003, 117)

Paraphrasing Adorno and transferring his question and answer to a time that is shaped by information society discourse, one can hypothesize that a fundamental question of the present structure of society is about the alternatives: capitalism or information society. In terms of critical, dialectical theory, we would like to propose as an initial, necessarily abstract answer that contemporary society is an information society according to the state of its *forces* of production. In contrast, however, contemporary society is capitalist in its *relations* of production. People are still what they were in Marx's analysis in the middle of the nineteenth century. Production takes place today, as then, for the sake of profit and for achieving this end it to a certain extent makes use of knowledge and information technology in production.

Productive forces and relations of production are interlocking phenomena, they contain each other. The informational forces of production (knowledge labour, information technology, science, theoretical knowledge) and the capitalist class relations should not be seen as polar opposites and the discussion about the existence or non-existence of an information society should neither be reduced to the level of the productive forces nor to the level of the relations of production. The first reduction will result in the assumption that we live in a new society, the information society, the second reduction will result in the response that nothing has changed and we still live in a capitalist society. The informational forces of production (just like the non-informational ones) are mediated by class relations, which means that the establishment of information technologies (as part of the instruments of production) and knowledge work (which is characterized by a composition of labour, where mental and communicative features dominate over manual features) as features of economic production are strategies for advancing surplus value exploitation, the reduction of variable and constant capital. Capital thereby hopes to achieve higher profit rates. The idea that the notion of society can today solely be constructed by reference to the informational forces of production is an ideological illusion. The counterclaim that nothing has changed because we still live in a society dominated by capitalist class relations is an understandable reaction and a strategy of ideology critique. A dialectical analysis cannot leave out that there are certain changes taking place that are intended to support the deepening of the class structure, but also contain what Marx termed *Keimformen* (germ forms of an alternative society). That the development of the informational productive forces is itself contradictory and comes in conflict with the capitalist relations of production can be observed by phenomena such as file sharing on the Internet, the discussions about intellectual property rights, the emergence of pirate parties in the political landscape of advanced capitalist countries, or the popularity of free software (Fuchs 2008, 2009).

Marx predicted the emergence of informational productive forces as the result of the development of fixed capital, i.e. the increasing technical and organic composition of capital that is characterized by an increase of the role of technology in production at the expense of living labour power.

> The development of fixed capital indicates to what degree general social knowledge has become a direct force of production, and to what degree, hence, the conditions of the process of social life itself have come under the control of the general intellect and been transformed in accordance with it. To what degree the powers of social production have been produced, not only in the form of knowledge, but also as immediate organs of social practice, of the real life process. (Marx 1857/1858, 706)

Marx argued that by technological development "the entire production process" becomes "the technological application of science" (1857/1858, 699). The "transformation of the production process from the simple labour process into a scientific process [. . .] appears as a quality of fixed capital in contrast to living labour" (1857/1858, 700). So for Marx, the rise of informational productive forces was immanently connected to capital's need for finding technical ways that allow accumulating more profits. That society has to a certain degree become informational is just like the discourse about this circumstance a result of the development of capitalism.

1.2   SOCIAL MEDIA?

By using the term "social media" in the title of this book, we want to signify several things that are reflected in the contributions in this volume:

- All media stand in the context of society. Neglecting the analysis of the media together with society often results in deterministic, administrative research.
- Contemporary media on the one hand are, as the contributions in this book show, entangled in numerous forms with the commodity form and private property. On the other hand they also have certain potentials and germ forms of advancing the social character of production and ownership.
- Special consideration is given in this book to what are today often misleadingly called "social media": blogs (e.g. Blogspot, Wordpress), social networking sites (e.g. Facebook), microblogs (e.g. Facebook, LinkedIn, Weibo), wikis (e.g. Wikipedia, WikiLeaks), user-generated content and file sharing sites (e.g. YouTube, the Pirate Bay). This does not mean that we share the social media hype that mainly is aimed at attracting investors and often celebrates contemporary capitalist culture as participatory, democratic and creative without giving enough consideration to realities of precarity, exploitation, inequalities and power asymmetries. But it means that we think the analysis of the mentioned kind of media is important, should be taken seriously and conducted in a critical way that goes beyond hype and ideology.

What is social about social media? The discussions about these terms started when Tim O'Reilly (2005) introduced the term "web 2.0" in 2005. Although O'Reilly surely thinks that "web 2.0" denotes actual changes and says that the crucial fact about it is that users, as a collective intelligence, co-create the value of platforms like Google, Amazon, Wikipedia, or Craigslist in a "community of connected users" (O'Reilly and Battelle 2009, 1), he later admitted that the term was mainly created for identifying the need of new economic strategies of Internet companies after the "dot.com" crisis, in which the bursting of financial bubbles caused the collapse of many Internet companies. In a paper published five years after the creation of the term "web 2.0", O'Reilly stated that this category was "a statement about the second coming of the Web after the dotcom bust" and that it was used at a conference that was "designed to restore confidence in an industry that had lost its way" (O'Reilly and Battelle 2009, 1). This is just another formulation for saying that "web 2.0" is a capitalist marketing ideology aimed at attracting venture capital investments for newly founded Internet companies.

Michael Mandiberg argues that the notion of "social media" has been associated with multiple concepts: "the corporate media favorite 'user-generated content', Henry Jenkin's media-industries-focused 'convergence culture', Jay Rosen's 'the people formerly known as the audience', the politically infused 'participatory media', Yochai Benkler's process-oriented 'peer-production', and Tim O'Reilly's computer-programming-oriented 'Web 2.0'" (Mandiberg 2012, 2).

The question of if and how social the web is or has become, depends on a profoundly social theoretical question: What does it mean to be social? Are human beings always social or only if they interact with others? In sociological theory, there are different concepts of the social, such as Émile Durkheim's social facts, Max Weber's social action, Karl Marx's notion of collaborative work (as also employed in the concept of computer-supported collaborative work—CSCW), or Ferdinand Tönnies's notion of community (Fuchs 2010). Depending on which concept of sociality one employs, one gets different answers to the questions regarding if the web is social or not and if sociality is a new quality of the web or not. Community aspects of the web have certainly not started with Facebook, which was founded in 2004, but was already described as characteristic of 1980s bulletin board systems like The WELL. Collaborative work (e.g. the co-operative editing of articles performed on Wikipedia) is rather new as a dominant phenomenon on the world wide web (WWW), but not new in computing. The concept of CSCW became the subject of a conference series that identifies multiple dimensions of sociality (such as cognition, communication, and co-operation), based on which the continuities and discontinuities of the development of the Internet can be empirically studied. The first ACM Conference on CSCW was held in Austin, Texas, in December 1986. Neither is the wiki-concept new itself—the WikiWikiWeb was introduced by Ward Cunningham in 1984. All computing systems, and therefore all web applications and also all forms of media, can be considered as social because they store and transmit human knowledge that originates in social relations in society. They are objectifications of society and human social relations. Whenever a human uses a computing system or a medium (also if s/he is alone in a room), then s/he cognizes based on objectified knowledge that is the outcome of social relations. But not all computing systems and web applications support direct communication between humans, in which at least two humans mutually exchange symbols that are interpreted as being meaningful. Because Amazon mainly provides information about books and other goods one can buy, it is not primarily a tool of communication, but rather a tool of information, whereas Facebook has in-built communication features that are frequently used (mail system, walls for comments, forums, etc.).

The discussion shows that it is not a simple question to decide if and how social the WWW actually is. Therefore a social theory approach of clarifying the notion of "social media" can be advanced by identifying three social information processes that constitute three forms of sociality (Hofkirchner 2013):

* Cognition
* Communication
* Co-operation

According to this view, individuals have certain cognitive features that they use to interact with others so that shared spaces of interaction are created. In some cases, these spaces are used not just for communication, but for the co-production of novel qualities of overall social systems and for community-building. The three notions relate to different forms of sociality (Fuchs 2010): The notion of cognition is related to Emile Durkheim's concept of social facts, the communication concept to Max Weber's notions of social actions and social relations, the co-operation concept to the notions of communities and collaborative work. According to this model, media and online platforms (1) that primarily support cognition (e.g. the websites of newspapers) are social media, (2) that primarily support communication (e.g. e-mail) are social media, and (3) that primarily support community-building and collaborative work (e.g. Wikipedia, Facebook) are social media. This means that social media is a complex term and that there are different types of social media. Empirical studies show that the most recent development is that there is a certain increase of the importance of social media on the Internet (Fuchs 2010), which is especially due to the rise of social networking sites such as Facebook, wikis like Wikipedia, and microblogs such as Twitter and Weibo.

If one compares lists of the most accessed websites from 1995–2000 to 2006–present for certain countries or the world, the rise of Facebook, YouTube, Twitter, Tumblr, Blogspot, Wordpress, and LinkedIn among the most accessed platforms will be evident. These platforms are especially focused on communication, collaboration, community-building and community-maintenance. There is a special focus on the critical study of such platforms in this book, i.e. the analysis of how they stand in the context of power, exploitation, domination, oppression, class, digital labour and ideology, as well as protest and struggles.

1.3 CRITIQUE

This book came about as a consequence of the fourth ICTs and Society Conference "Critique, Democracy and Philosophy in 21st Century Information Society. Towards Critical Theories of Social Media" (Uppsala University. May 2 to 4, 2012, see http://www.icts-and-society.net/events/uppsala2012/). Its task was to provide an opportunity to discuss and reflect on the role of critique, critical theory, and philosophy in the information society and in relation to the Internet and social media. The conference focused on discussing questions such as:

* What are the meanings and roles of critique and critical theory today?
* What are the conditions of critique today?
* What does it mean to study media and communication critically today?
* What does it mean to study digital media and the Internet critically today?
* In what society do we live today and what is the role of information in it?
* What is the role of crisis, capitalism, power, struggles, and democracy in contemporary society and how are they connected to digital media?
* What kind of theories and what philosophies do we need for understanding all of these phenomena?
* How can we bring about a just society?

The ICTs and Society Network (http://www.icts-and-society.net) was founded in 2008. It is an international group of scholars that focuses on fostering discussions and networking between scholars who conduct research about the role of ICTs and the Internet in the information society. The first conference took place in June 2008 at the University of Salzburg (Austria), the second in June 2009 at the University of Trento (Italy), the third in July 2010 at the Internet Interdisciplinary Institute of the Open University of Catalonia in Barcelona (Spain). In 2012, the ICTs and Society Conference was held in Sweden at Uppsala University. It was thus far the largest of the four conferences: There were approximately 170 attendees, 100 talks in parallel sessions, and 15 keynote talks in 7 plenary sessions. A generous funding of the event by Vetenskapsrådet (The Swedish Research Council) enabled the invitation of the keynote speakers. Besides Uppsala University and the ICTs and Society Network, scholars from the following institutions were also involved in the organisation of the conference: the European Sociological Association's Research Network 18: Sociology of Communications and Media Research; *tripleC: Communication, Capitalism, and Critique. Journal for a Global Sustainable Information Society*; the Unified Theory of Information Research Group (Austria); Aarhus University's Department of Information and Media Studies (Denmark); the Vienna University of Technology's Institute for Design & Assessment of Technology (Austria); and Jönköping University's School of Education and Communication (Sweden).

Overall, the conference presentations showed a strong interest in critical media and communication studies; a profound engagement with philosophy, critical theory, and social theory; and an interest in the critical study of media, communication and digital media in the context of society, capitalism, and domination. Many conference participants pointed out the large presence of PhD students and younger scholars coming from various countries, who were conducting critical studies of media and communication and were inspired by and engaging with critical social theory and critical political economy. There was a diverse range of critical theories and critical philosophies that were employed in the presentations. A significant observation is that there was a large presence of political economy and Karl Marx's works in the presentations. The conference showed that there is a significant interest in critical media and communication studies as well as critical theory and critical political economy of media, communication, ICTs, culture and the information society.

The following news clippings indicate that with the new global crisis of capitalism, we seem to have entered new Marxian times:

- "Marx makes a comeback" (*Svenska Dagbladet*, October 17, 2008)
- "Crunch resurrects Marx" (*The Independent*, October 17, 2008)
- "Crisis allows us to reconsider left-wing ideas" (*The Irish Times*, October 18, 2008)
- "Marx exhumed, capitalism buried" (*Sydney Morning Herald*, October 23, 2008)
- "Marx Renaissance" (*Korea Times*, January 1, 2009)
- "Was Marx Right All Along?" (*The Evening Standard*, March 30, 2009).
- "'Marx is fashionable again,' declares Jorn Schutrumpf, head of the Berlin publishing house Dietz, which brings out the works of Marx and his collaborator Friedrich Engels. Sales have trebled—albeit from a pretty low level—since 2005 and have soared since the summer. [...] The Archbishop of Canterbury, Rowan Williams, gave him a decent review last month: 'Marx long ago observed the way in which unbridled capitalism became a kind of mythology, ascribing reality, power and agency to things that had no life in themselves.' Even the Pope has put in a good word for the old atheist—praising his 'great analytical skill'" (*The Times*, "Financial crisis gives added capital to Marx' writings", October 20, 2008).
- "No one claims that we're all Marxists now but I do think the old boy deserves some credit for noticing that 'it's the economy, stupid' and that many of the apparently omniscient titans who ascend the commanding heights of the economy are not so much stupid as downright imbecilic, driven by a mad exploitative greed that threatens us all. Marx' work is not holy writ, despite the strivings of some disciples to present it as such" (*The Evening Standard*, "Was Marx Right All Along?" March 30, 2009).
- "Karl Marx is back. That, at least, is the verdict of publishers and bookshops in Germany who say that his works are flying off the shelves" (*The Guardian*, "Booklovers Turn to Karl Marx as Financial Crisis Bites in Germany", October 15, 2008).
- "Policy makers struggling to understand the barrage of financial panics, protests and other ills afflicting the world would do well to study the works of a long-dead economist: Karl Marx. The sooner they

recognize we're facing a once-in-a-lifetime crisis of capitalism, the better equipped they will be to manage a way out of it" (*Bloomberg Business Week*, "Give Karl Marx a Chance to Save the World Economy", August 28, 2011).

- *Time* magazine showed Marx on its cover on February 2, 2009, and asked in respect to the crisis: "What would Marx think?" In the cover story, Marx was presented as the saviour of capitalism and was thereby mutilated beyond recognition: "Rethinking Marx. As we work out how to save capitalism, it's worth studying the system's greatest critic" (*Time Magazine Europe*, February 2, 2009).

That there is suddenly a surging interest in Karl Marx's work is an indication for the persistence of capitalism, class conflicts, and crisis. At the same time, the bourgeois press tries to limit Marx and to stifle his theory by interpreting him as the new saviour of capitalism. One should remember that he was not only a brilliant analyst of capitalism, he was also the strongest critic of capitalism in his time:

In short, the Communists everywhere support every revolutionary movement against the existing social and political order of things. In all these movements, they bring to the front, as the leading question in each, the property question, no matter what its degree of development at the time. Finally, they labour everywhere for the union and agreement of the democratic parties of all countries. The Communists disdain to conceal their views and aims. They openly declare that their ends can be attained only by the forcible overthrow of all existing social conditions. Let the ruling classes tremble at a Communistic revolution. The proletarians have nothing to lose but their chains. They have a world to win. Proletarians of all lands unite! (Marx and Engels 1848/2004, 94)

In 1977, Dallas Smythe published his seminal article "Communications: Blindspot of Western Marxism" (Smythe 1977), in which he argued that Western Marxism had not given enough attention to the complex role of communications in capitalism. Thirty-five years have passed and the rise of neoliberalism has resulted in a turn away from an interest in social class and capitalism. Instead, it became fashionable to speak of globalization, postmodernism, and, with the fall of Communism, even the end of history. In essence, Marxism became the blind spot of all social science. Marxist academics were marginalized and it was increasingly career threatening for a young academic to take an explicitly Marxist approach to social analysis.

The declining interest in Marx and Marxism is visualized in Figures 1.1 and 1.2, which show the number of articles in the Social Sciences Citation Index that contain one of the keywords Marx, Marxist, or Marxism in the article topic description and were published in the five time periods,

1968–1977, 1978–1987, 1988–1997, 1998–2007, and 2008–2012. Choosing these periods allows one to determine if there has been a change since the start of the new capitalist crisis in 2008 and also makes sense because social upheavals in 1968 marked a break that also transformed academia.

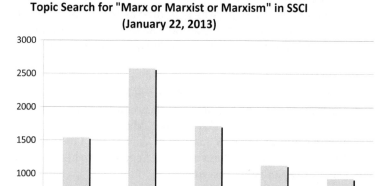

Topic Search for "Marx or Marxist or Marxism" in SSCI (January 22, 2013)

	1968–1977	1978–1987	1988–1997	1998–2007	2008–2012
Number of articles	1537	2574	1713	1127	931

Figure 1.1 Number of articles published about Marx and Marxism that are listed in the Social Sciences Citation Index in ten year intervals.

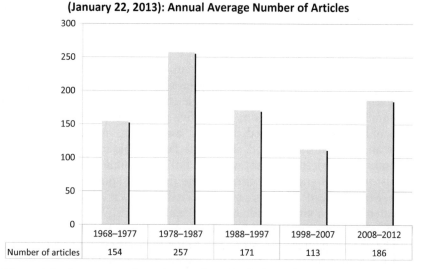

Topic Search for "Marx or Marxist or Marxism" in SSCI (January 22, 2013): Annual Average Number of Articles

	1968–1977	1978–1987	1988–1997	1998–2007	2008–2012
Number of articles	154	257	171	113	186

Figure 1.2 Average number of annually published articles in ten year intervals about Marx and Marxism that are listed in the Social Sciences Citation Index.

Figure 1.1 shows that there was a relatively large academic article output about Marx in the period 1978–1987 (2,574). Given that the number of articles published increases historically, interest in the period 1968–1977 also seems to have been high. One can observe a clear contraction of the output about articles focusing on Marx in the periods 1988–1997 (1,713) and 1998–2007 (1,127). Given the earlier increase of published articles, this contraction is even more pronounced. This period has also been the time of the intensification of neoliberalism, the commodification of everything (including public service communication in many countries), and a strong turn towards postmodernism and culturalism in the social sciences. There are multiple reasons for the disappearance of Marx, including:

* The rise of neoliberal and neoliberal class struggle from above.
* The commodification of everything, including the commons and public universities.
* The rise of postmodernism.
* The lack of trust in alternatives.
* The low presence and intensity of struggles.
* The climate of conservative backlash and commodification of academia, which was not opportune or conducive for an academic career and academic reputation to conduct Marxist studies.

In Figure 1.2, one can see that the annual average number of articles published about Marxism in the period 2008–2012 (186) increased in comparison to the periods 1998–2007 (113 per year) and 1988–1997 (171 per year). This circumstance is an empirical indicator for a renewed interest in Marx and Marxism in the social sciences, most likely an effect of the new capitalist crisis. The question is whether and how this interest can be sustained and materialised in institutional transformations.

Due to the rising income gap between the rich and the poor, widespread precarious labour, and the new global capitalist crisis, neoliberalism is no longer seen as common sense. The dark side of capitalism, with its rising levels of class conflict, is now recognized worldwide. Eagleton (2011) notes that never has a thinker been so travestied as Marx and demonstrates that the core of Marx's work runs contrary to common prejudices about his work. But since the start of the global capitalist crisis in 2008, a considerable scholarly interest in the works of Marx has taken root. Žižek argues that the antagonisms of contemporary capitalism in the context of the ecological crisis, intellectual property, biogenetics, new forms of apartheid and slums show that we still need the Marxian notion of class and that there is a need to renew Marxism and to defend its lost causes in order to "render problematic the all-too-easy liberal-democratic alternative" that is posed by the new forms of a soft capitalism that promises but fails to realize ideals like participation, self-organisation, and co-operation (Žižek 2008, 6). Moreover, Žižek (2010) argues that the recent world economic crisis has resulted in a renewed interest in the Marxian critique of political economy. Hobsbawm (2011, 12f) argues that for understanding the global dimension of contemporary capitalism, capitalism's contradictions and crises and the existence of socio-economic inequality we "must ask Marx's questions" (2011, 13). "Economic and political liberalism, singly or in combination, cannot provide the solution to the problems of the twenty-first century. Once again the time has come to take Marx seriously" (Hobsbawm 2011, 419). Jameson argues that global capitalism, "its crises and the catastrophes appropriate to this present" and global unemployment show that "Marx remains as inexhaustible as capital itself" (Jameson 2011, 1) and make *Capital. Volume 1* (Marx 1867/1990) a most timely book.

İrfan Erdogan (2012) has analysed 210 articles that mentioned Marx and that were published in seventy-seven selected media and communication journals between January 2007 and June 2011. He found that "Mainstream studies ignore and liberal-democrats generally appreciate Marx", whereas the main criticisms of Marx come from "so-called 'critical' or 'alternative' approaches", whose "'alternatives' are 'alternatives to Marx'" and critical in the sense of a "criticism directed against Marx" (Erdogan 2012, 382). At the same time as there are sustained attempts to downplay the importance of Marx for the study of society, media and communication, there are indicators of a certain degree of new engagement with Marx. One of them is the special issue of *tripleC* (http://www.triple-c.at) "Marx is Back—The Importance of Marxist Theory and Research for Critical Communication Studies Today" (Fuchs and Mosco 2012) that features twenty-nine articles on more than five hundred pages. Another one was the aforementioned conference "Critique, Democracy and Philosophy in 21st Century Information Society. Towards Critical Theories of Social Media", during which a sustained engagement with Marx and communication today took place, especially by and among PhD students.

Whereas Marx was always relevant, this relevance has not been much acknowledged in media and communication studies in recent years. It has been rather common, as Erdogan (2012) shows, to misinterpret and misunderstand Marx, which partly came also from a misreading of his works or from outright ignorance of his works. Terry Eagleton (2011) discusses ten common prejudices against Marx and Marxism and shows why Marx was right and why these prejudices are wrong. We have added to the following overview a media and communication dimension to each prejudice. These communication dimensions point towards common prejudices against Marx within media and communication studies.

1.4   CAPITALIST CRISIS

The chapters in this book were written in a time of capitalist crisis and so reflect the specific experience of life in times of crisis and change.

1.4.1 Crises and the Antagonisms of Capitalism

Most commentators agree that the economic crisis of the late 2000s was triggered by financialization and the burst of a housing bubble. However, rather than arguing that the crisis was caused by a lack of regulation of finance capital, critical political economists stress that the crisis needs to be understood in the context of the antagonistic character of capitalism. Karl Marx not only knew that an economy that is largely based on credit is crisis prone, but also that a resulting crisis, although it at the first sight might appear as a financial crisis, has its real causes in the expansive and contradictory character of capitalism:

> In a system of production where the entire interconnection of the reproduction process rests on credit, a crisis must evidently break out if credit is suddenly withdrawn and only cash payment is accepted in the form of a violent scramble. At a first glance, therefore, the entire crisis presents itself as simply a credit and monetary crisis. And in fact all it does involve is simply the convertibility of bills in exchange for money. The majority of these bills represent actual purchases and sales, the ultimate basis of the entire crisis being the expansion of these far beyond social need. On top of this however, a tremendous number of these bills represent purely fraudulent deals which now come to light and explode; as well as unsuccessful speculations conducted with borrowed capital, and finally commodity capitals that are wither devalued or unsaleable, or returns that are never going to come. (Marx 1894/1991, 323)

Marx described a number of antagonisms that shape capitalist economy and therefore make it prone to crises:

- *Antagonistic class relationships* that result in an antagonism between the accumulation of wealth and relative pauperisation. Marx and Engels described all history as a history of class struggles: "The history of all hitherto existing society is the history of class struggles" (1948/1991, 35). Marx highlighted that under capitalism the distribution of wealth is unequal and the accumulation of capital is only possible at the cost of workers: "Political economy starts from labour as the real soul of production; yet to labour it gives nothing, an to private property everything" (1844/2007, 81). He argued that as productivity increases the relative share of workers of the total value produced decreases: "the increasing productivity of labour is accompanied by a cheapening of the worker, as we have seen, and it is therefore accompanied by a cheapening of the worker, even when the real wages are rising. The latter never rise in proportion to the productivity of labour" (1867/1990, 753). Marx's analysis has frequently been interpreted as a hypothesis of impoverishment of the dominated

classes, i.e. that the development of the productive forces will result
in impoverishment, which will cause social revolution. Marx however
was speaking not about absolute, only about *relative* relationships.
With the overall increase of wealth, the social situation of the dominated classes might improve although at the same time the relative
share they get tend to decrease. Class struggle can result in a relative lowering of wages so that ever more capital is present that cannot be invested (overaccumulation/overproduction of capital) or that
commodities are available on the market that workers are not able
to buy (overproduction/underconsumption of commodities). But class
struggle can also increase the relative share of wages and decrease the
relative share of profits. Marx therefore writes that "crises are always
prepared by a period in which wages generally rise, and the working
class actually does receive a greater share in the part of the annual
product destined for consumption. [...] It thus appears that capitalist production involves certain conditions independent of people's
good or bad intentions, which permit the relative prosperity of the
working class only temporarily, and moreover always as a harbinger
of crisis" (1885/1992, 486f). Crisis explanations that stress that rising wages result in falling relative profits have come to be known as
profit-squeeze crisis theories.

- *The antagonism between producers and means of production*, which
  results in the degradation of human beings "to the level of an appendage of a machine" (Marx 1867/1990, 799). Marx argued that "[e]
  very kind of capitalist production, in so far as it is not only a labour
  process but also capital's process of valorization, has this in common,
  but it is not the worker who employs the conditions of his work, but
  rather the reverse, the conditions of work employ the worker. However, it is only with the coming of machinery that this inversion first
  acquires a technical and palpable reality. Owing to its conversion into
  an automaton, the instrument of labour confronts the worker during
  the labour process in the shape of capital, dead labour, which domi-
  nates and soaks up living labour-power" (1867/1990, 548).

- *The antagonism between necessary and surplus labour.* This antagonism is connected to the one between producers and means of production. A certain amount of labour is needed in every society for
  its reproduction. The alienation of labour in capitalism results in
  the antagonism between attempts to increase surplus value by methods that decrease necessary labour and herewith (at least temporarily) destroy the foundation of accumulation. Marx argued that
  "Capital itself is the contradiction [in] that, while it constantly tries
  to suspend *necessary labour time* (and this is at the same time the
  reduction of the worker to a minimum, i.e. his existence as mere
  living labour capacity), *surplus labour time* exists only in antithesis
  with necessary labour time, so that capital posits necessary labour

time as a *necessary* condition of its reproduction and realization" (1857/1858, 543).

- *The antagonism between use-value and exchange-value.* Products satisfy basic needs in all societies. Capitalism however requires the domination of this satisfaction by the logic of commodity and exchange. Already in the *Grundrisse* Marx described the doubling of the commodity into use-value and exchange-value causes crises (1857/1858, 147–150). In *Capital*, Marx argued: "There is an antithesis, immanent in the commodity, between use-value and value, between private labour which must simultaneously manifest itself as directly social labour, and a particular concrete kind of labour which simultaneously counts as merely abstract universal labour, between the conversion of things into persons and the conversion of persons into things; the antithetical phases of the metamorphosis of the commodity are developed forms of motion of this immanent contradiction. These forms therefore imply the possibility of crisis, though no more than the possibility" (1867/1990, 209).

- *The antagonism between productive forces and relations of production.* Marx argued: "The *true barrier* to capitalist production is *capital itself*. It is that capital and its self-valorization appear as the starting and finishing point, as the motive and the purpose of production; production is production only for *capital*, and not the reverse, i.e. the means of production are not simply means for a steadily expanding pattern of life for the *society* of producers. The barriers within which the maintenance and valorization of the capital value has necessarily to move—and this in turn depends on the dispossession and impoverishment of the great mass of the producers therefore come constantly into contradiction with the methods of production that capital must apply to its purpose and which set its course towards an unlimited expansion of production, to production as an end in itself, to an unrestricted development of the social productive powers of labour. The means—the unrestricted development of the forces of social production—comes into persistent conflict with the restricted end, the valorization of the existing capital" (Marx 1894/1991, 358f). The realization of the full social potential that arises from the development of productive forces is constrained by the capitalist relations of production that employ them for the sole purpose of expansion of capital.

- *The antagonism between single production and social need*—an antagonism between the organisation of production in the individual factories or offices and the "anarchy" of production in society, i.e. the uncoordinated form of production. Marx described this antagonism in such a way that "within capitalist production, the proportionality of the particular branches of production presents itself as a process of passing constantly of and into disproportionality, since the interconnection of production as a whole here forces itself on the agents of production as a blind law, and not as a law which, being grasped and therefore mastered by their combined reason, brings the productive process under their common control" (1894/1991, 365). This anarchy of production can result in overproduction or underconsumption: "Since capital's purpose is not the satisfaction of needs but the production of profit, and since it attains this purpose only be methods that determine the mass of production by reference exclusively to the yardstick of production, and not the reverse, there must be a constant tension between the restricted dimensions of consumption on the capitalist basis, and a production that is constantly striving to overcome these immanent barriers" (1894/1991, 365).

- *The antagonism between socialised production and capitalistic, private appropriation.* While production is necessarily based on social relations, the accumulation of capital requires the private ownership of the means and results of production: "The contradiction between the general social power into which capital has developed and the private power of the individual capitalists over these social conditions of production develops ever more blatantly, while this development also contains the solution to this situation, in that it simultaneously raises the conditions of production into general, common, social conditions" (Marx 1894/1991, 373).

- *The antagonism between the fictitious value of financial capital and the actual profits that this capital achieves on the commodity markets, i.e. the antagonism between virtual/fictitious values and real values of capital.* Finance capital does not itself produce profit, it is only an entitlement to payments that are made in the future and derive from profits or wages (the latter for example in the case of consumer credits). Marx therefore characterizes finance capital as fictitious capital (1894/1991, 596). "All these securities actually represent nothing but accumulated claims, legal titles, to future production" (1894/1991, 599). "The market value of these securities is partly speculative, since it is determined not just by the actual revenue but rather by the anticipated revenue as reckoned in advance. [. . .] the rise or fall in value of these securities is independent of the movement in the value of the real capital that they represent" (1894/1991, 598, 599, see also 608, 641). The result is a high risk system of speculation that resembles gambling: "Profits and losses that result from fluctuations in the price of these ownership titles [. . .] are by the nature of the case more and more the result of gambling" (1894/1991, 609). For Marx (1894/1991, 621, 649), the system of fictitious capital that produces a relative independence of stock values and profits is inherently crisis-prone.

David Harvey highlights that while understanding the "general laws of motion of capital" is important, explanations of economic crises also need to take historically specific circumstances into account (2011a, 8). Critical political economists put forward different analyses of the causes of the crisis that started in 2008. These explanations are expressions of certain specific antagonisms that Marx saw as characteristic for capitalism in general and that we just described or are combinations of several of these contradictions. A specific crisis is a manifestation of an interaction of general factors of crisis (Fuchs 2004)

There are several Marxist explanations of the capitalist crisis that started in 2008:

- A first approach stresses that class antagonism between workers and capital results in an antagonism between the accumulation of wealth and relative pauperisation. This explanation focuses on the intersubjective relationships between classes, i.e. class struggle. An example is Resnick and Wolff's approach.
- A second explanation stresses objective laws of capitalism that result in crisis. Such an objective law is the tendency of the rate of profit to fall, which as an expression of the antagonisms between a) producers and the means of production and b) necessary and surplus labour time. An example is Kliman's approach.
- A third kind of explanation combines intersubjective and objective antagonisms. One version explains the crisis as a combination of wage repression and financialization, i.e. a combination of the class antagonism and the antagonism between fictitious and real values. McNally is a representative of this approach. A second version sees the crisis as the result of wage repression and overaccumulation, i.e. a combination of the class antagonism on the one hand and, on the other hand, an interaction of a) the class antagonism and b) the antagonisms between b1) necessary and surplus labour and b2) producers and means of production that results in overaccumulation. David Harvey as well as Foster and McChesney are representatives of the second version.

Overaccumulation of capital means that capital has growth rates higher than investment possibilities in the key industries that it operates in. It is "a condition in which idle capital and idle labour supply [. . .] exist side by side with no idle way to bring these idle resources together to accomplish socially useful tasks" (Harvey 1990, 180). Overaccumulation results, according to Harvey, from a combination of three factors:

a) The need to accumulate.
b) The exploitation of labour, the "class relation between capital and labour" (Harvey 1990, 180).
c) The need for rising productivity by technological innovations: "Capitalism is necessarily technologically and organizationally dynamic" (Harvey 1990, 180).

In situations of overaccumulation, high levels of productivity and exploitation allow more capital to be accumulated than can be invested. Marx did not speak of overaccumulation as a specific antagonism, rather Harvey explains overaccumulation as a combination of a) the class antagonism and b) the antagonisms between b1) necessary and surplus labour and b2) producers and means of production. We will now describe examples of these crisis explanations.

1.4.2   Marxist Crisis Explanation Number 1: The Intersubjective Class Antagonism

These approaches are intersubjective because they stress aspects of class struggle. An example is the approach of Richard Wolff and Stephen Resnick. They highlight that the crisis that started in 2008 needs to be understood in the context of neoliberal developments since the 1970s and the resulting intensification of *class antagonisms*. According to Wolff (2008) "the current crisis emerged from the workings of the capitalist class structure". Resnick and Wolff (2010, 176) argue that in the United States after the crisis of the 1970s productivity levels kept rising while wages stagnated which allowed for increasing surplus value by increasing the rate of exploitation. In order to maintain high levels of consumer spending despite stagnating wages, worker borrowing was encouraged (Wolff 2008; Resnick and Wolff 2010, 176f). Wolff therefore argues that the boom between 1970 and 2006 in the US became possible due to a "double squeeze on workers": "In effect, US capitalism thereby substituted rising loans for rising wages to workers. It took from them twice: first, the surplus their labor produced; and second, the interest on the surpluses lent back to them" (2008). In 2008, a growing number of highly indebted families became unable to pay back their loans and defaults on debts increased. Banks were hit hard as securities that were based on worker debt became worthless (2008). Resnick and Wolff's explanation of the current crisis focuses on the subjective situation of workers whose wages stagnated since the 1970s and who therefore were susceptible to a variety of new consumer credit offers and finally became unable to pay back their debt.

1.4.3   Marxist Crisis Explanation Number 2: The Objective Law of the Rate of Profit to Fall

In contrast to Resnick and Wolff, Kliman provides an explanation of the crisis that is centred on *objective contradictions that are inherent to capital*. Kliman is a representative of the second type of explanations of the crisis that started in 2008. He argues that US wages did not stagnate after the 1970s: "U.S. workers are not being paid less in real terms than they were paid decades ago. Their real pay has risen. And their share of the nation's income has not fallen. It is higher now than it was in 1960, and it has been stable since 1970" (Kliman 2012, 6). According to Kliman, statistics about the development of wages that are based on US government data are flawed because these would only capture wages and exclude other parts of worker's income such as nonwage benefits and net government social benefits (2012, 153f).

Kliman thus argues that rather than class antagonisms, falling profit rates caused the current crisis (2012, 3). He points out that confronting the tendency of profits to fall requires the destruction of capital and argues that during the crisis of the 1970s economic policies were introduced that prevented the destruction of capital. Because not enough capital was destroyed, "the decline in the rate of profit was not reversed" (Kliman 2012, 3). Therefore profitability levels remained low, which held off a new boom. Kliman stresses that due to a lack of profit, investments declined, which led to low output and income. The resulting stagnation of the economy was confronted with policies that encourage the expansion of debt (Kliman 2012, 3): "These policies have artificially boosted profitability and economic growth, but in an unsustainable manner that has repeatedly led to burst bubbles and debt crisis" (2012, 4).

Kliman's analysis of falling profit rates exclusively focuses on the US. McNally points out that in times of globalization and multinational corporations it is however necessary to look at global developments rather than national economic indicators: "throughout the neoliberal era capitals in the core economies of the world system have increased social inequality while also shifting investment outside their national economies in the search for higher rates of return" (2011, 38). McNally stresses that even if exceptional growth rates of the Great Boom (1948–1973) remained out of reach, neoliberal capitalism "performed at or above the norm" and the world economy tripled in size between 1982 and 2007 (2011, 39).

Kliman's argument questions the view that neoliberalism resulted in increased social inequality, compromised social welfare and led to the reduction of social benefits and thereby helped capitalism to recover from the crisis of the 1970s. Most critical commentators (McNally 2011; Foster and McChesney 2012; Harvey 2011a, 2011b) disagree with Kliman and stress that increased rates of exploitation since the 1980s have allowed to temporarily restore profitability. They stress multiple factors that lead to increased financialization and debt including objective contradictions that are inherent to capital as well as class antagonisms.

1.4.4 Marxist Crisis Explanation Number 3: A Combination of Intersubjective and Objective Factors

As explained previously, there are explanations that combine several of the factors that Marx stressed.

1.4.4.1 *Explanation Number 3, Version 1: the Crisis as Result of the Combination of the Class Antagonism and the Antagonism between Fictitious and Real Values of Capital*

David McNally argues that after a slump that lasted from 1973 to 1982, neoliberal capitalism went through another period of recovery and growth (2011, 26). According to him this period of economic growth was achieved by an attack on working class organisations that resulted in a relative lowering of wages. The development would have been at the cost of countries in the global south. In addition, the rate of exploitation would have been raised by spatial reorganisation, primitive accumulation and the creation of new global labour reserves, foreign direct investment, new forms of work organisation and labour intensification as well as new technologies (McNally 2011, 40).

Besides wage repression, for McNally financialization also was an important cause of the crisis. A factor that promoted financialization, according to McNally, was the breakdown of the Bretton Woods agreement and the deregulation of financial markets. McNally points out that not only consumer borrowing increased since the 1980s, but financial sector debt increased even more: he argues that consumer debt relative to the GDP doubled between 1980 and 2007, while financial sector debt quadrupled (2011, 86). McNally stresses that after the breakdown of the dollar, gold convertibility and the fact that money was no longer tied to an underlying commodity, high exchange volatility created a market for currency trading (2011, 92f): "Currency markets thus seemed to offer a capitalist utopia in which money breeds money; it seemed to be a question of guessing which currencies would be winner and which losers. The extraordinary growth of forcing exchange trading thus drove the financialization of late capitalism" (2011, 95). Speculative financial products—such as derivates (McNally 2011, 97), securitization (McNally 2011, 99), credit-default swaps (McNally 2011, 103f)—increased financialization and created a financial bubble that burst in 2008.

Despite the importance of speculative finance as trigger of the 2008 crisis, McNally highlights that it cannot only be explained as a financial crisis. Understanding the crisis would require looking beyond financialization and giving attention to capitalist exploitation. Financialization would "still depend[s] on exploiting labour in workplaces" and therefore "opposition to banks must be joined to a politics that challenges all the sites of capitalist exploitation" (2011, 88).

1.4.4.2   Explanation Number 3, Version 2: the Crisis as Result of the Combination of the Class Antagonism and the Overaccumulation of Capital

John Bellamy Foster and Robert McChesney argue that a "long-term economic slowdown [. . .] preceded the financial crisis" (2012, 4). According to their analysis, overaccumulation of capital resulted over time in stagnating growth rates of capital (Foster and McChesney 2012, 12). Foster and McChesney highlight that excess capital was invested into financial markets in order to counter stagnation and to prevent profits from falling (2012, 42). Financialization thus served as a "desperate and ultimate dangerous savior" (Foster and McChesney 2012, 15). They refer to Paul

Sweezy and Paul Baran and their work on monopoly capital. According to this view, monopolistic corporations have high amounts of surplus capital available but have difficulties in finding investment opportunities (Foster and McChesney 2012, 11). In this situation sustaining economic growth is only possible based on external stimuli such as higher government spending or financialization (Foster and McChesney 2012, 12).

Based on this analysis, Foster and McChesney argue that the relationship between stagnation and financialization is interdependent. They describe "the stagnation-financialization trap" as "a dangerous feedback loop between stagnation and financial bubbles" (Foster and McChesney 2012, 4). They regard an "underlying stagnation tendency" that characterizes advanced capitalist economies as "the reason why the economy became so dependent on financialization" (2012, 4).

At the same time, Foster and McChesney argue, stagnating wages and rising productivity led to increased rates of exploitation and rising profits. This however restricted consumption and thus also created barriers for investment (2012, 33f). Consumer debt provided a solution to this problem, as it allowed keeping consumption levels high (Foster and McChesney 2012, 45).

Similarly David Harvey states: "With real wages stagnant or falling after 1980, the deficit in effective demand was largely bridged by resort to the credit system" (2011b, 100). Harvey points at the need of capital to continuously accumulate, which means that part of the profits need to be reinvested in order to ensure growth: "Any slowdown or blockage in capital flow will produce a crisis" (2011b, 90–91). He discusses potential blockage points that can potentially result in a crisis including a lack of investment opportunities, scarce or well organised labour, scarcity of natural resources or other means of production, excess productivity, worker resistance or insufficient effective demand (2011b, 92–101). Harvey highlights that any of these "potential blockage points [. . .] has the potential to be a source of crisis. There is, therefore, no single causal theory of crisis formation" (2011b, 101).

For David Harvey (2009), the crisis is rooted in the over-accumulation of capital, which is "any situation in which the surplus that capitalists have available to them cannot find an outlet". Harvey (2010, 26) argues that the "capital surplus absorption problem" is that capitalists are always "forced by competition to recapitalise and reinvest a part of" the produced profit and that "new profitable outlets" can be found. Spatio-temporal fixes for the capital surplus absorption problem have to be found, such as new spaces or new temporalities of accumulation. Otherwise, overaccumulation of capital is the result. Overaccumulation according to Harvey (2009, 2010) resulted in the financialization of the economy, which combined with a stagnation of real wages so that workers had to take out loans and go into debt. As a result, household debt and the volatility of the economy increased. Harvey (2010, 12) argues that since the 1970s wages have generally stagnated as a result of neoliberal wage repression attacks of capital on labour. "The gap between what labour was earning and what it could spend was covered by the rise of the credit card industry and increasing indebtedness. [...] Financial institutions, awash with credit, began to debt-finance people who had no steady income" (2010, 17). Asset losses are, for Harvey, forms of "dispossession that can be turned into further accumulation as speculators buy up the assets cheaply today with an eye to selling them at a profit when the market improves" (2010, 49).

1.4.5   An Explanation of the Capitalist Crisis

The rise of neoliberalism resulted in relative stagnation and wage losses, whereas profits rapidly increased. Neoliberalism therefore is a class struggle project of the ruling class aiming at increasing profits by decreasing wages with the help of strategies such as deregulation of labour laws, precarious labour conditions, welfare and public expenditure cuts, tax cuts for the rich and companies, the privatization of public goods, the global offshoring and outsourcing of labour, etc. Many working families had to take out loans, consumer credits and mortgages in order to be able to pay for their everyday life requirements. At the same time, capital investment into high-risk financial instruments boomed because the growing profits needed to be reinvested. Workers' debts were packaged into new financial instruments, so-called Asset Backed Securities (ABS), Mortgage Backed Securities (MBS), Collateralized Debt Obligations (CDOs) and Credit Default Swaps (CDS). The financial market promised high financial gains, but the profits in the non-financial economy in long run could not fulfil these growth expectations, which created a mismatch between financial values and the profits of corporations and the expectations of shareholders and the reality of capitalist accumulation. The results were financial bubbles that burst in the 2008 crisis. The share rapidly increased from around 10 per cent in 2000 to 57.5 per cent in 2008. It dropped after the start of the global capitalist crisis. The data show the tremendous growth of high-risk financial capital.

Critical observers of the crisis do not agree what its exact structural causes are, but see it not as a failure of regulation, rather as the outcome of capitalism's immanent fundamental contradictions: The relative disparity between the rich and companies on the one hand and the mass of people on the other hand is an expression of the class antagonism between capital and labour. The financialization of the capitalist economy is based on an *antagonism between* the fictitious value of financial capital and the actual profits that this capital achieves on the commodity markets, i.e. the antagonism between virtual/fictitious values and real values of capital. A third dimension is the overaccumulation of capital: The need to accumulate capital, the exploitation of labour and capital's technological progress and organisational dynamics tend to result in idle capital that is crisis-prone if it cannot find spheres of investment. The overaccumulation tendency is an antagonism between the production and consumption/ investment of capital. A crisis is the "manifestation of all the contradictions of bourgeois economy" (Marx 1863, bk. 2, chap. 17). "The fact that the movement of capitalist society is full of contradictions impresses itself most strikingly [. . .] in the changes of the periodic cycle through which modern industry passes, the summit of which is the general crisis" (Marx 1867/1990, 103).

Table 1.1 shows the annual growth of labour productivity since the early 1970s in the G7 countries (Canada, France, Germany, Italy, Japan, UK, USA) and the whole Organisation for Economic Co-operation and Development (OECD). The combined annual growth of labour productivity in the G7 countries was 88.0 per cent in the years 1971–2011. This means that in forty years productivity has almost doubled.

Table 1.1 Annual Growth of Labour Productivity in the G7 and OECD Countries, 1971–2011

Year	Annual growth rate, G7, in %	Annual growth rate, OECD, in %
1971	4.0	
1972	4.8	
1973	4.3	
1974	1.7	
1975	2.2	
1976	3.4	
1977	2.7	
1978	2.8	
1979	2.1	
1980	0.8	
1981	2.5	
1982	0.9	
1983	2.6	
1984	2.6	
1985	2.8	
1986	2.0	
1987	1.6	
1988	2.3	
1989	2.2	
1990	2.5	
1991	1.6	

(continued)

Table 1.1   (continued)

Year	Annual growth rate, G7, in %	Annual growth rate, OECD, in %
1992	2.7	
1993	1.7	
1994	1.8	
1995	1.4	
1996	1.9	
1997	2.0	
1998	1.8	
1999	2.6	
2000	2.9	
2001	2.0	1.8
2002	2.4	2.1
2003	2.0	2.1
2004	1.9	2.4
2005	1.5	1.7
2006	1.3	1.5
2007	1.2	1.7
2008	0.2	-0.1
2009	0.5	-0.3
2010	2.3	2.1
2011	1.5	1.5

Source: OECD iLibrary

Who has benefited from the strong productivity growth? In order to answer this question, we need to have a look at the development of the power relation between labour and capital. The rise of neoliberalism has been accompanied by a deregulation of financial markets, an encouragement of financial speculation and a massive redistribution of wealth from wages to profits. By class struggle from above, capital managed to increase its profits by relatively decreasing wages. The resulting profits were to a certain degree invested into financial markets and high-risk financial instruments, which increased the crisis-proneness, instability and volatility of capitalism. Comparing the years 1970 and 2013, the wage share, which is the share of wages in the GDP, decreased in the following way in selected European countries (adjusted wage share as percentage of GDP at current market prices. *Source*: AMECO).

Table 1.2   Adjusted Wage Share as Percentage of GDP at Current Market Prices

Country	2013	2007	2000	1990	1980	1970
EU15	58.4%	56.8%	58.9%	61.0%	65.7%	63.4%
Germany	58.6%	55.1%	60.6%	58.8%	63.7%	61.1%
Ireland	49.3%	50.3%	48.2%	59.4%	70.0%	67.2%
Greece	47%	53.5%	55.6%	62.4%	60.3%	64.8%
Spain	52.3%	55.3%	58.9%	60.7%	66.8%	64.2%
France	58.9%	56.8%	57.2%	59.3%	68.5%	63.0%
Italy	54.7%	53.7%	53.2%	61.9%	66.6%	65.4%
Cyprus	52.4%	55.0%	56.2%	N/A	N/A	N/A
Portugal	55.6%	57.2%	59.2%	55.0%	66.7%	72.5%
United Kingdom	64.2%	61.9%	62.5%	65.0%	66.0%	65.5%
Finland	58.8%	53.7%	53.8%	63.5%	63.6%	63.1%
USA	58.2%	60.6%	63.2%	63.1%	65.1%	65.9%
Japan	61.0%	58.6%	64.4%	64.3%	72.8%	64.4%
Canada	55.1%	56.4%	56.4%	59.7%	59.3%	61.0%

Source: AMECO

The data show that in the past forty years, capitalist class struggle from above has resulted in a relative decrease of wages in many countries. In Europe this struggle has especially been intense in countries such as Greece, Spain, Ireland and Cyprus, where the wage share dropped from values around 65 per cent in 1970 to values around 50 per cent in 2013. But the wages in almost all European countries and many others were affected, although to different degrees. Wages in the USA were undergoing a similar development as in Europe.

How have profits developed in parallel with the relative fall of wages? Net operating surplus is a variable that measures the gross value added of an economy minus fixed capital investments minus wage costs minus capital taxation. Calculating the share of net operating surplus in the value of GDP gives an estimation of capital's net share in an economy's total wealth.

Profit share = Net operating surplus / GDP

Tables 1.3, 1.4 and 1.5 show the development of the profit shares in the EU 15 countries, the UK and the USA.

Table 1.3   The Development of the Profit Share in the EU 15 Countries

Year	Net operation surplus (NOS): total economy in national currency (in billion €)	GDP in current market prices in national currency (in billion €)	Profit share
1975	321.3	1426.3	22.5%
1980	555.4	2537.8	21.9%
1990	1357.1	5449.1	24.9%
2000	2115.1	8760.3	24.1%
2007	2949	11531.8	25.6%
2008	2860	11478.6	24.9%
2009	2476.6	10876.9	22.8%
2010	2661.3	11332.9	23.5%
2011	2715	11650.6	23.3%
2012	2688.1	11898.9	22.6%
2013	2690.6	11990.7	22.4%

Source: AMECO.

Table 1.4   The Development of the Profit Share in the UK

Year	Net operation surplus (NOS): total economy in national currency (billion £)	GDP in current market prices in national currency (billion £)	Profit share
1975	15.8	106.9	14.8%
1980	36.9	233.7	15.8%
1990	115.4	574.1	20.1%
2000	203.6	975.3	20.9%
2007	335.7	1412.1	23.8%
2008	351.7	1440.9	24.4%
2009	309.9	1401.9	22.1%
2010	326.8	1466.6	22.3%
2011	339.5	1516.3	22.4%
2012	331.9	1546.2	21.5%
2013	335.4	1589.1	21.1%

Source: AMECO

Table 1.5 The Development of the Profit Share in the USA

Year	Net operation surplus (NOS): total economy in national currency (billion US$)	GDP in current market prices in national currency (billion US$)	Profit share
1975	351.1	1623.4	21.6%
1980	560.5	2767.5	20.3%
1990	1298.5	5754.8	22.6%
2000	2444.9	9898.8	24.7%
2007	3437.5	13961.8	24.6%
2008	3375.5	14219.3	23.7%
2009	3218.4	13898.3	23.2%
2010	3627	14419.4	25.2%
2011	3767.6	14991.3	25.1%
2012	4021	15589.6	25.8%
2013	4248.6	16123.5	26.4%

Source: AMECO

In 1980, the profit share was 20.3 per cent in the USA, 15.8 per cent in the UK and 21.9 per cent in the EU 15 countries. What followed was the rise of neoliberal politics in the USA and Europe. Thatcher came to power in the UK in 1979, Reagan in the USA in 1981. There were close bonds between Thatcherism and Reagonomics in terms of ideology and collaboration. Ten years later (in 1990), the profit share had risen to 22.6 per cent in the USA, 20.1 per cent in the UK and 24.9 per cent in the EU 15 countries, whereas the wage shares simultaneously decreased, which is an indication for successful neoliberal class politics that redistributed income from employees to companies and the rich. These developments further continued: in 2000 the profit shares increased to 24.7 per cent in the USA, 20.9 per cent in the UK and remained relatively constant in the EU 15 region. In 2007, a year before the crisis started, the profit share was 24.6 per cent in the USA, 23.8 per cent in the UK and 25.6 per cent in the EU 15, whereas the wage share had since 2000 fallen by 2.1 per cent USA, 0.6 per cent in the UK and 2.6 per cent in the EU 15. In the period 1980–2007, the wage share decreased in these countries/regions by 4.5 per cent (USA), 4.1 per cent (UK) and 8.9 per cent (EU 15), whereas the profit share increased by 4.3 per cent(USA), 8.0 per cent (UK) and 3.7 per cent (EU 15). Whereas capital had constantly high growth rates during the 1980s, 1990s and 2000s, wages stagnated or relatively declined. Neoliberalism increased the wealth of corporations at the expense of labour. In the USA, the profit share fell to 23.2 per cent in

2009 as an effect of the crisis, but was at a high of around 26 per cent in 2012 and 2013. In the EU 15 countries, high profit shares around 25 per cent before the crisis were reduced to around 22–23 per cent in the years after the crisis. In the UK, the profit share dropped from around 24 per cent before the crisis to a level of 21–22 per cent after the crisis.

The working class in many European and other countries was hit hard by austerity measures and a new round of neoliberalism in the aftermath of the crisis: The wage share decreased from 55 per cent in 2007 (before the crisis) to 52.4 per cent in 2013 in Cyprus, from 53.5 per cent to 47 per cent in Greece, from 52.9 per cent to 49.6 per cent in Hungary, from 70.1 per cent to 62.2 per cent in Iceland, from 50.3 per cent to 49.3 per cent in Ireland, from 53 per cent to 46.4 per cent in Latvia, from 49.7 per cent to 44.1 per cent in Lithuania, from 57.2 per cent to 55.6 per cent in Portugal and from 55.3 per cent to 52.3 per cent in Spain (*Source*: AMECO). In Poland and Slovakia, workers had already been relatively poor before the crisis: the wage shares were 46.5 per cent in 2007 and 46.1 per cent in 2013 in Poland. The respective values for Slovakia were 42.3 per cent in 2007 and 43.1 per cent in 2013.

Decreasing relative wages of employees increased the dependence of their families on consumer credits, loans and mortgages for financing basic needs such as housing and transport. In the Euro 17 countries, the gross debt-to-income ratio of households increased from 74.91 per cent in 2000 to 87.6 per cent in 2005, 94.96 per cent in 2008 and 99.36 per cent in 2011 (*Source*: Eurostat). In the UK, this value was 101.0 per cent in 2000, 138.6 per cent in 2005 and 155.34 per cent in 2008 (ibid.). In the USA, the household debt increased from US$1,396 billion in October 1980 to US$3,571.6 billion in October 1990, US$6,963.5 billion in October 2000, US$11,716.4 billion in October 2005 and US$13,711.6 billion in October 2007 (*Source*: Federal Reserve Economic Data, Household Credit Market Debt Outstanding).

The class struggle of capital against the working class that resulted in falling wage shares and high profits has been accompanied by a decrease of capital taxation. The available data on corporate taxation is relatively incomplete. In the EU 27 countries, corporate taxes accounted in 2013 for only 0.3 per cent of the GDP. In the United States the value was 0 per cent, meaning that treated as a collective capitalist, companies in the USA do not pay taxes. Table 1.6 shows some of the limited available data. It indicates that capital taxation has since the 1970s in general been low in European and North American capitalism, never reaching 1 per cent of the GDP of a country and varying in most countries between 0 per cent and 0.3 per cent of the GDP. It is interesting to observe that in 1970 the UK (0.8 per cent) and the USA (0.5 per cent) taxed capital higher than Germany (0.1 per cent) and the Netherlands (0.2 per cent). The rise of neoliberalism has resulted in a subsequent lowering of capital taxation in both the UK and the USA. Overall the data in Table 1.6 shows that European and North American tax regimes are friends of capitalist interests, which have supported the neoliberal class struggle of capital against labour.

Table 1.6   Capital Taxes, Percentage of GDP at Market Prices

	2013	2007	2005	2000	1995	1990	1985	1980	1975	1970
Germany	0.2	0.2	0.2	0.1	0.1	0.1	0.1	0.1	0	0.1
Netherlands	0.3	0.3	0.3	0.4	0.3	0.2	0.2	0.2	0.2	0.2
Austria	0	0.1	0.1	0.1	0	0.1	0.1	0.1		
Portugal	0	0	0	0.1	0.1	0.1	0.2	0.1		
Finland	0.2	0.3	0.3	0.3	0.2	0.2	0.1	0.1	0.1	
United Kingdom	0.2	0.3	0.2	0.2	0.2	0.2	0.3	0.2	0.3	0.8
United States	0	0.2	0.3	0.4	0.3	0.3	0.2	0.3	0.4	0.5

Source: AMECO

The working class' wages have been attacked by neoliberal policies. The resulting profits were invested in finance because capital is driven by the need to accumulate ever more profits and financial speculation promised high returns. The volatility of the economy steadily increased, which resulted in a big explosion in 2008. The result was more of the same: hyper-neoliberalism, which means the intensification of neoliberalism. Banks were bailed out with taxpayers' money, which means a bailout by taxes predominantly paid by employees because companies hardly pay taxes. The discourse of austerity wants to make people believe that they have lived beyond their means, that austerity is necessary because states have spent too much money, etc. The circumstance that profits have been growing, wages shrinking and that companies have hardly paid taxes is not mentioned in the dominant ideology. The working class was first exploited by capital and the reaction to the crisis is an intensification of exploitation and the attempt to legitimize this form of exploitation, which works by redistribution from workers to companies, cuts of public expenditures, wage cuts, tax support for banks and companies. The working class is constantly being dispossessed of the wealth it produces. Austerity measures bring much more of the same.

Rising profits resulted in the need to invest them in order to avoid over-accumulation crisis. This circumstance spurred the financialization of capitalist economies. Table 1.7 shows the development of the share of the finance industry in the total value added of selected countries. A general increase can be observed that has been especially strong in the USA, where the share has doubled from 1970 until 2005, when it made up 8.1 per cent of the US economy's total value added. The data indicate an increased financialization of capitalism.

Table 1.7   Share of the Financial Industry in the Total Economy's Value Added (in Current Prices) of Selected Countries

Year	Canada	France	Germany	Italy	Japan	UK	USA
1970	5.3%	4.1%	3.4%	4.4%	4.3%	N.A.	4.2%
1980	4.8%	4.5%	4.4%	5.7%	5.2%	N.A.	4.9%
1990	6.0%	5.4%	4.8%	5.0%	5.9%	6.6%	6.0%
2000	7.1%	5.1%	4.2%	4.7%	5.8%	5.2%	7.7%
2005	7.4%	4.9%	4.7%	4.8%	6.7%	7.1%	8.1%
2008	N.A.	4.6%	3.6%	5.3%	5.8%	N.A.	7.7%
2009	N.A.	N.A.	4.3%	5.4%	5.7%	N.A.	8.3%

Source: OECD iLibrary, STAN, financial industry=ISIC Rev. 3: C65-C67

Derivatives are relatively high-risk financial instruments that derive their value from other assets. Over-the-counter derivatives are traded directly between two partners. They include instruments such as foreign exchange contracts, forwards and forex swaps, currency swaps, interest rate contracts, forward rate agreements, interest rate swaps, equity-linked contracts or credit default swaps. They are high-risk because they are not direct ownership titles, but derived from the value of other assets. Figure 1.3 shows the development of the share (in per cent) of the global gross market value of over-the-counter derivatives in world GDP.

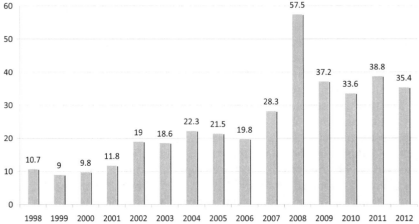

Share of gross market value of over-the-counter derivatives in world GDP(data sources: derivates - Bank for International Settlements, GDP - IMF World Economic Outlook), in %

Figure 1.3   Share of the global gross market value of OTC derivatives in world GDP (in %).

The data show that capitalist economy has since the middle of the 1970s been shaped by the capitalist class' neoliberal struggle against the working class, increasing inequality between capital and labour, an increase of household debts, a decrease of capital taxation, a rising financialization of the economy and as a consequence an increased crisis volatility. The contradictions between capital and labour, fictitious value and actual profit, the production and consumption/investment of capital were heightened by the development dynamics of neoliberal capitalism and finally resulted in a new world economic crisis and a crisis of capitalist society.

1.4.6   The Crisis and the Media

The Crisis impacts the media in several ways:

- Media report on the crisis, either in a critical or a distorted way. Crisis explanations are mainly communicated over the mass media to the population. As the preceding discussion shows, the causes of the crisis are complex. Given that the logic of the capitalist mass media is itself driven by capital interests, it is rather unlikely that they give a lot of voice to explanations that see the crisis as immanent to capitalism and as a consequence draw the political conclusion that capitalism needs to be abolished. There is therefore a tendency that crisis reporting in capitalist mass media is ideological, simplified and reductionist. A lot of mass media referred to Marx when explaining the crisis, but truncated his crisis analysis and turning him in an ideological reversal and complete distortion into Keynes and arguing that Marx shows that capitalism needs to be reformed. Alternative media tend to give more complex and critical explanations of the crisis. Due to the fact that they are often non-commerical, they however have problems to reach a broad public.
- In situations of crisis, many capitalist businesses go bankrupt, which results in lay-offs. Also in the media industries, the crisis results in large layoffs. So for example Hewlett-Packard laid-off 24,600 employees in September 2008,[1] Verizon Wireless 39,000 in 2009, AT&T more than 18,000 between 2008 and 2010, Sun Microsystems around 14,000 during the same time period.[2] In the US newspaper industry, almost 1,000 workers lost their job within one month in June 2008.[3] The website http://newspaperlayoffs.com reported 1,850 layoffs at US newspapers in 2012; 4,190 in 2011; 2,920 in 2010; 14,828 in 2009 and 15,993 in 2008.
- Times of crisis are also potential times for revolutions, social unrests, rebellions and protests. It is no accident that the Arab spring; major protests in Greece, Spain and Portugal; student protests all over the world; the rise of Occupy movements and other uprisings took place in the course of the crisis. Social movements are using and confronted with media in various ways. They communicate among themselves,

with the public and other media report about them. The mentioned movements used various commercial and non-commercial media. The usage of "social media" such as YouTube, Facebook and Twitter especially received a lot of attention. Whereas some claimed that there were Twitter of Facebook revolutions, others argued that revolutions take place on the streets and are made by humans, not by technologies. Communication technologies are tools that are articulated in various ways with struggles, they neither determine them nor are they unimportant (Fuchs 2012b, 2014).

- Commercial media are largely or partly advertising-financed. Crises of capital accumulation impact advertising revenues and advertising investment decisions because advertising is a crucial mechanism that establishes the structural coupling of the capitalist media industry and the rest of the capitalist economy.

All of these factors are important dimensions of the media in the crisis of capitalism. We want to give a little bit more attention to aspects of advertising in the crisis because this factor is particularly important in the capital accumulation models of so-called social media like Facebook, Google/YouTube, Twitter, LinkedIn, Pinterest, Foursquare, Weibo, VK, etc. That these platforms are social media is an euphemism that distracts from the circumstance that most "social media" are advertising corporations that use targeted advertising as their capital accumulation model and as part of this model exploit users' labour (see the contributions in Scholz 2013 and Burston et al. 2010).

As many media, in particular radio, TV, print and online media depend on and generate large shares of their profits based on advertising, they are likely to be affected by economic downturns as these might result in decreased advertising spending. McChesney and Nichols showed empirically that there is a tendency that advertising moves "in the same direction as business activity" (2010, 3).

The development of global advertising revenues between 2007 and 2011 (see Figure 1.4) shows that during the crisis most media types were confronted with a decline of advertising income. From 2008 to 2009 advertising revenues declined for all media types except for Internet media. While TV and print media still have the largest shares of total advertising revenues, the shares of the Internet sector have been growing the fastest. Between 2007 and 2011 advertising revenues of Internet media have increased on average by 16 per cent per year, followed by cinemas with a compound annual growth rate of 4 per cent and television growing on average by 2.5 per cent. The advertising revenue of all other media types, including outdoor, radio and print media, is decreasing. In 2007, Internet advertising accounted for 8.7 per cent of the global advertising revenues of the media. In 2011 this share had risen to 16.1 per cent, which is nearly a doubling. Radio, magazines, newspapers and outdoor advertising had negative annual

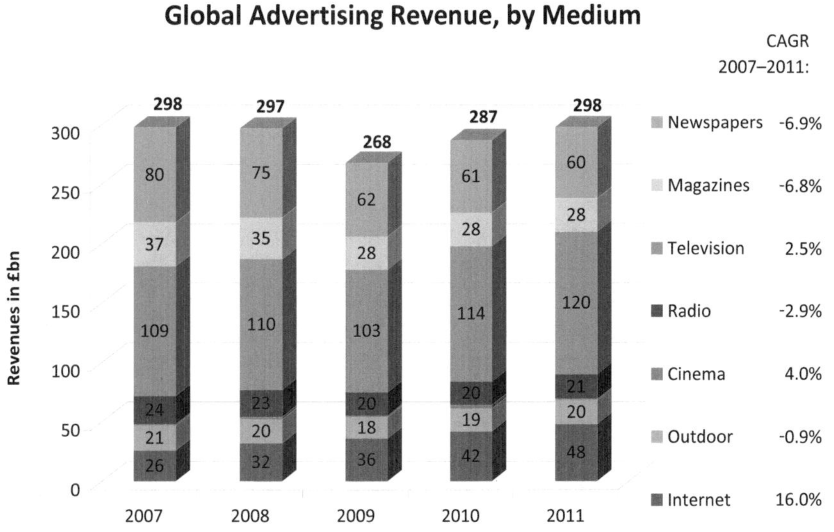

Global Advertising Revenue, by Medium

CAGR
2007–2011:

Revenues in £bn

Year	2007	2008	2009	2010	2011
Total	298	297	268	287	298
Newspapers	80	75	62	61	60
Magazines	37	35	28	28	28
Television	109	110	103	114	120
Radio	24	23	20	20	21
Cinema	21	20	18	19	20
Outdoor	26	32	36	42	48

CAGR 2007–2011:

- Newspapers -6.9%
- Magazines -6.8%
- Television 2.5%
- Radio -2.9%
- Cinema 4.0%
- Outdoor -0.9%
- Internet 16.0%

Figure 1.4 Global advertising revenue, by medium 2007–2011. *Source*: Ofcom 2012, 21 (Data based on ZenithOptimedia), CAGR=compound annual growth rate.

growth rates, with print industries having dramatic declines of more than 6 per cent per year, which has not only reduced profits, but also increased layoffs. Cinema and television had modes annual growth rates in the years 2007 to 2011.

Targeted advertising on social media is based on a constant surveillance of the users' online behaviour, profiles, communications and social networks. Therefore advertising can be highly individualised and targeted to personal interests. Total surveillance in online advertising promises more effective and efficient advertising, which may be one of the reasons why in situations of crisis advertisers tend to invest more into forms of advertisement that they perceive to be more effective and efficient. It is however unclear, if high targeting of advertising results in more sales of the advertisers because it is not self-evident that the presentation of targeted ads results a) in clicks on these ads and b) in purchases after users have been redirected to the advertisers' webpages. The promise of high returns has also resulted in high financial investments in social media corporations such as Google and Facebook. These investments have not only been driven by the crisis, but in addition also been advanced by ideologies that present "web 2.0" and "social media" as new, revolutionary and great business opportunities. If it however turns out that social media returns are not as high as expected, this can result in a) the withdrawal of financial capital investments and b) the decrease of advertising investments into social media. The ultimate effect would be the burst of a new financial bubble and possibly the next financial crisis. So another coupling of the media to the current crisis is that the investment of advertising budgets into social media and Internet corporations may result in yet another financial bubble.

In 2011 global advertising revenues had again reached the level of 2007. However, even if companies have been able to restore profits the crisis is far from over. Its consequences are still visible and are likely to have a strong impact on social, political and economic life in the years to come. McNally highlights that generating "a small economic bounce" was only possible through "the most massive bailout ever undertaken", while "profound economic problems persist" (2011, 21). Through bank bailouts the bank debt was transferred to governments. Thus, "[p]rivate debt became public debt" (McNally 2011, 4). As recent examples of state bailouts in Greece and Cyprus show, the increase of public debt poses a serious challenge to governments.

David Harvey describes the spiral between wage repression, increasing private debt, crisis, increasing government debt and austerity as follows: "Wage repression produces a deficit of effective demand, which is covered by increasing indebtedness, which ultimately leads into financial crisis, which is resolved by state interventions, which translates into a fiscal crisis of the state, which can best be resolved, according to conventional economic wisdom, by further reductions in the social wage" (2011b, 101). Reductions in the social wage, austerity measures and attacks on public services especially affect the poor, who are the most dependent on public social services such as education, health care, pensions, unemployment benefits etc. The poor are thus paying the debts of the rich (McNally 2011, 4). Social problems are thus likely to be accelerated. McNally (2011) projects a decade of austerity, a "prolonged global slump".

While the impacts of the crisis are being passed on to the poor, "business as usual" seems to continue. Foster and McChesney highlight that "there seems no way out of the present economic malaise that is acceptable to the vested interests, but to restart the financialization process" (Foster and McChesney 2012, 30). The reaction to the crisis illustrates that "capital never solves its crisis tendencies; it merely moves them around" (Harvey 2011b, 101).

By 2013 the economic crisis has largely disappeared from mainstream media headlines. McNally (2011, 16f) observes a shift from great panic to great denial. After the outbreak of the crisis mainstream media, economists and policy makers panicked and raised questions about the future of capitalism. After the first shock the rhetoric shifted: "our planet's rulers are hurriedly sweeping their fear and panic under the boardroom carpets" (McNally 2011, 21). It is therefore a major challenge for critical scholars and critical media to point at the unresolved crisis tendencies of capitalism, to show how current austerity measures are a means for shifting the costs of the crisis from the rich to the poor and to highlight that alternatives to capitalism are necessary in order to prevent more misery and suffering created through capitalist crises. Harvey points out that in the aftermath of the crisis there is the potential to promote such alternatives: "It could be that 2009 marked the beginning of a prolonged shakeout in which the question of grand far reaching alternatives to capitalism will step by step bubble up to the surface in one part of the world or another" (2011b, 109). In order to foster a debate about and the creation of alternatives it is necessary that critical scholarship connects to the social struggles that emerged in the context of the crisis and that are an expression of a deep dissatisfaction with social inequality and injustice (e.g. Occupy, the Indignados movement in Spain or protests in Greece).

1.5   THE CHAPTERS IN THIS BOOK

The chapters are organised in three sections that reflect the overall focus of the book:

- Critical Studies of the Information Society
- Critical Internet- and Social Media-Studies
- Critical Studies of Communication Labour

The contributions stand and speak for themselves. We therefore do not adhere to the common practice of summarising their main contents in the introduction, but rather want to motivate the readers to engage with all of the chapters and are confident that this is an intellectually rewarding endeavour. We want to give a brief overview of how the chapters relate to one specific question that we consider to be of particular importance, namely: What is the relevance of Karl Marx' works today for understanding and changing society, the media and politics?

Section I: Critical Studies of the Information Society

Christian Fuchs argues that the surging interest in Marx should, in the study of media and communication, lead to a reconsideration and unification of the approaches of the Frankfurt School and Critical Political Economy. Marxian analysis would be relevant for discussing the role of the information society and capitalism, criticising ideologies of the Internet and the media, understanding and critically conceptualising commodification, labour and exploitation on the Internet and social media and as inspirations for the struggle for a commons-based Internet in a commons-based society.

Wolfgang Hofkirchner stresses that the ecological, economic, political and ideological structures of society have become threats to the survival of society and humans. He thereby reflects the Marxian idea that modernity's creative and productive forces turn into destructive forces due to the logic of accumulation and domination. The choice humanity would have to make today would again be, as Fredrick Engels and Rosa Luxemburg already said, the one between barbarism on the one hand and socialism on the other hand. The task for the latter would be to reappropriate the technological, ecological, economic, political and cultural commons of society that are produced by all, but today are enclosed by a dominant class. Hofkirchner, based on Slavoj Žižek, argues that Marx' communist principle "from each according to their ability, to each according to their need" must today take on the form of a commons-based information society.

Sebastian Sevignani, Robert Prey, Marisol Sandoval, Thomas Allmer, Jernej Amon Prodnik and Verena Kreilinger argue that critical social science is influenced by Marx and that Marx's thinking is very important today. They maintain that the value chain of media technologies and content involves various forms of the exploitation of labour that can best be analysed with the help of Marx's theory. Also Marx's dialectical notion of contradiction would be helpful for understanding the ambiguous character that ICTs have in capitalism as well as struggles that emerge from capitalism and that make use of ICTs. The authors point out that the logic of commodification has shaped higher education and academia and that neoliberalism poses manifold problems for young critical scholars in the form of constant raises of tuition fees, unpaid internships, precarious academic jobs, cuts of university and higher education budgets, the competitive logic of publish or perish, the private companies' influence on universities. This would be accompanied by a hostile climate towards Marxists in some countries. Young scholars would therefore face problems, ambivalences and difficult choices. The authors point out that students, young scholars and people are angry about the situation they have to face and that this circumstance has resulted in protests in many countries. They hereby reflect the circumstance that Marxist thinking focuses on potentials and actualities of social struggles against injustices and that Marxism is a theory that strives towards political praxis and a theoretically reflected political praxis.

Gunilla Bradley argues that work in the ICT industry is characterised by a decreasing privileged core workforce and an increasing peripheral workforce that is facing precarious conditions. Work would today be too much individualised and expect too much responsibility of the single individual in an economy, where the single person can hardly control his/her own fate. ICTs would be connected to major changes in private and work life. They would bring about an acceleration of actions and decisions in both realms. This would bring about more flexible and networked organisations, but also more social problems, such as increased stress. Convergences would take place in the realms of ICTs, life roles, the life environment and globalization, resulting in ubiquitous technologies, virtual roles, virtual environments and virtual worlds, phenomena that all would have complex impacts on humans.

Section II: Critical Internet- and Social Media-Studies

Andrew Feenberg argues that Marx provides several elements for a critical theory of technology:

* He shows that technology is embedded in class structures and struggles.
* He provides an approach that allows technologies to be seen as historical artefacts that change during their own history and have various layers of organisation.
* He points out that capitalism alienates individuals by transferring their knowledge to machines and deskilling their labour and that socialism therefore implies not only the collective control of the means of production, but also the well-rounded development of human capacities enabled by the means of production.
* He argues that technologies only have meaning and functions in the context of specific context and social relations, into which they are embedded. Therefore the way technologies are used can be changed by changing the social relations to which they refer.

An application of Marx and critical theory to understanding the Internet would mean to see it a system that is facing a contradiction and struggle between commodification and community-orientation. Marx could furthermore inspire thoughts about the role of contemporary struggles in transforming society and how an alternative Internet could look.

Graham Murdock argues that Marx is the most important thinker for understanding contemporary society and culture. Marx would have shown that there is a dialectic of production and consumption, that commodities come along with ideologies of consumption and commodity fetishism as ideology, that commodification and exploitation are foundational processes of capitalism, that capitalism is inherently crisis-ridden. The notion of commodity fetishism would allow understanding the ideologies that shape the history of advertising and shape consumers' desires. Prosumption means that consumption becomes productive and produces use-values and economic value. The Marxian dialectic of production and consumption would today take on the form of prosumption that shapes web 2.0, where user labour and ideologies constitute two aspects of commodification. In the history of commodity culture, specific media would be typical for retail environments that use certain central principles: newspapers would be associated with local shops and utility, cinemas with department stores and display, commercial TV with supermarkets and flows, multi-channel TV with malls and immersion, and web 2.0 with retail destinations and integration.

Marisol Sandoval takes up Marx' distinction between the productive forces and the relations of production. She argues that discussions about "social media" such as Facebook, Twitter and YouTube often reduce the understanding of the social to the technical productive forces, where being social indicates communication, participation and sharing. She extends the meaning of the sociality of the media to the realm of the productive forces that according to Marx are in capitalism exploitative class relations.

She analyses the working conditions at Foxconn, Google's exploitation of unpaid user labour, News Corporation's right wing ideology, the monopoly-capitalist practices of Microsoft and the poisoning of nature and humans by HP's e-waste. Reflecting Marx's distinction between capitalism and communism, Sandoval discerns between the logic of property and the logic of the commons. Media that are based on the logic of property, such as Foxconn, Google, News Corporation, Microsoft and HP, are according to Marisol Sandoval "unsocial media"—they are governed by a particularistic logic that generates profit that is owned by a small group of individuals and harms both society and nature. Karl Marx (1867/1990, 638) wrote in *Capital. Volume 1*: "Capitalist production, therefore, only develops the techniques and the degree of combination of the social process of production by simultaneously undermining the original sources of all wealth—the soil and the worker." Marisol Sandoval's chapter shows that the dialectic of social production and individual appropriation that harms nature and society that Marx identified applies to twenty-first century capitalist media.

The practices of these companies result in the commodification of the eco-social commons, the labour commons and the networked commons, elite control of decision-making in media companies and ideologies advanced by these media. Sandoval concludes that corporate media are unsocial media and that there is a need for truly social media—commons-based media.

Nick Dyer-Witheford discusses the changes the working class has been undergoing in the past decades. He situates Marx's notion of Gesamtarbeiter (collective/total worker) in the context of contemporary capitalism, globalization, offshoring, outsourcing, deindustrialization, digital media and knowledge labour and coins the notion of Weltgesamtarbeiter (world total worker). This worker would be transnational, embedded into a global division of labour, feminized, mobile and migrant, precarious, earth-changing and connected. He describes an antagonism between the hacker model and the capital model of digital media and the Internet. Especially since 2001, the hacker model would have become the foundation of new capital accumulation strategies. "Immaterial" labour would thereby have become subsumed under communicative capital. The crisis of this model would not have been the result of labour's struggles, but of the antagonisms of the financial system that have been connected to capital's neoliberal struggle against labour. The resulting crisis would have driven the emergence of new struggles. Social and mobile media would not have caused these struggles, but supported decision-making in and networking of the new movements in close connection with street protests taking place in physical spaces. Capital was however fighting back, including austerity measures and the monitoring of digital media. The challenge would be to build new forms of associations that make use and re-appropriate digital media.

Mark Andrejevic discusses the relationship of alienation and exploitation on social media. He criticises approaches that argue that social media result in exploitation without alienation. There would be no death of alienation,

alienation and exploitation would rather be entwined. Andrejevic argues for a Marxist use of both terms. The private ownership and control of the ICT infrastructure and the generation of data doubles that are used for capitalist purposes would play a crucial role in online alienation. The notion of immaterial labour would be problematic because the physical infrastructure of the Internet would be decisive for its operation and under capitalist conditions constitute an infrastructure of alienation. Fixed capital would still matter and it would not just be mass intellectuality and skills that matters, but also the infrastructure of knowledge and communication. Alienation on the Internet would increasingly take on the form of algorithmic alienation, where algorithms mine data and automate decision-making.

Peter Dahlgren points out that social media do not automatically result in politics, protest and political participation, but have a potential to foster political struggles and engagement. He argues that the realities of politics, participation and protest are shaped by discourses. He thereby reflects a basic analytical domain of Marx, namely that power structures do not naturally or in a deterministic manner develop, but are shaped by and shape ideologies and worldviews. Dahlgren discusses the notion of political participation and relates it to the media and social media. He shows that the focus on the accumulation of visibility and reputation on social media can limit. Here he implicitly uses the Marxian notion of accumulation applied to the realm of a specific cultural phenomenon, reputation. Reputation plays a crucial role, so that political participation is disadvantaged in comparison to consumption. One could say that he applies two Marxian approaches, ideology critique and political economy, to the realm of social media politics and argues that the logic of social media can easily ideologically deflect political participation and that those who engage in political activism supported by social media are facing power asymmetries.

Tobias Olsson points out that a Marxist position in discussions of "web 2.0" and "social media" argues that capitalism and commodification are central contexts of these phenomena. Other positions would stress possibilities for consumer participation. Olsson argues that they advance an ideology that celebrates new technologies as harbingers of change. Implicitly Tobias Olsson here reflects Marx's analytical assumption that commodities have two aspects—one of value and capital accumulation and one of ideological (commodity fetishism). A third position would be that social media advance political engagement. Olsson argues for empirical studies of social media production and use and presents three case studies. We can add that Marx would ask in the context of specific cases, how far they represent a capitalist model or a public service model of social media, how political they are, how well or not they are represented in the overall power structure of the Internet and to which extent users' online politics confirm overall liberal values immanent in capitalism or engage in more fundamental power struggles (and if the latter is the case, how long this activism is tolerated by corporations or liberal politicians on their platforms, and how long it takes until they are censored).

Section III: Critical Studies of Communication Labour

Catherine McKercher argues that Marx's concept of piece work allows understanding the exploitation of freelance journalists. She presents data that shows that Marxian proletarianisation today often takes on the form of the feminisation of work, cultural work, freelance journalism and higher education as well as the forms of the layoff of journalists, free labour conducted by citizen journalists, and unpaid or underpaid internship work. The Marxian notion of contradiction would allow understanding the dialectic of resistance and exploitation that cultural workers are facing. Also contradictions of success and loss would shape the struggles of proletarianised cultural workers. McKercher's chapter shows the inherent connection of capitalism and patriarchy. Women have historically been confronted with a gendered division of labour that has assigned housework, family work and reproductive work to them. This means that often there is no pay for this work, no end of the work, but rather constant availability to serve others and care for others. In capitalism, this division has taken on new forms and in contemporary capitalism, patriarchy also shapes, as McKercher shows, media work.

Margareta Melin uses the theories of Pierre Bourdieu and Michel de Certeau, especially their concepts of struggles, to analyse the war-like practices in everyday life in journalism. She shows that in journalism there are certain unquestioned dominant male-dominated rules, values, thought patters and behaviours—what with Bourdieu can be called a journalistic doxa. Struggles would also focused on changing the ruling doxa. Women journalists often have to face status hierarchies, low skill activities, sexual harassment or the problem of finding a job, or freelance jobs. Bourdieu discusses how women journalists struggle against patriarchal structures in journalism and which tactics and strategies they use. She also shows how the rise of the Internet and social media has influenced the careers of women journalists. Bourdieu has generalised Marx's concepts of capital and struggles, stressing the importance of accumulation of economic, political and cultural capital and the inequalities that result from it. Margareta Melin uses Bourdieu's generalised version of Marxian theory and combines it with a feminist analysis in order to show how economic, social and cultural capital structures discriminate women journalists and how the they fight back in creative forms of struggles.

Vincent Mosco argues that there is a return of the interest in Marx. The mainstream media would report on Marx's relevance for understanding the crisis. The Marx of the *Grundrisse* that coined the notion of the "General Intellect" would be needed for understanding communication labour. He would have shown that communication technologies are part of the

productive forces and that communication is inherently connected to globalization. The notion of the General Intellect would be a remarkable fore-
sightful analysis of knowledge work and the knowledge economy. Marx,
the journalist, would be a role model for critical journalism. He would have
fought for freedom of speech with his pen, which resulted in the censorship
and ban of the newspapers he wrote, trials and his ban from Germany. This
makes clear that besides equality freedom was also a very important value
for Marx. Marx saw the newspaper as an inherently political medium that
should intervene in struggles. This was at a time before the news media
were heavily commercialised and can remind us that commercialisation
goes along with the value of (pseudo-)objectivity and just like political censorship negatively impacts the freedom of speech that Marx struggled for.
Marx, the politician and communist, would be needed as inspiration for
knowledge workers to unite as a class that struggles against their exploitation. Mosco points out that the convergence of capital and the communication technologies it controls can best be answered by the convergence of
communication workers' trade unions, which allows struggles to be more
powerful. Mosco, by engaging with Marx, reminds scholars that the topic
of labour is of special importance because there is a strong focus on technology, platforms and companies in the research landscape, knowledge
labour has economic significance and this kind of analysis allows scholars
to connect to political struggles that matter in the twenty-first century.

1.6 KARL MARX AND THE CHAPTERS IN THIS BOOK

For analysing media, digital media, social media and the information society, the authors in this book employ theory, empirical research, ethical
and political reasoning and a historical method. Not every author employs
a combination of all four methods, which is hardly possible in a single
book chapter and has today become rare because academia does not foster wholism, but rather particularistic methods. An integrated method
that makes use of theory, empirical research, ethics and historical analysis
requires time and resources, which are both structures that are rare in contemporary academia because of neoliberal deregulation, cuts and spending
priorities that discriminate critical research approaches. If we read the epistemological approaches that are employed for generating new knowledge
in this book, then this is precisely Marx's method—a unity of a) theory, b)
empirical research, c) historical analysis and d) ethics/politics.

Take as an example Marx's *Capital. Volume 1* (Marx 1867/1990): it is a) a
theoretical analysis and critique of capitalism that starts with the category of
the commodity as the most abstract notion and then subsequently makes the
analysis more concrete by connecting the already developed categories subsequently to others such as use-value, value, concrete labour, abstract labour,
the forms of value, money, the fetishism of commodities, surplus-value,

capital, the unity of the labour and valorisation process, constant capital, variable capital, rate of surplus-value, mass of surplus-value, the method of absolute surplus-value production, the method of relative surplus-value production, co-operation, machinery, wages, the overall process of capital accumulation, capital concentration, surplus population, primitive accumulation, crisis, and colonialism. Marx has a general concept of developing a theory that he termed the advancement from the abstract to the concrete: one starts with a certain category and then develops out of this category another relational category that contradicts the previous one so that this contradiction gives rise to a third category that again stands in relation to another category, etc. This method develops a system of categories, which is exactly the definition of a theory. The underlying assumption is that this system is not arbitrary, but describes actual parts of the world.

b) Marx also employed empirical research for illustrating and validating his theoretical concept. In *Capital. Volume 1*, the main data he employed are fabric inspectors' reports of working conditions in British companies. Marx uses this material for illustrating his theoretical assumptions. This is most apparent in Chapter 15 "Machinery and Modern Industry" (that is actually Chapter 13 "Maschinerie und große Industrie" in the most widely read German edition of the book, [Marx 1867], which shows that in preparing the English edition a serious mistake was made, namely the one of not maintaining the same numbering of chapters). This is longest chapter in the book and probably also the one that is most illustrative of the horrible conditions that workers in industrializing capitalism had and have (!) to face. Marx's thinking is not only dialectical and realistic, it is also c) historical: he sees capitalism as a historical system that has a beginning and an end, contradictions as drivers of history and revolutions and conceives capitalism as the historical sublation (Aufhebung) of previous modes of production (feudalism, ancient slavery, patriarchy) that are no longer dominant, but preserved and transmogrified in capitalism.

Marx's language and analysis is d) inherently ethical and political. He did not believe in the myth of the objectivity of science, but rather tried to show in *Capital. Volume 1*, and other works that the most bourgeois theory of capitalism (classical political economy) is ideological by declaring phenomena that are specific for capitalism or class societies in general (such as class, exploitation, profit, money, accumulation, competition, the division of labour, etc.) as natural properties of all societies. Marx criticises that these approaches are devoid of history, which turns them into ideology: they do not see the historical character of existing phenomena and cannot imagine and do not desire an alternative to capitalism. Marx, in contract, is aware that every academic approach is shaped by the political values of its authors and does, in contrast to bourgeois thinkers who try to morally justify capitalism by scientific laws, make no secret out of the fact that he sees capitalism as a morally unjust system that should be abolished. This becomes apparent in categories such as the rate of exploitation or the characterisation of surplus value as the reality of exploitation that are not just analytical and theoretical, but at the same time communicate that injustice is an inherent feature of capitalism. Consider for example the following passage:

> Capital is dead labour which, vampire-like, lives only by sucking living labour, and lives the more, the more labour it sucks. The time during which the worker works is the time during which the capitalist consumes the labour-power he has bought from him. If the worker consumes his disposable time for himself, he robs the capitalist. (Marx 1867/1990, 342)

Marx deliberately chose categories such as the vampire, blood-sucking, robbing and stealing for characterising capital in order to not only express the analytical circumstance that capital requires the appropriation of workers' unpaid labour time for accumulating capital and profit, but also for expressing that this societal circumstance is unjust and should be abolished by a political revolution. Marx used the figure of the vampire for illustrating the monstrosity of capital accumulation: "Capital is dead labour, that, vampire-like, lives only by sucking living labour, and lives the more, the more labour it sucks" (1867/1990, 342). This characterisation of capital resembles Bram Stoker's description of the vampire that "can flourish and fatten on the blood of the living. Even more [. . .] his vital faculties grow strenuous, and seem as though they refresh themselves when his special pabulum is plenty" (Stoker 1897, 211). Like the kiss of the vampire turns a human being into another vampire, capital works as an "animated monster" (Marx 1867/1990, 302) that turns ever more living labour power into ever more capital. Both capital and the vampire follow only one purpose: While capital's single purpose is its constant accumulation, that is to turn living labour into dead capital (Marx 1867/1990, 253), the only purpose of the vampire is to suck the blood of the living: "as his [count Dracula's] intellect is small and his action based on selfishness, he confines himself to one purpose. That purpose is remorseless" (Stoker 1897, 302).

The authors in this book agree that the Internet and social media have a contradictory character and pose positive potentials and risks, potentials for deepening domination and practicing attempts to liberate humanity from domination. They stress aspects of domination and liberation to different degrees and also in ways that partly contradict each other, which is first and foremost an indication of a lively academic debate. The discourse shows overall that the Internet and social media form a dialectic system: it is full of contradictions that reflect and transpose the actual contradictions of society. If we consequently apply Marx' way of thinking as an epistemological method, then we can formulate the overall insights of this book in an integrated manner: The Internet and social media are systems of cognition, communication and cooperation that are embedded into contemporary society's power structures. This means that on the one hand they pose potentials for making society and social reality more participatory, cooperative and sustainable, but on the other hand the reality is that corporate social media and the corporate Internet are embedded, shaped by and shaping structures of exploitation and domination. The Internet and social media are highly contradictory: They represent the potential for a more just world, in which property, decision power, reputation and meaning making are social in character, i.e. controlled by all in participatory and cooperative processes, and the reality of particularism. "Social media" have social potentials for fostering the common interest and a particularistic reality under capitalism that favours private interests and the interests of the few and the privileged. This contradiction of the simultaneous common sociality and exploitative and dominative particularism of the Internet and "social media" translates today into struggles and discussions about the opportunities and risks of these communication forms. This book contributes to these debates and wants to inform these struggles.

1.7 CONCLUSION

The new global crisis has shown that global capitalism has difficulties to continue to exist in the neoliberal mode of existence that it has acquired in the past decades. Accumulation by dispossession has strongly increased inequality and the finance-based regime of accumulation, coupled with the redistribution of wealth from the working class to companies and the rich, has increased the crisis-proneness of capitalism and resulted in a new world-economic crisis of capitalism.

New struggles and rebellions as well as attempts to introduce an even more brutal neoliberal regime have emerged. It is unclear what the future of capitalism will look like. For the social sciences, it is also unclear what their own future will look like. There are both opportunities and great risks: the opportunity to renew the critical spirit of the social sciences that has suffered under the hegemony of neoliberalism, as well as the risk that the social sciences, in general, and critical approaches, in particular, will be even more cut back, structurally discriminated, and weakened due to the potential emergence of a hyper-neoliberal regime of regulation.

Much will depend on how the political situation develops in the coming years in various countries and regions of the world. In our view, the critical spirit and the interest in critical research that has guided the Uppsala conference, are signs that there is an interest in a renewal of critical media and communication studies. It is unclear, how large this potential is, if it can constitute a counter-hegemony to the hegemony of administrative research, and if new opportunities for institutionalizing critical research exist and can be fostered. All we can say is that there are indicators for a certain renewed critical potential. What we need to do next, in our opinion, is to find creative ways and projects to realize and institutionalize these potentials. This is definitely easier said than done. If those, who are interested in fostering critical research, join forces and create collective spaces for critical research, then we are definitely on the right way. The Uppsala conference and this book as well as many other contributions are first steps for renewing critical media and communication studies in times of neoliberal capitalism, global crisis, and uncertainty. Much remains to be accomplished and to be done.

NOTES

1. Douglas A. McIntyre, 2011, "The Biggest Corporate Layoffs Of All Time," December 7, accessed April 5, 2013, http://jobs.aol.com/articles/2011/12/07/the-biggest-corporate-layoffs-of-all-time/.
2. Douglas A. McIntyre, 2010, "The Layoff Kings: The 25 Companies Responsible for 700,000 Lost Jobs," August 18, accessed April 5, 2013, http://www.dailyfinance.com/2010/08/18/the-layoff-kings-the-25-companies-responsible-for-700–000-lost/.
3. Mark Potts, 2008, "Death of Almost 1,000 Cuts," June 26, accessed April 5, 2013, http://recoveringjournalist.typepad.com/recovering_journalist/2008/06/death-of-almost-1000-cuts.html.

REFERENCES

Adorno, Theodor W. 1968/2003. "Late capitalism or industrial society? The fundamental question of the present structure of society." In *Can one live after Auschwitz?*, edited by Rolf Tiedemann, 111–125. Stanford, CA: Stanford University Press.
Bell, Daniel. 1974. *The Coming of Post-Industrial Society*. London: Heinemann.
Burston, Jonathan, Nick Dyer-Witheford, and Alison Hearn, eds. 2010. "Digital labour: workers, authors, citizens." *Ephemera* 10 (3/4).
Eagleton, Terry. 2011. *Why Marx was right*. London: Yale University Press.
Erdogan, İrfan. 2012. "Missing Marx: The place of Marx in current communication research and the place of communication in Marx' work." *trifleC* 10 (2): 349–391.
Foster, John Bellamy, and Robert McChesney. 2012. *The endless crisis. How Monopoly-finance capital produces stagnation and upheaval from the USA to China*. New York: Monthly Review Press.
Fuchs, Christian. 2004. "The antagonistic self-organization of modern society." *Studies in Political Economy* 73: 183–209.
———. 2008. *Internet and society. Social theory in the information age*. New York: Routledge.
———. 2009. "Information and communication technologies and society. A contribution to the critique of the political economy of the Internet." *European Journal of Communication* 24 (1): 69–87.
———. 2010. "Social software and web 2.0: their sociological foundations and implications." In *Handbook of research on web 2.0, 3.0, and X.0: technologies, business, and social applications. Volume II*, edited by San Murugesan, 764–789. Hershey, PA: IGI-Global.

———. 2012a. "Capitalism or information society? The fundamental question of the present structure of society." *European Journal of Social Theory*. First published November 20, 2012, doi:10.1177/1368431012461432.

———. 2012b. "Some reflections on Manuel Castells' book 'Networks of outrage and hope. Social movements in the Internet age'." *tripleC: Cognition, Communication, Cooperation. Open Access Journal for a Global Sustainable Information Society* 10 (2): 775–797.

———. 2014. *Social media. A critical introduction*. London: Sage.

Fuchs, Christian and Vincent Mosco, eds. 2012. Marx is back. The importance of Marxist theory and research for Critical Communication Studies Today. *tripleC: Communication, Capitalism & Critique* 10 (2): 127–632.

Harvey, David. 1990. *The condition of postmodernity*. Malden, MA: Blackwell.

———. 2009. "Interview." *Socialist Review* (4).

———. 2010. *The enigma of capital*. London: Profile Books.

———. 2011a. The urban roots of financial crisis: Reclaiming the city for anticapitalist struggle. *Socialist Register* 48: 1–25.

———. 2011b. "The enigma of capital and the crisis this time." In *Business as usual. The roots of the financial meltdown*, edited by Graig Calhoun and Georgi Derluguian, 89–112. New York: New York University Press.

Hobsbawm, Eric. 2011. *How to change the world. Marx and Marxism 1840–2011*. London: Little, Brown.

Hofkirchner, Wolfgang. 2013. *Emergent information. An outline unified theory of information framework*. Hackensack, NJ: World Scientific.

Jameson, Frederic. 2011. *Representing Capital*. London: Verso.

Kliman, Andrew. 2012. *The failure of capitalist production. Underlying causes of the great recession*. New York: Pluto.

Mandiberg, Michael. 2012. "Introduction." In *The social media reader*, edited by Michael Mandiberg, 1–12. New York: New York University Press.

Marx, Karl. 1844/2007. *Economic philosophic manuscripts*. Mineola, New York: Dover Publications.

———. 1857/1858. *Grundrisse*. London: Penguin.

———. 1863. *Theories of surplus value. Books I, II, and III*. Amherst, NY: Prometheus Books.

———. 1867/1990. *Capital. Volume 1*. London: Penguin.

———. 1867. *Das Kapital. Band 1. MEW, Band 23*. Berlin: Dietz.

———. 1885/1992. Capital. Volume II. London: Penguin.

———. 1894/1991. *Capital Volume III*. London: Penguin.

Marx, Karl, and Friedrich Engels. 1848/1991. "Manifesto of the communist party." In *Selected Works in One Volume*, 35–90. London: Lawrence & Wishart.

———. 1848/2004. *The Communist manifesto*. Peterborough: Broadview.

McChesney, Robert and John Nichols. 2010. *The death and life of American journalism*. New York: Nation Books.

McNally, David. 2011. *Global slump. The economics and politics of crisis and resistance*. Oakland: PM Press.

Ofcom. 2012. *International communications market report 2012*. Accessed April 5, 2013. http://stakeholders.ofcom.org.uk/binaries/research/cmr/cmr12/icmr/ICMR-2012.pdf.

O'Reilly, Tim. 2005. "What is web 2.0?" O'Reilly. http://www.oreilly.de/artikel/web20.html.

O'Reilly, Tim and John Battelle. 2009. *Web squared. Web 2.0 five years on*. Special report. http://assets.en.oreilly.com/1/event/28/web2009_websquared-whitepaper.pdf.

Resnick, Stephen and Rick Wolff. 2010. "The economic crisis. A Marxian interpretation." *Rethinking Marxism* 22 (2). Reprinted in *SocialistWorker.org*. Accessed

March 13, 2013. http://socialistworker.org/blog/critical-reading/2011/12/26/ marxist-explanation-crisis..

Scholz, Trebor, ed. 2013. *Digital labor. The Internet as playground and factory.* New York: Routledge.

Smythe, Dallas W. 1977. "Communications: Blindspot of Western Marxism." *Canadian Journal of Political and Social Theory* 1 (3): 1–27.

Stoker, Bram. 1897. *Dracula. A mystery story.* Amazon Kindle edition.

Wolff, Rick. 2008. "Capitalism's crisis through a Marxian lens." *MRZine*, December 14. Accessed March 13, 2013. http://mrzine.monthlyreview.org/2008/wolff141208.html.

Žižek, Slavoj. 2008. *In defense of lost causes.* London: Verso.

———. 2010. *Living in the end times.* London: Verso.

Part I

Critical Studies of the Information Society

2 Critique of the Political Economy of Informational Capitalism and Social Media

Christian Fuchs

2.1 INTRODUCTION

The conference "Critique, Democracy and Philosophy in 21st Century Information Society" (Uppsala University, May 2–4, 2012, http://www.icts-and-society.net/events/uppsala2012/; see also Fuchs 2012c) that took place at the University of Uppsala has shown that there is a big interest in critical studies of digital media and the information society. And by critical studies, the majority of the participants at the conference actually mean Marxist studies of digital media and the information society. The term "Marxist studies of digital media and the information society" for me encompasses several dimensions, namely that digital media and information, communication, and media in society are analysed in respect to:

a) processes of capital accumulation (including the analysis of capital, markets, commodity logic, competition, exchange value, the antagonisms of the mode of production, productive forces, crises, advertising, etc.),
b) class relations (with a focus on work, labour, the mode of the exploitation of surplus value, etc.),
c) domination in general (based on the insight that in capitalism forms of domination—such as racism or patriarchy—are always connected to exploitation, i.e. class),
d) ideology (both in academia and everyday life), as well as the analysis of and engagement in
e) struggles against the dominant order, which includes the analysis and advancement of
f) social movement struggles and
g) social movement media that
h) aim at the establishment of a democratic socialist society that is based on communication commons as part of structures of commonly-owned means of production.

Since the start of the global economic crisis in 2008, there has been a surging interest in the analysis of capitalism and the works of Karl

Marx (Fuchs and Mosco 2012). At the same time, the actual rise of inequality in most Western societies has resulted in a certain return of the public discussion of class and exploitation. So for example the self-description of the Occupy movement as a movement that fights "back against the richest 1% of people that are writing the rules of an unfair global economy that is foreclosing on our future" shows a focus on class and class struggle.[1] In a survey published in July 2012, 65 per cent of the US respondents (N=2,508) said that in the past ten years the income gap between the rich and the poor has gotten larger.[2] In January 2012, 66 per cent of the US respondents said in a survey (N=2,048) that there are strong or very strong conflicts between the rich and the poor in comparison to 47 per cent in 2009 (N=1,701).[3] One can infer from these data that although the Occupy movement has been evicted from Wall Street by the US government and the police, one of its big successes was that it has helped to raise public awareness of class divisions.

2.2   FRANKFURT SCHOOL AND CRITICAL POLITICAL ECONOMY

Two of the main schools that have studied the media, communication and culture critically are Frankfurt School Critical Theory (see Wiggershaus 1995) and Critical Political Economy of the Media (see Mosco 2009). For Horkheimer and his colleagues, critical theory "was a camouflage label for 'Marxist theory'" (Wiggershaus 1995, 5) when they were in exile from the Nazis in the USA, where they were concerned about being exposed as Marxist thinkers. Representatives of Critical Political Economy have considered their approach as being Marxist in character (e.g. Murdock and Golding 2005, 61; Smythe 1981, xvi–xviii; 1994, 258). Besides the grounding in Marx's works, both approaches also share the focus on commodity exchange as a crucial starting point or grounding category of analysis (Adorno 2000, 32; Smythe 1994, 259). Marx said in respect to the analysis of modern society that the commodity is the cell form of capitalism (Marx 1867, 125), so both Critical Theory and Critical Political Economy of the Media have a genuinely Marxian approach.

A common prejudice against both approaches, especially formulated by cultural studies scholars, is that there is no or little focus on agency, that no alternatives to capitalist media are seen and that audiences are seen as passive (e.g. Grossberg 1995, Hall 1986, 1988). These views are shortsighted because they neglect the fact that scholars like Smythe stressed the potentials of resistance to capitalism (Smythe 1981, 270) and the potentials for and need of alternatives (see Fuchs 2012b for a detailed discussion). For example, both Adorno (2005) and Smythe (1994, 230–244) imagined an alternative system of television. Adorno (1977, 680) also stressed the positive role that TV could play in anti-fascist education in Germany after Auschwitz.

Both approaches have given attention to the analysis of the commodity form of the media and ideology critique, although to different extents (Fuchs 2012b). A difference between Critical Political Economy of the Media and Critical Theory is that the first is strongly rooted in economic theory and the second in philosophy and social theory. There has been a stronger focus on ideology critique in the Frankfurt School approach for historical reasons: in order to understand German fascism, an explanation was needed as to why the revolutionary German working class followed Hitler, which brought up the interest in the analysis of the authoritarian personality and media propaganda.

The Marxist analysis of media and communication is grounded in a double-understanding of what Lukács (1923) termed reification, Horkheimer (1947, 2002) called instrumental reason and Marcuse (1964) termed technological rationality: capitalism a) reduces humans to the status of being instruments for capital accumulation in the form of their role as wage workers and consumers and b) tries to make them believe in the feasibility of the overall system by using ideology as an (attempted) silencing instrument.

2.3 INFORMATION SOCIETY OR CAPITALISM?

The fundamental question of a theory of contemporary society is: in what kind of society do we live today and what are the main tendencies in the development of contemporary society (Fuchs 2012a)? A classification of information society theories can be achieved by combining the degree of novelty and the kind of sociological theorizing as distinguishing criteria. The information society theory discourse can then be theoretically categorised by distinguishing two axes: the first axis distinguishes aspects of societal change, the second one the informational qualities of these changes. There are theories that conceive the transformations of past decades as constituting radical societal change. These are discontinuous theories. Other theories stress the continuities of modern society. Subjective information society theories stress the importance of human knowledge (thought, mental activities) in contemporary society, whereas objective information society theories emphasise the role of information technologies such as the mass media, the computer, the Internet, or the mobile phone (Fuchs 2012a). Figure 2.1 shows a typology of information society theories.

If one applies a dialectical methodology, one can argue that knowledge in contemporary society has both objective and subjective aspects that are mutually constitutive, they transform the means of production and the relations of production (Fuchs 2012a). The search of capital for

54   *Christian Fuchs*

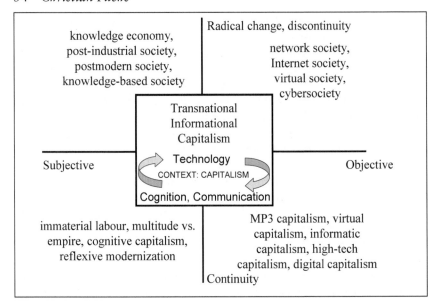

Figure 2.1   A typology of information society theories.

new strategies and forms of capital accumulation transforms labour in such a way that cognitive, communicative and co-operative labour forms a significant amount of overall labour time (a development enforced by the rise of the ideology of self-discipline of "participatory management"), but at the same time this labour is heavily mediated by information technologies and produces to a certain extent tangible informational goods (as well as intangible informational services). There is a subject-object-dialectic that allows conceptualizing contemporary capitalism based on the rise of cognitive, communicative and co-operative labour that is interconnected with the rise of technologies of and goods that objectify human cognition, communication and co-operation. There is a dialectical interconnection of subjective knowledge and knowledge objectified in information.

Transnational informational capitalism is the result of the dialectic of continuity and discontinuity that shapes capitalist development (Fuchs 2012a). Surplus value, exchange value, capital, commodities and competition are basic aspects of capitalism, how such forms are exactly produced, objectified, accumulated, and circulated is contingent and historical. They manifest themselves differently in different capitalist modes of development. In the informational mode of capitalist development, surplus value production and capital accumulation manifest themselves increasingly in symbolic, "immaterial", informational commodities and cognitive, communicative, and co-operative labour.

Informational capitalism is a tendency of and relative degree in the development of contemporary capitalism. This does not mean that it is the only or the dominant tendency.. Capitalism is many things at the same time, it is to a certain degree informational, but at the same time it is also to a certain degree finance capitalism, imperialistic capitalism, hyperindustrial capitalism, etc. We have many capitalisms today existing within one overall capitalist mode of organising society. Capitalism is at the same time a general mode of production and exploitation and a specific realisation, co-existence and interaction of different types and forms of capitalist production and exploitation.

In 1968, Theodor W. Adorno (1968/2003) gave an introductory keynote talk on the topic of "Late capitalism or industrial society?" at the annual meeting of the German Sociological Association. He said that the "fundamental question of the present structure of society" is "about the alternatives: late capitalism or industrial society" (1968/2003, 111). We can reformulate this question today and say that the fundamental question about the present structure of society is about the alternatives: capitalism or information society (Fuchs 2012a). The answer to this question can be given, by paraphrasing and transforming Adorno's (1968/2003, 117) answer to his question: In terms of critical, dialectical theory, contemporary society is an information society according to the state of its *forces* of production. In contrast, however, contemporary society is capitalist in its *relations* of production. People are still what they were in Marx's analysis in the middle of the nineteenth century. Production takes place today, as then, for the sake of profit and for achieving this end it, to a certain extent, makes use of knowledge and information technology in production.

2.4   COMMUNICATION POWER AND PARTICIPATORY CULTURE: MANUEL CASTELLS AND HENRY JENKINS

Two particularly popular approaches in the study of digital media and the Internet in the information society have been advanced by Manuel Castells and Henry Jenkins.

Castells (2009) argues in his book *Communication Power* that social media are tools of communication power and network-making power that would be the central form of power in what he terms the network society (for a detailed discussion and critique of this book, see Fuchs 2009). In his book *Networks of Outrage and Hope: Social Movements in the Internet Age*, Castells (2012) applies the idea of communication power to contemporary social movements: he argues with the help of examples from Tunisia, Iceland, Egypt, Spain and the USA that contemporary social movements' use of the Internet has facilitated the creation of occupied spaces, that the Internet allows movements to communicate the emotions of outrage and hope that are needed for switching from collective emotions to collective action and that contemporary social movements are online and offline socially networked movements, for which social media are of crucial importance, and that these movements were born on, conveyed by and are based on the Internet (for a detailed discussion and critique of this book, see Fuchs 2012e).

Claims about social media that are similar to the ones made by Castells have been present in popular political discourses, e.g. when activists argue that the Egyptian revolution was due to Twitter and Facebook, a "revolution 2.0" (Wael Ghonim),[4] when conservative bloggers claim that "the revolution will be twittered" (Andrew Sullivan),[5] or when tabloids simplify reality by writing that the 2011 UK riots were Twitter and Facebook mobs.[6] Such claims focus on technology without taking into account its embeddedness into power structures. They are expression of what Vincent Mosco terms the digital sublime, in which the Internet is "praised for its epochal and transcendent characteristics and demonized for the depth of the evil it can conjure" (Mosco 2004, 24).

When asked who the main theorist is in their field, quite some scholars in the fields of Internet Studies and Information Society Studies will answer: Manuel Castells. But Castells's approach is not a social theory because such a theory starts from giving systematic answers to questions like: What is a society? What is the role of humans in society? What is the role of structure and agency in society? How can we explain the dynamics and historicity of society? Based these models, one can apply them to answering the same questions, first for a) modern society and then for b) contemporary society, which then gives a foundation for the study of digital media in contemporary society. Castells' does not advance from the abstract to the concrete, has no sense for the philosophical grounding of sociological analysis and does not engage with the history and meanings of concepts (such as power, see Fuchs 2009).

Henry Jenkins argues that increasingly "the Web has become a site of consumer participation" (2008, 137) and that fans are "preparing the way for a more meaningful public culture" online and offline (2008, 239). Then he describes the emergence of what he terms "participatory culture".

The Internet is not only a space of commercialism, everyday communication, and relatively progressive communication (WikiLeaks, Indymedia, Democracy Now!, Alternet, OpenDemocracy, etc.), it is also a space of online fascism. So for example the forum ultras.ws provides a discussion board for soccer fans. Fascism is an everyday phenomenon in this forum. For example when the German soccer team Hallescher FC had to pay a fine because its fans shouted anti-Semitic paroles in a match, 56 per cent answered to a survey conducted on ultras.ws that they thought this fine was unjust.[7] Fascist jokes are also part of the everyday life on these forums. For example, "How do you get 30 Jews into a Trabi [small car produced in the former GDR]? 2 in the front, 3 in the back, and the rest in the ashtray. I forgot that one does not make jokes about Jews? But Wehrmacht [in German "wer macht" is translated who makes, and it sounds similar to Wehrmacht, the armed forces of Nazi Germany] something like this?"[8] Right-wing extremism is especially on the rise since the start of the new world economic crisis, which likely intensifies and extends online fascism. Is online fascism "preparing the way for a more meaningful public culture" and expression of a "participatory culture"? Participation is not only an analytical, but also a normative term that implies that the analysed phenomenon is developing in a democratic manner. One should not assume that fan culture (online and offline) is always progressive and an expression of participation, but rather view its expressions critically.

Manuel Castells and Henry Jenkins have advanced uncritical and administrative studies of social media and the Internet. It is time to discard their approaches and to focus on Marxist studies of communication, digital media and the information society instead.

2.5   MARXIST STUDIES OF THE INTERNET AND SOCIAL MEDIA

A Marxist analysis of the Internet and social media starts with the analysis of exploitation, class, and commodification on the Internet and generates based on this analysis insights about the actual and potential role of the Internet in social struggles and the establishment of alternatives (Fuchs 2008, 2011a, 2014).

Dallas Smythe (1977; 1981, 22–51) suggests that in the case of media advertisement models, the audience is sold as a commodity to advertisers (audience commodity). In the case of social media, users are much more active and to a certain degree create user-generated content. It is therefore feasible to speak in the case of commercial online media like Facebook and Google, which use targeted advertising as their business model, not of audience commodification as the specific model of commodification, but rather of Internet prosumer commodification (Fuchs 2010, 2012b). Users' digital labour generates value that is appropriated by capital: online work time is time that generates profile data, social network data and browsing behaviour data. Facebook, Google and similar companies sell this user-generated data as a commodity to advertising clients that present targeted advertisements to users.

The time that users spend on commercial social media platforms for generating social, cultural and symbolic capital is in the process of prosumer commodification transformed into economic capital. Labour time on commercial social media is the conversion of Bourdieuian social, cultural and symbolic capital into Marxian value and economic capital. Users work without pay and produce content, communications, social relations, and transaction data that become part of data commodities (collection of individuals with specific user demographics) that are sold to advertisers. Targeted advertising is a process, in which advertisers pay money to ad-serving companies (like Facebook and Google) and thereby get access to specific user groups that have certain demographic features and interests.

Most commercial social media services are free to use. They are not commodities.

User data and the users form the social media commodity. The exploitation of digital labour involves three elements:

* Coercion: Users are ideologically coerced to use commercial platforms in order to be able to engage in communication, sharing, and the creation and maintenance of social relations, without which their lives would be less meaningful.
* Alienation: companies, not the users, own the platforms and the created profit.
* Expropriation: The value (work time) of data commodities is turned into money that is privately owned by corporations.

Surveillance of users' interest and activities is a crucial process in social media commodification. It is subsumed to political economy and involves the surveillance of personal profile data, produced content, browsing and clicking behaviour, social relations and networks and communication. Surveillance on social media is targeted, highly rationalised (it is not an estimation, but an exact observation of online behaviour on certain platforms), it works in real time and makes use of a convergence of social roles (for example between private, professional and public roles that converge in one profile) and social activities (the convergence of information, communication, community-maintenance, and collaboration in one space) that these platforms mediate.

According to Marx, the law of value says that "the greater the labour-time necessary to produce an article, [. . .] the greater its value" (Marx 1867, 131). Some authors claim that we are experiencing an end of the law of value due to the rise of the social worker (value is not only produced by wage workers, but also by non-wage workers, including users of commercial Internet websites) and knowledge work. Hardt and Negri formulate this assumption by saying that "biopolitical production is [. . .] immeasurable, because it cannot be quantified in fixed units of time [. . .] This is why we have to revise Marx's notion of the relation between labor and value in capitalist production" (2004, 146). The more time a user spends on commercial social media, the more data about her/his interests and activities are available and the more advertisements are presented to her/him. Value as the average number of hours humans spend to produce a commodity is measurable as long as capitalism exists, although due to rising productivity the amount of value of a commodity tends to decrease historically and phenomena like the rise of the social worker, financialization, and branding create differences between the value and price of commodities, which increases the crisis-proneness of capitalism.

Sut Jhally (1987) has argued that due to the rise of the audience commodity, the living room has become a factory. Mario Tronti (cited in Cleaver 1992, 137) has taken this idea one step further by arguing that society has become a social factory and that the boundaries of the factory extend beyond the traditional factory that is the space of the exploitation of wage labour. Nick Dyer-Witheford (2010, 485) speaks in this context of the emergence of the "factory planet". The exploitation of user labour on commercial Internet platforms like Facebook and Google is indicative for a phase of capitalism, in which we find an all-ubiquitous factory that is a space of the exploitation of labour. Social media and the mobile Internet make the audience commodity ubiquitous and the factory no longer limited to your living room and your work place—the factory and work place surveillance are also in all the in-between spaces. Almost the entire planet and all of its spaces today form capitalist factories.

Internet user commodification is part of the tendency of the commodification of everything that has resulted in the generalisation of the factory and of exploitation. Neoliberal capitalism has largely widened the boundaries of what is treated as a commodity.

Internet labour and its surveillance are based on the surveillance, blood and sweat of super-exploited labour in developing countries. Stories about the highly precarious, non-unionised hardware producers in the Foxconn factories, who face working conditions so terrible that some of them commit suicide, and African slave workers, who extract "conflict minerals" that are needed for producing ICTs, show how the Western use of ICTs is based on what Alain Lipietz (1995) termed "bloody Taylorism", which is a contemporary capital accumulation regime that is coupled to two other accumulation regimes (peripheral Fordism, post-Fordism). "To the traditional oppression of women, this strategy adds all the modern weapons of anti-labour repression (official unions, absence of civil rights, imprisonment and torture of opponents)" (Lipietz 1995, 11). Taylorism has not been replaced, we do not live in an age of post-Taylorism, rather we are experiencing an extension and intensification of Taylorism that is complemented by new ideological forms of workforce control. The emergence of work/play places is a tendency in contemporary capitalism that interacts with established forms of work, play, and toil. The corporate Internet requires for its existence the exploitation of the labour that exists under bloody Taylorist conditions. On top of this foundation, we find various work/play places on the Internet, where users work without payment and deterritorialise the boundaries between play and work. iPhones, iPads, iMacs, Nokia phones, etc. are also "blood phones", "blood pads", and "blood Macs". Many smartphones, laptops, digital cameras, mp3 players, etc. are made out of minerals (e.g. cassiterite, wolframite, coltan, gold, tungsten, tantalum, tin) that are extracted from mines in the Democratic Republic of Congo and other countries under slave-like conditions.

The existence of the Internet in its current dominant capitalist form is based on various forms of labour: the relatively highly paid wage work of software engineers and low-paid proletarianised workers in Internet companies, the unpaid labour of users, the highly exploited bloody Taylorist work and slave work in developing countries producing hardware and extracting "conflict minerals". There is a class conflict between capital and labour that is constituted through exploitation. The rate of exploitation varies depending on the type and location of activity. In the case of the salaried knowledge workers that are employed by companies like Google in Western countries, capital pays relatively high wages in order to try to gain their hegemonic consensus, whereas low-paid knowledge workers, users, hardware and software producers, and mineral extractors are facing precarious working conditions and varying degrees and forms of slavery and exploitation that as a whole help to advance the profits of capital by minimizing the wage costs. Free-labouring Internet users and the workers in conflict mines have in common that they are unpaid—the difference is that the first gain pleasure through their exploitation, whereas the latter suffer pain and die through their exploitation and enable the pleasure of the first. The main benefit from this situation is monetary and goes to companies like Google, Apple and Facebook that are contemporary slaveholders and slave masters.

Different forms of control are needed for exploiting digital labour. Self-control and play labour (playbour) that feels like fun, but creates parts of the value, is only one part of the labour process that has its foundation in a racist mode of production and exploitation of workers in developing countries. The exploitation of play workers in the West is based on the pain, sweat, blood and death of workers in developing countries. The corporate Internet needs for its existence both playbour and toil, fun and misery, biopolitical power and disciplinary power, self-control and surveillance. The example of the Foxconn factories and Congolese conflict minerals shows that the exploitation of Internet playbour needs as a precondition and is coupled to the bloody Taylorist exploitation of workers in the developing world.

Based on the exploitation of slaves and Taylorist workers in developing countries, a new regime of play labour has developed in Western countries. The boundaries between work time and playtime tend to blur, alienation feels like play, play takes on characteristics of work. The Fordist separation between the Eros (pleasure) associated with free time and the pain associated with work time (Marcuse 1955) is sublated, in play labour time (like on commercial social media) surplus value generation appears to be pleasure-like, but serves the logic of private ownership of capital. In play labour, joy and play become toil and work, and toil and work appear to be joy and play. Leisure time becomes work time and work time leisure time.

One can conduct some easy empirical tests that show that commercial social media do not constitute a public sphere and a participatory web:

the top results for the search keyword "political news" on Google are mainly corporate media channels; the most popular Facebook groups are related to games, entertainment, and pop stars; the most viewed videos of all time on YouTube are music videos, for which the rights are owned by global multimedia corporations; the top trends on Twitter are much more related to sports and entertainment than to politics; and most blogs are covering mundane everyday activities, not politics. Social media are mainly commercial and mundane spaces—politics is the exception from the rule. Certainly those moments, where social media become tools that support politics, are interesting, but commercial social media's democratic and political potentials should not be overestimated. Not technologies, but people living under certain social conditions and power relations make rebellions and revolutions.

But what about the potential for an alternative Internet? Wikipedia advances the common character of knowledge, co-operative knowledge production, voluntary work with a common purpose, and is a non-profit organisation. It is facing the contradiction that only highly educated people with enough free time contribute and that its knowledge can be commodified and sold, which shows the difficulties and contradictions of trying to operate based on alternative principles within a stratified world. WikiLeaks is an alternative whistleblowing medium that provides knowledge to the public that shall make power transparent. It is mainly a government watchdog that has a rather liberal self-understanding and lacks focus on corporate crime and corporate irresponsibility (Fuchs 2011b). Anonymous is a complex and dynamic form of hacktivism that has a strong liberal bias (it stresses freedom of speech and assembly and not so much inequality) that is to a certain extent contradicted by socialist orientations that supported the Occupy movement, not only because it wants to advance freedom of assembly and speech, but also because it wants to show solidarity with people that protest against socio-economic inequality. Both WikiLeaks and Anonymous affirm liberal values, but also constitute an immanent critique of these values by showing how liberal institutions violate the liberal values of the system that they represent. Anonymous and WikiLeaks see themselves as today's enlightenment, but are in fact the immanent dialectic of the contemporary enlightenment. They should be advocates of socialist enlightenment, which means that they have the potential to act as socialist movements.

The Occupy movement is a new socialist movement because it fights against socio-economic inequality in the world and perceives capitalism as the source of this inequality. It is connected to the new capitalist crisis and makes use of social media for co-ordinating occupations and communicating to the public. On the one hand it employs corporate social media (such as Facebook, Twitter and Tumblr), which entails the risk of censorship and police surveillance. Given that they are part of the 1 per cent, why should social media capitalists like Mark Zuckerberg, Dick Costolo and

Jack Dorsey be friends of the Occupy movement? The Occupy movement's use of corporate social media furthermore stands in the context of capital accumulation with the help of targeted advertising, which helps the 1 per cent to get richer by exploiting the digital labour of the 99 per cent. But the Occupy movement has also advanced the creation and growth of new alternative social media, such as the social networking sites occupii.org and N-1, as well as alternative online news sites, such as the Occupy News Network, the Occupied Times, the Occupied Wall Street Journal, occupy. com or Occupied Stories.

2.6   CONCLUSION: THE NEED FOR ALTERNATIVES AND STRUGGLES

Marxist Studies of the media, the Internet, and technology are not just interested in analysing how class structures, power structures, and domination are embedded into and manifested on the Internet, they are also interested in helping to create an alternative, just and participatory world and in creating and supporting media that participate in struggles for such a society.

Communism is "not a state of affairs which is to be established, an ideal to which reality [will] have to adjust itself", but rather "the real movement which abolishes the present state of things" (Marx and Engels 1844, 57). Communism needs spaces for materialising itself as movement. The contemporary names of these spaces for the movement of communism are not Facebook, YouTube or Twitter, but rather Tahrir Square, Syntagma Square, Puerta del Sol, Plaça Catalunya, or Zuccotti Park.

Raymond Williams (1983) stressed the connection of commons—communism—communication. To communicate means to make something "common to many" (Williams 1983, 72). Communication is part of the commons of society.

Denying humans to communicate is like denying them to breathe fresh air; it undermines the conditions of their survival. Therefore the communicative commons of society should be available for free (without payment or other access requirements) for all and should not be privately owned or controlled by a class.

The commons of society are needed for all humans to exist. They involve communication, nature, welfare, health care, education, knowledge, arts and culture, food, and housing. Basing the commons on the logic of markets, commodities, competition, exchange and profit results in fundamental inequalities of access to the commons.

For strengthening the communication commons, we need commons-based media and a commons-based Internet in a commons-based participatory society. Commons-based media have common access for all and common ownership, they are common spaces of communication, common spaces for the creation of shared meanings and knowledge, common spaces of co-operation, common spaces for political debate, common spaces for co-forming collective values and identities, and common spaces for struggles against the colonisation and commodification of the world.

Another Internet is possible. Another Internet is needed. Another society is possible. Another society is needed. Both require another communism. Another communism is possible.

NOTES

1. "About Us," Occupy Wall Street, accessed May 11, 2012, http://occupywallst. org/about/.
2. "Pew Research Poll Database" Pew Research Center, accessed May 11, 2012, http://www.pewresearch.org.
3. Ibid.
4. TEDTalks, *Wael Ghonim: Inside the Egyptian revolution*, March 5, 2011, accessed accessed July 23, 2013, http://www.youtube.com/watch?v= SWvJxasiSZ8.
5. The Daily Dish, "The Revolution Will Be Twittered," June 13, 2009, accessed accessed July 23, 2013, http://www.theatlantic.com/daily-dish/ archive/2009/06/the-revolution-will-be-twittered/200478/.
6. "Roll up and loot: Rioting thugs use Twitter to boost their numbers in thieving store raids," *The Sun*, August 8, 2011; "How technology fuelled Britain's first 21st century riot," *The Telegraph*, August 8, 2011; For an analysis of social media in the UK riots, see Fuchs 2012d.
7. "Ultras.ws Forum,", accessed accessed July 23, 2013, http://www.ultras.ws/ umfrage-juden-jena-rufe-und-die-strafe-t4414.html.
8. Translation from German: "Wie passen 30 Juden in einen Trabi? 2 Vorne, 3 Hinten und der Rest im Aschenbecher. Ich vergaß man macht keine Judenwitze Aber Wehrmacht denn auch so etwas?" (http://www.ultras.ws/ viewtopic.php?t=9436&start=104&postdays=0&postorder=asc&highlight).

REFERENCES

Adorno, Theodor W. 2005. "Prologue to television." In *Critical models*, 49–57. New York: Columbia University Press.
———. 2000. *Introduction to sociology*. Cambridge, UK: Polity.
———. 1977. *Kulturkritik und Gesellschaft II*. Frankfurt am Main: Suhrkamp.
———. 1968/2003. "Late capitalism or industrial society? The fundamental question of the present structure of society." In *Can one live after Auschwitz?*, edited by Rolf Tiedemann, 111–125. Stanford, CA: Stanford University Press.
Castells, Manuel. 2009. *Communication power*. Oxford: Oxford University Press.
———. 2012. *Networks of outrage and hope. Social movements in the Internet age*. Cambridge: Polity Press.
Cleaver, Harry. 1992. "The inversion of class perspective in Marxian Theory. From valorisation to self-valorisation." In *Open Marxism. Vol. 2*, edited by Werner Bonefeld, Richard Gunn, and Kosmos Psychopedis, 106–144. London: Pluto.
Dyer-Witheford, Nick. 2010. "Digital labour, species being and the global worker." *Ephemera* 10 (3/4): 484–503.

Fuchs, Christian. 2008. *Internet and society. Social theory in the information age.* New York: Routledge.

———. 2009. "Some reflections on Manuel Castells' book 'Communication Power'." *tripleC: Communication, Capitalism & Critique. Open Access Journal for a Global Sustainable Information Society* 7 (1): 94–108.

———. 2010. "Labor in informational capitalism and on the Internet." *The Information Society* 26 (3): 179–196.

———. 2011a. *Foundations of critical media and information studies.* London: Routledge.

———. 2011b. "The political economy of WikiLeaks: Power 2.0? Surveillance 2.0? Criticism 2.0? Alternative media 2.0?" *Global Media Journal—Australian Edition* 5 (1).

———. 2012a. "Capitalism or information society? The fundamental question of the present structure of society." *European Journal of Social Theory.* First published November 20, 2012, doi:10.1177/1368431012461432.

———. 2012b. "Dallas Smythe Today—The Audience Commodity, the Digital Labour Debate, Marxist Political Economy and Critical Theory. Prolegomena to a Digital Labour Theory of Value." *tripleC: Communication, Capitalism & Critique. Open Access Journal for a Global Sustainable Information Society* 10 (2): 692–740.

———. 2012c. "New Marxian Times! Reflections on the 4th ICTs and Society Conference 'Critique, Democracy and Philosophy in 21st Century Information Society. Towards Critical Theories of Social Media'." *tripleC: Communication, Capitalism & Critique. Open Access Journal for a Global Sustainable Information Society* 10 (1): 114–121.

———. 2012d. "Social media, riots, and revolutions." *Capital & Class* 36 (3): 383–391.

———. 2012e. "Some reflections on Manuel Castells' book 'Networks of outrage and hope. Social movements in the Internet age'." *tripleC: Communication, Capitalism & Critique. Open Access Journal for a Global Sustainable Information Society* 10 (2): 775–797.

———. 2014. *Social media: A critical introduction.* London: Sage.

Fuchs, Christian, and Vincent Mosco. 2012. "Introduction: Marx is back—The importance of Marxist theory and research for Critical Communication Studies today." *tripleC: Communication, Capitalism & Critique. Open Access Journal for a Global Sustainable Information Society* 10 (2): 127–140.

Grossberg, Lawrence. 1995. Cultural Studies vs. Political Economy: Is anybody else bored with this debate? *Critical Studies in Mass Communication* 12 (1): 72–81.

Hall, Stuart. 1986. The problem of ideology—Marxism without guarantees. *Journal of Communication Inquiry* 10 (2): 28–44.

Hall, Stuart. 1988. The toad in the garden. Thatcherism among the theorists. In *Marxism and the intepretation of culture*, ed. Cary Nelson and Lawrence Grossberg, 35–73. Urbana, IL: University of Illinois Press.

Hardt, Michael, and Antonio Negri. 2004. *Multitude.* New York: Penguin,

Horkheimer, Max. 1947. *Eclipse of reason.* New York: Continuum.

———. 2002. *Critical theory.* New York: Continuum.

Jenkins, Henry. 2008. *Convergence culture.* New York: New York University Press.

Jhally, Sut. 1987. *The Codes of advertising.* New York: Routledge.

Lipietz, Alain. 1995. "The post-fordist world. Labour relations, international hierarchy and global ecology." *Review of International Political Economy* 4 (1): 1–41.

Lukács, Georg. 1923/1972. *History and class consciousness.* Cambridge, MA: MIT Press.

Marcuse, Herbert. 1955. *Eros and civilization*. Boston, MA: Beacon Press.
———. 1964. *One-dimensional man*. New York: Routledge.
Marx, Karl. 1867. *Capital: critique of the political economy*. Volume 1. London: Penguin.
Marx, Karl and Friedrich Engels. 1844. *The German ideology*. Amherst, NY: Prometheus Books.
Mosco, Vincent. 2004. *The digital sublime*. Cambridge, MA: MIT Press.
———. 2009. *The political economy of communication*. Second edition. London: SAGE.
Murdock, Graham, and Peter Golding. 2005. "Culture, communications and political economy." In *Mass media and society*, edited by James Curran and Michael Gurevitch, 60–83. London: Hodder.
Smythe, Dallas W. 1977. "Communications: blindspot of Western Marxism." *Canadian Journal of Political and Social Theory* 1 (3): 1–27.
———. 1981. *Dependency road*. Norwood, NJ: Ablex.
———. 1994. *Counterclockwise*. Boulder, CO: Westview Press.
Wiggershaus, Rolf. 1995. *The Frankfurt School. Its history, theories, and political significance*. Cambridge, MA: MIT Press.
Williams, Raymond. 1983. *Keywords*. New York: Oxford University Press.

3 Potentials and Risks for Creating a Global Sustainable Information Society

Wolfgang Hofkirchner

3.1 INTRODUCTION

Spontaneously ever newer communities of action germinate. One example is the multifold "Occupy" movements around the world. All of them face the following challenge: They share noble aims, but their common fate seems to be exhaustion and expiration. Thus the question is: Can these communities be supported by means of Information and Communication Technologies (ICTs)in order to have a lasting positive impact on society?

Currently in the IT sector vast numbers of engineers concentrate on designing things we do not need, whereas things we would need are not designed. The inertia of the economic system creates an obstacle to building meaningful technologies. What a meaningful technology is, derives from the need for societal change. A Global Sustainable Information Society (GSIS) is the overall framework of conditions promising a future without the danger of anthropogenic breakdown. A GSIS is a society, in which information is used to safeguard sustainable development on a global scale.

Informatisation—the spread of ICTs, computers and the Internet—has to be reshaped as a means for informationalisation. This involves raising the problem-solving capacity of world society to a degree of collective intentionality, to a level of collective intelligence and to an intensity of collective action that successfully tackles the problems that arise from society's own development. Informationalisation helps to establish computer-supported communities of action in contrast to mere communities of practice or communities of interest. Communities of action can share common goals for the development of world civilisation and can act collectively to alleviate global challenges.

This chapter is a theoretical discussion and a contribution to fundamental issues dealt with in the field of ICTs and society. It is theoretical in character and will therefore not refer to concrete empirical studies or include concrete design suggestions.

3.2 THE GREAT BIFURCATION

We are living in the age of global challenges. Since the second half of the last century the dominant way of using technological, environmental and human resources has been turning out to be increasingly incompatible with a peaceful and harmonious future of societies. There are forceful impediments on our way to establish sustainable international as well as intra-national relations (which exclude the use of military violence and other technological means that are detrimental to a good life), to establish ecologically sustainable relations to nature (which excludes the overuse of resources and their abuse as sinks for harmful waste), and to establish sustainable relations amongst humans in the cultural, political and socio-economic context (which includes all of the producers and users in a fair production and usage of whatever is commonly produced). If we fail to establish these relations, the humane development of civilisation and even the survival of humankind is at stake.

3.2.1 CHALLENGE IN COMPLEXITY

Global challenges are global because they affect humanity as a whole and because it is only humanity as a whole that can treat them successfully. Complex thinking means to recognise that real-world systems are built up by two levels at least. The higher level is not the mere aggregation of agents located on the lower level (which increases the degree of complexity) but a leap in quality that is characteristic of rather stable relations that are the outcome of the interaction of agents by a process of bottom-up self-organisation. The higher level, in turn, qua organisational relations that channel the interaction on the lower level constrains and enables agency by a top-down process inherent in self-organisation (which simplifies the degree of complexity).

According to this definition, global challenges are complex problems. "Humanity as a whole" means an entity that has at least two levels: a higher level on which sustainable relations reside that sustain the whole; and a lower level consisting of diverse social agents ranging from transnational corporations, other supranational institutions and NGOs, to nation states, to individual civil society members that all form part of humanity.

However, humanity as a whole does not yet exist. It is in statu nascendi. A multitude of particular societies, having spread over the globe and having populated the entire habitable biosphere, have been developing interdependencies and are on the point of recognising the fact that they have to take into account each other, because effects external to one society turn out to become internal for other societies. The environment of a society is made up of all the other societies. This situation calls for a change. The principles of societal development that have been effective so far, cannot any longer be effective without resulting in serious disadvantages to the maintenance of society. Rules for governance need to be established on a higher level, and such a change cannot be the unilateral action of a sole system but necessitates the joint operation of all affected systems. It is a task that exceeds the problem solving capacity of any currently existing system.

3.2.2   The Nascent Global Sustainable Information Society

We are witnesses, if not agents, of change never seen before—of a possible and morally necessary meta-system transition, in which a supra-system is on the point of emerging. This supra-system would be a real world society which turns the current systems into its components. As this new supra-system would have the task to alleviate and master the global challenges by the higher complex order its organisation would represent, it would bear some essential features. Among those features are three worth stressing:

1. Globality: It would exist on a planetary scale, that is, it would be global.
2. Sustainable: It would, by establishing its organisational relations, be capable of acting upon the dangers of anthropogenic breakdown, that is, it would be sustainable.
3. Information: It would, by means of ICTs, be capacitated to create requisite wisdom, knowledge, data, that is, it would be informational.

Being global implies being sustainable implies being informational. Informationality means there is information needed for sustainability; sustainability means there are sustainable relations needed for globality. Thus a societal system that meets these criteria can be called a Global Sustainable Information Society (GSIS) (Hofkirchner 2011). It is a framework of conditions that must be fulfilled for society to survive, rather than a detailed blueprint. It is a vision that can guide social actors, if they are willing and ready to contribute to the continuation of human life on earth that is worth living.

The alternative to an integrative GSIS is the increase in heterogeneity, fragmentation and decoherence—the falling apart of social systems, the falling back into barbarism, if not the fall of humanity at all. The evolution of human social systems has reached a critical point. The evolutionary process has paved the way for an organisation of higher order of social systems such that they are enabled to catch up with the complexity that ensues from their own development. On the other hand, human actors might fail to face up to that complex challenge. That's the Great Bifurcation.

3.3   THE COMMONS

Self-organising systems exist, because their elements produce synergy effects that hold these elements together. This is advantageous for these elements. The systems obtain in the course of evolution ever-increasing complexity and reinforce co-operative solutions in the long run (Corning 2003). Actually, systems may even be defined as collections of elements that interact in such a way that relations emerge because synergy effects dominate their interaction (Hofkirchner 2013a, 105). Synergy effects are emergent as well as dominant properties of systems. The elements participate in the generation as well as in the utilisation of these effects.

3.3.1 The Enclosure of the Commons

In human social systems (which are a variety of self-organising systems) human social agents (which are individual or collective social actors) produce and use synergy effects that are different material goods or different kinds of what is deemed an ideational good. Social systems form a multiplex which makes up a societal system. The same social actor participates in different social systems at the same time. Social systems can be ordered along a specification hierarchy (Hofkirchner et al. 2007):

1. Techno-eco-social systems form the basis of that hierarchy. In these systems, actors produce scientific-technological innovations that enhance human self-actuation.
2. Eco-social systems, in which actors produce adaptations to or of the natural environment that supports human self-preservation.
3. Social systems, in the narrow sense, include products that make sense and are provided for human self-actualisation. Basically, they have three varieties:
   a) In economic systems, it is resources that are produced to be allocated for the sake of self-realisation.
   b) In political systems, it is decisions that are produced to regulate self-determination.
   c) In cultural systems (the topmost level system), it is rules that are produced to define self-expression.

The more one moves to a higher level system, the more ideational and the less material the shared good is. Every material good is a materialisation of an ideational good. As every ideational good exists in the form of a relation—namely, it connects actors by connecting them to (an idea they share about) the social system—every good is a relational good (Donati 2010), regardless of whether it is more or less embodied in matter.

In each system the good is a common product. As an emergent entity, it is commonly produced and commonly used. It is produced through a common action although the actors can contribute to the common action in different ways. And although the use of the good by the actors might differ, it is, in principle, provided for common use. The good is produced by a co-operation of actors for the usage of actors who long for it, who demand it and who need it. So one can argue that every good is a common good that emerges from the relations of humans. For the same reason, it can be classified as a commons.

The commonness of the common good or the commons is an emergent feature that is a characteristic of the macro-level relations of the system in question. However, historically the commons were enclosed—a terminology that goes back to Karl Marx's *Capital. Volume 1* where he writes about the primitive accumulation (Marx 1890/1972). Competition prevailed over co-operation and domination prevailed in societal formations, in which actors could pursue their self-centred aims at the cost of the aims of other actors.

3.3.2   The Current Crises

"From each according to their ability, to each according to their need" is often quoted to be the principle of a humane organisation of production and usage of the commons. The revolutionary labour movement focused on the contradiction between the productive forces and the relations of production. The socialisation of the means of production as expropriation of the expropriators was seen as a precondition for the fulfilment of the principle.

The demise of the so-called societies of Real Socialism and the so-called victory of the free West was accompanied by an amplification of the global challenges, which was reflected by a shift in political campaigning. The New Political Thinking revolved around universal human values instead of allegedly restricted class struggle slogans. For Slavoj Žižek, however, the global challenges of today are nothing else than enclosures of commons. He lists as what should belong to all of us and what is endangered by increasing trends of privatisation (Krishnakumar 2010):

1. the field of the external nature (ecology),
2. the field of our inner nature regarding biogenetics,
3. the field of knowledge in intellectual property, and
4. the whole social field we should be included in.

On can interpret the idea of the enclosure of the commons as the common denominator of Karl Marx and Žižek. In line with the social systems specification given above, the commons can be specified as follows: on the level of the techno-eco-social system, the common good is science and technology; on the level of the eco-social system, it is the human nature and the natural environment; in social systems, it is the space of society as inclusive community, which is the field of resources in economy, the agora in polity, and the realm of values in culture.

The current crises are expressions of the progressive enclosure of all these commons. As a result, there are battles over reclaiming the commons on each level:

1. On the science and technology battlefield, there is a struggle for science as a "communist", universal, disinterested and organised sceptical endeavour, as Robert K. Merton put it in "The normative structure of science" (Merton 1942/1973, 267–278), as well as a struggle for

technology assessment and for designing meaningful technologies that questions research and development funded by the military-industrial-complex.

2. On the battlefield of the external and internal nature, there is a struggle for a cautious treatment of the bio-physical bases of human life that is directed against their extensive and intensive colonisation.

3. On the battlefield of sociality at large, there is a struggle for inclusion and against exclusion, which differentiates into three struggles:
   a) On the resources battlefield, there is a struggle for unalienated working conditions and a fair share for all that is directed against the erosion of the labour force, against the pressure exerted by financial capital, against corruption, against the rich-get-richer mechanisms inherent in capitalist economies, etc.
   b) On the agora battlefield, there is a struggle for participatory democracy that opposes right-wing, technocratic or populist authoritarian rule.
   c) On the battlefield of the community of values, there is a struggle for inclusive definitions of selves that is based on the principle of unity through diversity and challenges parochial ways of living, nationalism and fundamentalist ideologies.

It is not difficult to understand that the enclosures of the commons have aggravated to such a degree that all of them morphed into global challenges. As long as social systems could externalise the negative effects, their self-organisation was compatible with the enclosure of the commons. But being interconnected as they are, the enclosure of the commons is not tenable any more.

3.4 THE DIALECTICS OF INFORMATISATION

Self-organising systems have a certain ability to re-organise themselves when there are external pressures. In order to establish new organisational relations, old ones have to be deconstructed. So in times of crises, elements and subsystems decouple from each other, thus marking a period of disintegration. In this phase of the development of systems, weak links between distant nodes of the network in a system can provide a minimum stability and creative elements can provide novel options for the future. When these creative elements bring about new strong ties, they usher in another phase—the phase of re-integration, re-organisation and re-ontologisation of the whole system (Csermely 2009).

3.4.1 Informationalisation in the Context of Transformations

In human social systems, this re-organisation is mediated by human actors' conscious interventions. Consciousness is the special form that information processes assume in human systems. Human collective intelligence is a specific form of consciousness. The global challenges—disparities in the development of the relations amongst humans, between humans and nature, and between humans and technology—can be viewed as expressions of a human deficiency, i.e. an incapability to control and regulate the systems in question by information. The problems are problems in controlling and regulating society, the environment and technology in such a way as to ensure the maintenance of the systems and their functions critical for the survival of humanity (Hofkirchner 1995). They can be interpreted "as frictions in the functioning of the information generation of those systems that make up world society" (Hofkirchner 2000, translation from Vietnamese).

Thus, information proves the only remedy to the global problems, given the malfunctions in society, the environment and technology that continue to aggravate the global challenges and to create obstacles to keeping society as a whole on a stable, steady path of development. Information is what is required to alleviate and reduce the frictions in the functioning of the systems that make up humanity—from the individual to ethnicities to nations to world society, from economy to polity to culture, from society to ecology to technology, from the social realm to the biotic realm to the physical realm. Information is what is required to steer society and to re-organise humanity onto a higher level of organisation.

Thus, the continued existence of humanity may well be impossible without conscious and cautious interventions in its own development processes. This includes all spheres of intervention. Conscious intervention can optimise human self-organisation as well as self-organisation in other systems in which it intervenes and reduce frictions. This intervention is informational in nature, oriented toward relinking a world falling apart due to processes of heterogenisation, fragmentation and disintegration. This intervention might be in accord with the self-organisation capacities of the systems or might be dissonant, tending to disable their self-organisation capacities. In the first case, frictions will be decreased or, at least, not increased, whereas in the second case such frictions are not decreased, eventually running the risk of damaging the system. The aim is to regain the steering capability at least to the extent that a breakdown is avoided. This can be achieved by keeping the frictions in, among and in between the social, natural and artificial subsystems of the emerging world society below the threshold of causing a breakdown. This is the informational task of a GSIS.

Collective intelligence in the human sphere is then not only the result of less frictions in social terms but is, in turn, the starting point for reducing social and other frictions, a necessary step for a sustainable future of the supra-system and its component systems. The human race has all the capabilities to be the first species on earth to master the challenges that accrue from its own development. Society has this possibility because the agents it is made up of are endowed with reflexivity that enables them, in principle, to reflect on the causes for the rising complexity and the flexibly catch up with it (Hofkirchner 2013b):

1. *Cognition* is able to make the whole system the object of reflection and to extend the perspective from focusing on the immediate social system the agent is an element of to including the emerging world society. Every agent can reflect the whole they are possibly becoming part of.
2. *Communication* is able to deliberate upon the roles and functions of elements in the whole system and to take the perspective of other agents in the whole. Agents can reach an understanding by distancing themselves from their immediate immersion into their proximate social systems, by relativising their membership in these relations, and by adopting the perspective of world society.
3. *Co-operation* is able to set and seek common goals for the whole system and to share intentionality when anticipating world society. Every agent can reach a consensus with other agents on the outline of the new rules that are to structure the possible new whole and necessitate modification of the rules currently governing the structure of the component systems.

3.4.2 Antagonisms of Informatisation

The information revolution still going on turns out to provide new potentials for reducing frictions. Luciano Floridi (2007, 61) expounds that the "infosphere" will ultimately, by connecting systems to it one by one, turn into a "frictionless" cyberspace. Informationalisation provides the requirements for the creation of a GSIS. If informationalisation can be defined as the process of raising the problem-solving capacity to a level of collective intelligence that enables successfully tackling the problems arising from the social systems' and their component systems' own development, then informatisation as the diffusion of ICTs can be defined as a means in the context of informationalisation. Information/*Cognitive* technologies, *communication* technologies and technologies for *co-operation* all can support self-organisation processes and thus ease the frictions occurring in the systems they are applied to. ICTs inhere a potential for enhancing human collective intelligence that is required to cope with the global challenges by reducing imminent frictions. ICTs, however, can also be used to prolong exclusions and hinder the advent of a GSIS.

Informatisation can thus:

1. provide potentials for informationalisation, sustainabilisation and globalization in order to promote the advent of a GSIS, but also
2. quantitatively reinforce existing dislocations, or even
3. qualitatively span new dislocations.

Studies in the research field of ICTs and society provide empirical evidence for each of the conjectured tendencies. The potentials of informatisation for the good of society meet huge impediments and are instrumentalised for egotistic interests. Therefore the antagonisms on all the battlefields of the commons listed above are aggravated and transformed into antagonisms of the information society, as long as societal development is under capitalist rule:

1. There is an antagonism of the informed productivity of productive forces, on the one hand, and ICT-aided systems' vulnerability, on the other, that is inflicted upon the science and technology commons.
2. There is an antagonism of the informed reproductivity of work that reproduces the natural initial conditions needed for another cycle of production, on the one hand, and ICT-aided degradation, on the other, that is inflicted upon the commons of external as well as internal nature.
3. There is an antagonism of informed world netizenship, on the one hand, and the digital divide of several orders, on the other, that is inflicted upon the commons of sociality. This antagonism includes:
   a) an antagonism of unfettered information, on the one hand, and intellectual proprietarisation, commodification and commercialisation of information, on the other, that is inflicted upon the resource-commons of the economy;
   b) an antagonism of empowerment of all by information, on the one hand, and surveillance and information warfare, on the other, that is inflicted upon the agora- commons of politics; and
   c) an antagonism of wisdom through information, on the one hand, and media disinfotainment that hinders the development of global consciousness and global conscience, on the other, that is inflicted upon the value and lifestyle commons of culture.

3.5 CONCLUSION

ICTs, including social media, can have, and so far have had, ambiguous impacts on the social system they support: On the one hand there is a potential for reducing frictions in the functioning of social systems and their component systems that are biotic or physical in nature so that it is possible to sustain the continuation of nature and society. On the other hand, these systems can be and are—in the social world we live in—functionalised for purposes detrimental to reclaiming the commons. Thus they need to be designed deliberately in order to bring their potential to the fore, they need to be designed decidedly in service of the aim of assembling the GSIS. The inclusion of stakeholders in the genesis of technology can make the design process a participatory one and can ensure a discourse that will marginalise the exclusion of the affected.

Communities of action like the "Occupy" movements are examples of the use of ICTs for the reclaiming of the commons. At the same time as they are a realisation of the possibility to informationalise with informatised means, they demonstrate the need for the further design of ICTs so that they can better meet the demands of the network, including the design of social processes, because technology is socially embedded and a social system in itself.

REFERENCES

Corning, Peter. 2003. *Nature's magic. Synergy in evolution and the Fate of humankind*. Cambridge: Cambridge University Press.

Csermely, Péter. 2009. *Weak links. The universal key to the stability of networks and complex systems*. Berlin: Springer.

Donati, Pierpaolo. 2010. *Relational sociology. A new paradigm for the social sciences*. London: Routledge.

Floridi, Luciano. 2007. "A look into the future impact of ICTs on our lives." *The Information Society* 23 (1): 59–64.

Hofkirchner, Wolfgang. 1995. "'Information science'—an idea whose time has come." *Informatik Forum* 3: 99–106.

———. 2000. "Tin hoc va xa hoi [Informatics and Society, in Vietnamese]". In *Internet o Viet Nam va cac nuoc dang phat trien* [Internet in Viet Nam and other developing countries—Vietnamese], edited by Jörg Becker and Dang Ngoc Dinh, 73–84. Ha Noi, Viet Nam: Nha Xuat Ban Khoa Hoc Va Ky Thuat.

———. 2011. "Information and communication technologies for a good society." In *Information and communication technologies, society and human beings. Theory and framework*, edited by Darek M. Haftor and Anita Mirijamdotter, 434–443. Hershey, PA: Information Science Reference.

———. 2013a. *Emergent information. A Unified Theory of Information framework*. Singapore: World Scientific.

———. 2013b. "Self-organisation as the mechanism of development and evolution in social systems." In *Social morphogenesis*, edited by Margaret Archer. London: Springer.

Hofkirchner, Wolfgang, Christian Fuchs, and Bert Klauninger. 2007. "The dialectic of bottom-up and top-down emergence in social systems." *Systemica* 14 (1–6): 127–150.

Krishnakumar, R. 2010. "World according to Zizek." *Frontline* 27 (3). http://www.frontlineonnet.com/fl2703/stories/20100212270310400.htm.

Marx, Karl. 1890/1972. *Das Kapital. Kritik der politischen Ökonomie. Erster Band*. Berlin, DDR: Dietz Verlag.

Merton, Robert K. 1942/1973. *The sociology of science. Theoretical and empirical investigations*. Chicago, IL: University of Chicago Press.

4 Critical Studies of Contemporary Informational Capitalism
The Perspective of Emerging Scholars

*Sebastian Sevignani, Robert Prey,
Marisol Sandoval, Thomas Allmer,
Jernej A. Prodnik and Verena Kreilinger*

4.1 INTRODUCTION

As six young scholars from Europe and North America, we first met each other as a group of PhD students at a conference in Uppsala, Sweden, called "Critique, Democracy, and Philosophy in 21st Century Information Society. Towards Critical Theories of Social Media" (see http://www.icts-and-society.net/events/uppsala2012/). For us it was a new and inspiring experience to have discussions with other emerging critical scholars in an international context and to discover that co-operation through joint projects can be an appropriate answer to feelings of isolation and marginalisation.

The kind of criticism which unites us and that we want to promote does not contend itself with merely an academic critique of categories, but instead focuses on the material critique of society. We thus agree with Adorno who, in his confrontation with Popper (known as the Positivism Dispute in German sociology), argued that "the critical path is not merely formal but also material. If its concepts are to be true, critical sociology is, according to its own idea, necessarily also a critique of society" (Adorno 1962/1976, 114). This orientation situates our approach within a tradition of Marxian-inspired thinking.

Karl Marx's notion of critique is essentially humanist, it is based on the insight that "man is the highest essence for man", and it leads to the "categoric imperative to overthrow all relations in which man is a debased, enslaved, abandoned, despicable essence" (Marx 1844/1975a, 182). Marxist critique is directed against all forms of domination and oppression, which should not only be theoretically criticised but practically abolished. Influenced by Marx's approach, Theodor W. Adorno, Herbert Marcuse and Max Horkheimer made an important contribution to further conceptualizing this notion of critique: Critical thinking is characterised by dialectical reasoning that rejects one-dimensional logic and conceives of social phenomena as complex and dynamic. It considers social relations that lie behind mere appearances and analyses social phenomena in the context of societal totality. It is characterised by a humanist orientation, an interest in human emancipation and the desire to create a society without domination and oppression in which all human beings can live a self-determined life. It perceives social structures and phenomena as historically specific results of human practice and therefore as changeable (Marcuse 1937/1989; Horkheimer 1937/2002; Adorno 1962/1976).

This chapter is a first outcome of our cooperation and reflects our subjective experiences and basic views as emerging scholars. In what follows, we first want to point to the value and the importance of a critical approach to informational capitalism (Section 4.2.). We then identify principal challenges for critical thinking in today's higher education sector in Section 4.3. and in Section 4.4. we describe struggles against this situation and point to prospects that arise therein.

4.2   WHY IS CRITICAL THINKING IMPORTANT TODAY?

We live in a period of communicative and informational abundance. Never has it been easier to connect with friends, family or colleagues half a world away. Never has it been easier to find and participate in communities of affinity. It is perhaps the very richness and conveniences of our online lives however that obscures our simultaneous embeddedness in asymmetrical infrastructures of control and exploitative economies of accumulation.

But what do we mean by 'exploitation' in such a world? Exploitation presupposes that humans have to be alienated from the means of material and immaterial production by other humans. Exploitation is then, under capitalism, the legitimate appropriation of the fruits of human activities at the expense of their genuine producers (Marx 1867/1976, 729f). Informational capitalism still depends on the exploitation of double-free labourers who are free from personal dependence, but also free in terms of lacking the means of life production and therefore forced to sell their labour power (Marx 1867/1976, 270–272). The consequence of exploitation is ever widening social inequality.[1] Not only have asymmetries with the rise of the Internet remained, they have often been exacerbated and the gap between *the haves and have-nots* has subsequently widened (Bellamy Foster and McChesney 2011).

Informational capitalism's technological materials and infrastructure—natural resources like silicon, computer hardware, software and so on—are predominantly produced in traditional "sweat and blood" exploitative conditions in developing countries such as China and India as well as in Africa. Without these forms of labour no genuine knowledge work could exist. Frequently this fact is neglected by those who speak of today's knowledge economy. However we are starkly reminded of this when the biggest IT suppliers recurrently gain public attention and contempt for super-exploiting their employees,[2] or when we hear of, or experience ourselves, precarious working conditions in the media, education and service sectors. Nick Dyer-Witheford (2001) therefore suggests an integrative focus on "material", "immiserate", and "immaterial" labour and their exploitation by capital on a global scale.

These are clearly phenomenologically distinct forms of exploitation, but the point is that capital has retained traditional forms of exploitation while finding new ways to valorise knowledge and information. From supermarket loyalty programs to Facebook posts we increasingly leave behind digital footprints that are packaged and sold as commodities, and used to further rationalise production. Indeed, the basic principle of web 2.0 is the massive provision and storage of personal(ly) (identifiable) data that can be systematically evaluated, marketed and used for targeted advertising. With the help of legal instruments such as privacy policies, Facebook, for example, has the right to store, analyse, and sell personal data of their users to third parties for targeted advertising in order to accumulate profit.[3]

These developments necessitate re-evaluation of some of the most central debates within media and communication studies: for instance, the cultural studies vs. political economy battles of the 1990s (Grossberg 1995; Garnham 1995). In the early years of the twenty-first century, just as the smoke had settled on this infamous debate, the emergence of interactive "web 2.0" and participatory "new media" appeared at first glance to signal that proponents of "the active audience" had won the day. In line with popular discourse, academic scholarship became almost giddy in its celebration of the libratory, creative, and participatory dimensions of the digital transformation, with reception and consequently consumption assuming pole position within the communicative process.

In recent years this celebration has been interrupted by the realisation that perhaps there was another side to this story. Data mining through "interactive" practices associated with "web 2.0" has first and foremost caused widespread concern about personal privacy. However, several scholars (Andrejevic 2007; Fuchs 2012) have argued that interactivity should not only be understood through the "invasion of privacy" perspective. As Mark Andrejevic (2011, 615) puts it "the goal is to craft an interactive mediascape that triples as entertainment, advertising and probe." Indeed, the active audience is also active for capital. Intensive monitoring and surveillance means that consumption, whatever else it may also be, is at its core about production.

Within critical scholarship these new means of accumulation have been theorised with the help of concepts that, while often dating back to the pre-Internet period, have a renewed relevance today. Examples include theoretical concepts such as the general intellect (Marx 1939/1973), the exploitation of the commons (De Angelis 2007; Linebaugh 2008; Hardt and Negri 2009), the ongoing primitive accumulation of capital (Harvey 2003; Perelman 2000), the "housewifezation" of labour (Mies et al. 1988), the social factory (Tronti 1972; Negri 1984), immaterial labour

(Lazzarato1996; Negri 1992), the cybertariat (Huws 2003), audience commodity (Smythe 1977; Jhally and Livant 1986), and the panopticon (Foucault 1977), to name only a few.

One shouldn't get the impression that these new means of accumulation emerge uncontested. They certainly do not. Contradictions and antagonisms between the haves and the have-nots shape contemporary society. Such areas of contradiction and struggle in the media and communication system include: the enforcement of intellectual property rights vs. the possibility of collective knowledge resources and a shared and accessible culture; the promotion of destructive and conformist ideologies through commercial media vs. media that act as critical public watchdogs; environmental destruction through short-lived and toxic IT products that end up as dangerous eWaste vs. the prospect of sustainable ICTs; exploited and precarious labour as opposed to self-determined knowledge work.

Therefore struggles and contradictions are fought on behalf of (new) media but (new) media are also themselves embattled. The Internet is able to support both the commons and the commodification of the commons. New media are tools for exerting power, domination, and counter-power. Based on a Marxian dialectical perspective it is possible to grasp these contradictions that arise between the emancipatory potentials of new media, which entail a logic of the commons, and processes of commodification and enclosure that capture the commons and integrate them into the logic of capital.

Critical and Marxian-inspired media and information studies strive for the development of theoretical and empirical research methods in order to focus on the analysis of media, information, and communication in the context of asymmetrical power relations, resource control, and social struggles between the "Gesamtarbeiter" (collective worker) and capital. Critical media and communication studies want to overcome domination, exploitation, alienation, and the commodification of the commons in order to establish political processes and social transformations towards a participatory, democratic, and commons-based information society.

One of the main characteristics of critical political economy is praxis, through which this approach tries to transform the actually-existing social structures and processes, thus achieving the aforementioned goals. It therefore attempts to forego the usual dichotomy between theory and political practice. A radical interpretation of the world, after all, does not yet necessarily lead to actual social changes. Praxis was an important element of several philosophies, including those of Aristotle and Plato, but regained its importance with Marx and some Marxist interpretations in the twentieth century (most noticeably Gramsci and the Yugoslav "Praxis School"). The nucleus of this approach was perhaps most succinctly presented in the eleventh *Thesis on Feuerbach*, where Marx (1845/1976, 5) famously wrote that "philosophers have hitherto only interpreted the world in various ways; the point is to change it". Critical thinking both in and outside academia can however lead to actual social changes if it breaks into wider society and materialises itself in social struggles. As Marx (1844/1975a, 182, 187) forcefully pointed out:

> The weapon of criticism cannot, of course, replace criticism by weapons, material force must be overthrown by material force; but theory also becomes a material force as soon as it has gripped the masses. Theory is capable of gripping the masses as soon as it demonstrates *ad hominem*, and it demonstrates *ad hominem* as soon as it becomes radical. To be radical is to grasp the root of the matter. But for man the root is man himself. [. . .] As philosophy finds its *material* weapons in the proletariat, so the proletariat finds its *spiritual* weapons in philosophy.

4.3   CHALLENGES FOR CRITICAL SCHOLARS

As young scholars in the field of media and communication studies we are witnessing the unfolding of a contradiction between the importance and explanatory value of critical, Marxian-inspired research on the one hand, and the reduction of spaces for critical thinking within academia on the other hand. In what follows we would like to reflect on this tension and refer to our own experiences in struggling against the neoliberal orientation of universities. Supporting these struggles means supporting the need for spaces for future generations of scholars in media and communication studies to learn from Karl Marx as a theorist of contemporary informational capitalism.

Capitalism works to decouple reflection and action, brain and hand. Privileged scholars were traditionally set free in a double sense. They were free from economic pressure, free to pursue individual self-development but also relatively free from contact with those material processes that maintained social inequalities in a class-based society. Such privileged scholars are often ideologists as they are detached from material practices. Critical young scholars must be critical about the persistence of these conditions that separate theory from praxis, they should strive to learn from other forms of knowledge that do not follow the specific rules of academia, and they can't be satisfied with merely reaching a privileged position. They do not consider knowledge as a power-neutral value per se, instead they are concerned with how knowledge production and their own activity as intellectuals can contribute to abolishing societal power and structures of domination.

In the 1960s, when student protest movements joined other new social movements, the education-for-all demand was an attempt to erode the privileged social position of the few. In the following decades though, the critique of these privileges was simultaneously sublated and inverted within the neoliberal project of restructuring the educational sector. This neoliberal reform agenda is for instance manifest in the EU goal to become the most competitive knowledge-based economy in the world (the Lisbon Strategy). It also can be seen in the current focus on so-called "smart growth" (Europe 2020 strategy). Education and knowledge production is becoming completely subsumed under the goal of economic growth and capitalist profit orientation. The traditional idea of the privileged free-floating scholar, newer processes induced by neoliberalism, and post-fordist modes of production are all establishing the framework that critical scholars must deal with today.

At the same time we can observe budget cuts in the realm of public education throughout North America and in many EU member states. These states, on the one hand, explicitly call for private sector funding of research and education, which opens doors for corporations to more directly influence research questions and programmes. On the other hand, the principle of competition has been implemented in the educational sector. Far from a productive competition over the best ideas, this is instead a material competition that is oriented around quantitative measurability. It generates great pressure to publish academic outcomes in highly ranked journals, while marginalizing the critical analysis of society. Such changes in the mode of academic production were prompted by changed relations of production. A downsizing of democratic organisational structures within universities and other research institutions has been enacted. Decision-making structures have been personalised and reorganised from the top to the bottom. For instance, it is now extremely hard for critical scholars to build coalitions amongst themselves or with students when it comes to influencing appointments or study programmes.

Neoliberalism can be understood as the one-dimensional making of education. The privileged position of the scholar is eroded within this process. Educational labour, along with information, knowledge, and affective work, has become a crucial part of the post-fordist capitalist economy, collapsing former boundaries between "the brain" and "the hand" (Virno 2004). Knowledge production has tended to move from the superstructure to the base. This is a very similar process to what happened to (now fully industrialised) communicative and cultural production in the twentieth century. Raymond Williams (2005, chap. 2) famously observed three decades ago how the means of communication were being transformed into means of production (cf. Garnham 1979; Smythe 1981).

Similarly, pressures of the capitalist market and competition started to colonise the realm of knowledge production at the level of university education. Of course knowledge production and research was already (ab)used during the Cold War, when the United States lavishly financed research and development in communications technology through military investments, while also crucially influencing the shift toward the "information society" (H. Schiller 1969; D. Schiller 2007). However commodification in the realm of education is today even more all-encompassing, directly influencing the curricula of courses and study programmes.

The contemporary university is facing what can be called a "double crisis". The debut issue of the *EduFactory Journal* laid out this problem clearly: "On the one hand, this involves an acceleration of the crisis specific to the university, the inevitable result of its outdated disciplinary divisions and eroded epistemological status. On the other hand, it is the crisis of post-fordist conditions of labour and value, many of which are circuited through the university" (Edu-Factory Collective 2010, 4f). This situation is tremendously challenging.

The challenge is heightened by the normalisation of precarious jobs and temporary contracts in North American and European universities. The simple reality of a perpetually expendable labour force of PhD students, post-docs, and sessional instructors serves as the most effective disciplinary tool available to university administrators. It is difficult to expect young scholars to challenge dominant views when they do so without the security that tenure provides. For example, some of us tried to organise the non-professorial teaching and research staff as part of the Austrian student protests "unibrennt" in Salzburg that also fought for the provision of sustainable funding and against precarious working conditions in the education sector. However we were not successful. It was difficult to motivate university teachers to see similarities between their interests and the demands of students. The students' claims were seen by many teachers as potentially creating additional work that might prevent them from being successful in their struggle against precarity.

In this context we can see that teaching is being de-qualified and loaded onto precarious education workers. De-qualification implies a division between research and teaching, which has become ever more common. Generally, and unjustly, teaching does not count much when the career potential of young scholars is evaluated.

Besides the mentioned structural problems that critical young scholars are facing, they also remain dependent on existing spaces for their critical thinking. These spaces must actively be created by those critical scholars that have already gained resources, job security and reputation. In Germany and Austria there is currently no institutionalisation of Marxian-inspired critical theory within the field of communication, media and Internet studies. Although there is interest in critical theories among students and independent researchers, the fact is that two entire generations of German-speaking scholars do not engage with Marxist critical theory. On the contrary they support a hostile climate towards radical critical thinking by denouncing it as old-fashioned and outdated. They thereby completely neglect arguments for its pressing relevance, as presented in this volume. Emerging scholars from German-speaking countries are consequently forced to leave these regions and settle where better opportunities are provided or, alternatively, must focus on non-academic fields of activity, such as working for NGOs or political parties.

For critical young scholars it is particularly challenging to find a suitable way between the necessity to meet formal qualification requirements in order to get a job, and their desire to follow emancipatory goals that a critical analysis of society demands. For instance, to what extent is it meaningful to publish as much as possible instead of concentrating on real in-depth analysis? Or how meaningful is it to focus efforts on getting published in highly ranked commercial category A journals that are part of an exploitative knowledge industry, instead of giving full public access to one's work by publishing in alternative, non-commercial open-access journals? Critical young scholars must in these and other situations find a balance between adapting to a problematic educational and research system, and their will to transform this system.

4.4   STRUGGLES AND PROSPECTS FOR FOSTERING CRITICAL THINKING

In the previous section we tried to show how capitalism is increasingly encroaching upon research and teaching. Political economic pressures force the university to produce practically and technically exploitable knowledge. From a critical perspective the problem is not that scholarship is expected to be practically useful, but that it is expected to be practically useful for capital.

Of course, the university has never existed in isolation from society: societal developments have always shaped the university and the knowledge produced and taught at university has always had an impact on society. Marx stressed that above all, academic work necessarily is a social activity: "Even as I am active *scientifically*, etc.—an activity which I can seldom perform in direct community with others—I am *socially* active because I am active as a *man*. Not only is the material of my activity— such as the language in which the thinker is active—given to me as a social product, but my *own* existence *is* social activity; what I make from myself, I make of myself for society, conscious of myself as a social being" (1844/1975b, 298).

Rather than seeing the university as separated from society, critical scholarship wants to be connected to emancipatory political praxis. Marx emphasised that his work not only sought to theoretically criticise domination and oppression, but to abolish them. He argued that connected to political struggles "criticism is no passion of the head, it is the head of passion" (1844/1975a, 177).

As critical scholars we see it as our task to promote critical thinking and progressive change within academia and society in general. A first, and very defensive goal, is to keep alive the humanist idea that education is more than a business: it is a weapon for social emancipation. This may demand alliances with those scholars and political actors who bewail the fall of their privileged scholarly status.

Even if the dominant tendency today is the integration of the university into the logic of capital, there are still spaces in which critical thinking can arise and be fostered. The deterioration of work and study conditions at university might, for example, trigger critical reflection. In Section 4.3 we stressed that many young scholars are confronted with high teaching loads, which reduces their available time for reflection and research. However, teaching at the same time provides an opportunity to foster critical thinking. Not only scholars, but also students are experiencing pressures resulting from neoliberal education policy. Undergraduate students in many countries pay higher tuition rates every year while receiving fewer opportunities to actually learn from tenured professors. Most of them have little awareness of this reality until they are well into their degree. Those of us who have taught as sessional instructors have often been approached by students asking for reference letters for graduate school applications. When told that it would be better for them to ask a professor, they often reply that they don't know any professors.

While this is no doubt a sorry state of affairs, it also presents new opportunities for education. Instead of perpetuating the romantic image of the "life of the mind", we must seize the chance to connect the knowledge labour that we do to the jobs that many of our students will take upon graduation. For instance, many of our students have dreams of working in arts/culture/media sectors. In North America and Europe, it is impossible to even consider applying for such a job without having done one or more internships first. This is, for the most part, simply accepted as "paying one's dues". "This generation doesn't even look at it as exploitation" explains a member of Intern Labor Rights, a group that grew out of Occupy Wall Street:

> I don't know how a bunch of smart, highly educated, willing workers can walk into an office or onto a film set or into a gallery, contribute all that intelligence, energy, and enthusiasm to an organization [and its] bottom line, and then think they didn't have anything to contribute because they [haven't] already worked in the industry for five years [. . .] This whole idea that their contribution doesn't mean anything yet, has no value, they've completely internalized [it]. It's horrifying to watch. (Cohen et al. 2012)

The "creative class" has clearly learned how to capitalise on the passions, idealism and dreams of the generation behind them. As depressing as this may be, it once again points to the relevance and urgency of bringing Marx into the classroom. Encouraging students to talk about their individual experiences with internships is a perfect way to introduce a number of core Marxian concepts, such as value, ideology, exploitation, or "free labour".

Connecting to the experiences students are having while studying to get a degree is only one way to encourage critical thinking. It is also possible, and necessary, to try to connect to wider social struggles and protests. Today's students are often dismissed as politically apathetic and career-obsessed. However there are numerous examples around the world that demonstrate just how flimsy this generalisation is.

On October 22, 2009, a group of students squatted the assembly hall of the Academy of Fine Arts in Vienna in order to resist the restructuring of study programs according to the Bologna Declaration. This was the start of a wave of student protests in Austria that became known as the "unibrennt" movement and that continued throughout the fall of 2009. Between October 22 and October 29, lecture halls at the Universities of Vienna, Graz, Linz, Salzburg, Klagenfurt and Innsbruck were squatted. For several weeks, hundreds of students continued to occupy spaces and lecture halls at universities and used them for organising demonstrations, protest flash mobs, lectures, discussions and concerts as well as for reflecting on society, education and capitalism. The protests were directed against access restrictions to study programmes, tuition fees, the reduction of university education to professional training, undemocratic decision-making, the commodification of higher education and precarious working conditions at universities. On December 21, 2009, the police, by order of the vice-chancellor, cleared the largest squatted lecture hall at the University of Vienna.

As a moment of rupture the student protest was successful in initiating a public debate and critical reflection on the role of education in society. By occupying lecture halls, students not only created awareness about these issues, but furthermore re-appropriated parts of the university and created alternative spaces, characterised by democratic-decision making, critical thinking and debate. One important outcome of the protests at the University of Salzburg, for example, was that the university provided the necessary funds for a student-organised lecture series. Students from the University of Salzburg could attend the lecture series as part of their elective course modules. Throughout the 2010 summer term eleven invited speakers gave talks, which subsequently appeared in a collected volume (Sandoval et al. 2011). The lecture series inspired critical reflection about the role of the university in society, contemporary education policy as well as the role of student activism. A decisive question seemed to be how it would be possible to translate occasional protest waves into long term transformative movements that expanded spaces for critical thinking and critical scholarship.

At the University of Salzburg's department of communication studies, the struggle to strengthen the structural foundations for critical scholarship was in the end unsuccessful. In fact, the student protests coincided with the elimination of critical scholarship from the department. In fall 2009 a professor who was an exponent of a critical political economy approach retired and his chair was rededicated. At the same time the contract of another critically-minded professor was not extended and all members of his research group, who had temporary contracts, left the University of

Salzburg together with him. For critical young scholars the loss of these two professors ended all chances of receiving support or starting an academic career at the University of Salzburg. By fall 2010—one year after the student protests—critical Marxist thinking no longer existed in Salzburg's department of communication studies.

One limitation of the Austrian protest movement was that it failed to make connections beyond the university. Other student protests have been more successful in establishing alliances with wider social movements.

The Canadian province of Quebec saw one of the largest mass mobilisations of students over the first half of 2012. Dubbed "the Maple Spring", the uprising was stoked by opposition to the provincial government's proposal to raise tuition rates by CAD 325 per year over five years. When the government passed an emergency law that attempted to control the growing demonstrations Quebec's society joined forces with the students. Between 400,000 and 500,000 people marched through the streets of Montreal on May 22, 2012, transforming what had started as a student-led protest into what has been called "the largest act of civil disobedience in Canadian History".[4] The movement was able to expand because student protestors were able to effectively link their struggle to other struggles that resonated with the wider citizenry. One student participant told the Montreal daily *La Presse*, "We are fighting against the tuition hike, but we're also fighting against the Northern Plan (a proposal by the Quebec government to expand natural resource exploitation in the vast, north of the province) and against this corrupt government [. . .] We have succeeded in opening up a debate over the future of Quebec society. This is already a victory."[5]

In the end, the uprising succeeded in not only blocking the proposed tuition increases but it also helped force the ruling party from power in the provincial elections a few months later.

In Slovenia students have also played a large role in several recent protests. For example, Occupy Slovenia was initiated mostly by students and the younger generations who saw no bright prospects for the future. The first noticeable upsurge of political movements since the start of the global economic crisis started at the end of 2011. A multitude of several thousand people that organised itself through the Internet joined the 15-October (15O) global protests in Ljubljana. These global protests were inspired by the Arab Spring, the Greek protests, the Occupy movement, and especially the Spanish "Indignados" movement that started on May 15, 2011, (the 15M Movement). All of these movements fought for a redistribution of wealth and a different, more participatory form of democracy. The 15O protesters in Ljubljana decided to occupy the square in front of the Ljubljana Stock exchange. The protesters erased the "R" in *Borza* (Ljubljana Stock exchange) and renamed it *Boj_Za!* (meaning "a struggle for"). For several months Occupy Slovenia organised daily assemblies, where participants practiced "democracy of direct action", set up several workshops, and throughout the occupation stressed that "no one represents us" (Razsa and Kurnik 2012). A month later the *Mi Smo Univerza* movement ("We are the University") declared an occupation of the Faculty of Arts (a part of the University of Ljubljana). A sit-in started on November 22 and MSU organised several lectures, demanding education and scholarships for everyone, coupled with the democratisation of universities and curricula that encompass critique of the prevailing neoliberal order.

These were only the early signs of awakened political activism in Slovenia. A new wave of protests was set loose at the end of 2012 in Maribor, where an uprising began against corrupt political elites. The *Gotof je* movement ("He is finished", referring to the mayor of Maribor who later stepped down) then spread to other cities across Slovenia, most noticeably to Ljubljana, where several "all-Slovenian uprisings" against political and economic elites still continue into 2013. They involve all generations, including young students whose future prospects are the most difficult. In many cases the debates that started on the streets spread to the university in the form of lectures and seminars about the existing social situation.

The (student) protests in Austria, Canada and Slovenia are just some examples of the current wave of social activism that includes the wider Occupy movement, the Indignados movement in Spain and the social uprisings in Greece. Where possible, critical scholars should introduce their analyses into societal movements and social movements into the classroom. In this way both scholarly analyses and the movement may mutually benefit from emerging discussions. Protests have the potential to put certain topics on the public agenda. The Occupy movement was successful in initiating a debate about issues of class by pointing to the injustices of the capitalist system, which creates a minority of winners and a majority (99 per cent) of losers. Dissatisfaction and heightened public awareness of social problems such as inequality, domination, exploitation, environmental destruction, poverty, corporate irresponsibility, etc. may inspire critical reflection about capitalism both within and outside the university. This awareness may also provide renewed legitimacy to Marxian inspired theories and research.

The conference at Uppsala University that led to this book is a prime example of the renewed interest in Marxism and critical research in media and communication studies. Talks at this conference critically dealt with topics such as communication labour, surveillance, digital culture, commodification, exploitation, alienation and ideology in informational capitalism, alternatives, commons, the role of the Internet for protests and revolutions, etc. What seemed particularly promising was the strong presence of young scholars. Similarly a special issue published by *tripleC* (http://www.triple-c.at) in 2012 collected twenty-eight papers that give a rich account of Marxian-inspired theory and research, truly indicating that "Marx is Back" in media and communication studies.[6] The Uppsala conference, as well as *tripleC*'s special issue, illustrate that there certainly is the potential for building international networks among emerging as well as more established critical scholars in this field.

As young scholars, it is certainly difficult to maintain a critical stance in face of all the challenges discussed in this chapter. But for inspiration it may help to remember what another critical scholar once wrote in his youth:

[. . .] what we have to accomplish at this time is all the more clear: *relentless criticism of all existing conditions,* relentless in the sense that the criticism is not afraid of its findings and just as little afraid of the conflict with the powers that be. (Marx 1843/1967, 212)

NOTES

1. Global wealth distribution is such that Oxfam recently claimed that the world's richest one hundred people earned enough last year to end extreme poverty for the world's poorest people four times over (Oxfam 2013).
2. The European project makeITfair for example published numerous reports that document the existence of unacceptable working conditions in the supply chain of media hardware companies, "makeITfair," accessed February 14, 2013, http://makeitfair.org/en?set_language=en.
3. Facebook's annual profit was US$1 billion in 2011, Facebook SEC-Filings, "Form 8-k, 2012," accessed February 14, 2013, http://pdf.secdatabase.com/700/0001193125-12-316895.pdf. This number is comparable with the entire national budget of a small country like Slovenia.
4. Staff, 2012, "Biggest Act of Civil Disobedience in Canadian History" *Common Dreams,* May 23, accessed February 14, 2013, https://www.common-dreams.org/headline/2012/05/23-5.
5. Roger Annis, 2012, "Government Repression of Quebec Student Movement Sparks Massive Protests," *Global Research,* May 28, accessed February 14, 2013, http://www.globalresearch.ca/government-repression-of-quebec-student-movement-sparks-massive-protests/31079.
6. Critical conferences and journals such as *tripleC: Communication, Capitalism & Critique. Open Access Journal for a Global Sustainable Information Society*; *Javnost—The Public, Political Economy of Communication* (the journal of IAMCR's political economy section); *Democratic Communiqué*; and *Fast Capitalism* are essential for providing a platform for critical scholars in media and communication studies to network and exchange ideas.

REFERENCES

Adorno, Theodor W. 1962/1976. "On the logics of the social sciences." In *The positivist dispute in German sociology*, 105–122. London: Heinemann.
Andrejevic, Mark. 2007. *iSpy: Surveillance and power in the interactive era.* Lawrence: University Press of Kansas.
———. 2011. "The work that affective economics does." *Cultural Studies* 25 (4–5): 604–620.
Bellamy Foster, John, and Robert W. McChesney. 2011. "The Internet's unholy marriage to capitalism." *MRZine* 62 (10). Accessed February 14, 2013. http://monthlyreview.org/2011/03/01/the-internets-unholy-marriage-to-capitalism.
Cohen, Nicole, Greig de Peuter, and Enda Brophy. 2012. "Internet, unite! You have nothing to lose-literally!" *Briarpatch* 41 (6): 9–12. Accessed February 14, 2013.

http://briarpatchmagazine.com/articles/view/interns-unite-you-have-nothing-to-lose-literally.
De Angelis, Massimo. 2007. *The beginning of history: Value struggles and global capital.* London: Pluto Press.
Dyer-Witheford, Nick. 2001. "Empire, immaterial labor, the new combinations, and the global worker." *Rethinking Marxism: A Journal of Economics, Culture & Society* 13 (3/4): 70–80.
Edu-Factory Collective. 2010. "Intro: The double crisis of: Living on the borders." *EduFactory Web Journal* 0. Accessed February 14, 2013. http://www.edu-factory.org/wp/wp-content/uploads/2011/08/Edu-factory.pdf.
Foucault, Michel. 1977. *Discipline and punish.* New York: Vintage.
Fuchs, Christian. 2012. "The political economy of privacy on Facebook." *Television & New Media* 13 (2): 139–159.
Garnham, Nicholas. 1979. "Contribution to a political economy of mass-communication." *Media, Culture and Society* 1 (1): 123–146.
———. 1995. "Political Economy and cultural studies." *Critical Studies in Mass Communication* 12 (1): 60–71.
Grossberg, Lawrence. 1995. "Cultural studies vs. Political economy: Is anybody else bored with this debate?" *Critical Studies in Mass Communication* 12 (1): 72–81.
Hardt, Michael and Antonio Negri. 2009. *Commonwealth.* Cambridge: Belknap Press of Harvard University Press.
Harvey, David. 2003. *The new imperialism.* Oxford: Oxford University Press.
Horkheimer, Max. 1937/2002. "Traditional and critical theory." In *Critical Theory Selected Essays: Max Horheimer,* 188–243. New York: Continuum.
Huws, Ursula. 2003. *The making of a cybertariat: Virtual work in a real world.* New York: MR Press.
Jhally, Sut, and Bill Livant. 1986. "Watching as working: The valorization of audience consciousness." *Journal of Communication* 36 (3): 124–143.
Lazzarato, Maurizio. 1996. "Immaterial labour." In *Radical thought in Italy: A potential politics,* edited by Paolo Virno and Michael Hardt, 133–147. Minneapolis: University of Minnesota Press.
Linebaugh, Peter. 2008. *The Magna Carta manifesto: Liberties and commons for all.* Berkeley: University of California Press.
Marcuse, Herbert. 1937/1989. "Philosophy and critical theory." In *Negations. Essays in Critical Theory,* 134–158. London: Free Associations Books.
Marx, Karl. 1843/1967. "Marx to Ruge. Letters from the Deutsch-Französische Jahrbücher." In *Writings of the young Marx on philosophy and society,* 211–215. Indianapolis, IN: Hackett Publishing.
———. 1844/1975a. "Contribution to the critique of Hegel's philosophy of law: Introduction." In *Karl Marx and Frederick Engels: Collected Works, Vol. 3 (1843–1844),* 175–187. London: Lawrence & Wishart.
———. 1844/1975b. "Economic and philosophic manuscripts of 1844." In *Karl Marx and Frederick Engels: Collected Works: Vol. 3 (1843–1844),* 175–187. London: Lawrence & Wishart.
———. 1845/1976. "Theses on Feuerbach [Original version]." In *Karl Marx and Frederick Engels: Collected Works: Vol. 5 (1845–1847),* 3–5. New York: International Publishers.
———. 1867/1976. *Capital: A critique of political economy: Volume one.* Middlesex: Penguin.
———. 1939/1973. *Grundrisse.* Middlesex: Penguin.
Mies, Maria, Veronika Bennholdt-Thomsen, and Claudia von Werlhof. 1988. *Women: The last colony.* London: Zed Books.
Negri, Antonio. 1984. *Marx beyond Marx: Lessons on the Grundrisse.* London: Pluto Press.

————. 1992. "Interpretation of the class situation today: Methodological aspects." In *Open Marxism: Volume 2: Theory and practice*, edited by Werner Bonefeld, Richard Gunn, and Kosmas Psychopedis, 69–105. London: Pluto Press.

Oxfam. 2013. *Oxfam media briefing: The cost of inequality: How wealth and income extremes hurt us all.* Accessed February 11, 2013. http://www.oxfam.ca/sites/default/files/cost-of-inequality-briefing-note.pdf.

Perelman, Michael. 2000. *The invention of capitalism: Classical political economy and the secret history of primitive accumulation.* Durham: Duke University Press.

Razsa, Maple, and Andrej Kurnik. 2012. "The Occupy movement in Žižek's hometown: Direct democracy and a politics of becoming." *American Ethnologist* 39 (2): 238–258.

Sandoval, Marisol, Sebastian Sevignani, Alexander Rehbogen, Thomas Allmer, Matthias Hager, and Verena Kreilinger. 2011. *Bildung MACHT Gesellschaft.* Münster: Westfälisches Dampfboot.

Schiller, Dan. 2007. *How to think about information.* Urbana, IL: University of Illinois Press.

Schiller, Herbert I. 1969. *Mass communications and American empire.* Boston, MA: Beacon Press.

Smythe, Dallas W. 1977. "Communications: Blindspot of Western Marxism." In *Counterclockwise: Perspectives on communication*, edited by Thomas Guback, 266–291. Boulder: Westview Press.

————. 1981. *Dependency road: Communications, capitalism, consciousness, and Canada.* Norwood: Ablex.

Tronti, Mario. 1972. "Workers and capital." *Telos* 14: 25–62.

Virno, Paolo. 2004. *A Grammar of the multitude: For an analysis of contemporary forms of life.* Los Angeles: Semiotext(e).

Williams, Raymond. 2005. *Culture and materialism. Selected essays.* London: Verso.

5 Social Informatics and Ethics
Towards the Good Information and Communication Society

Gunilla Bradley

5.1 INTRODUCTION

The fourth ICTs and Society Conference "Critique, Democracy and Philosophy in 21st Century Information Society" in Uppsala offered me an opportunity to return to Uppsala University (after fifty years), where I studied French, Russian, psychology, sociology, pedagogics, and ethnography. Why did I study computing and work life? From childhood I knew what huge difference electricity could make. My father was an electrician and I went with him to farms that had not experienced electricity before. People around me started to take courses in computer programming, a new type of job in the '60s. I did my PhD in educational psychology at Gothenburg University. In 1972, after receiving my PhD degree, I was given a commission from the Swedish Central Trade Union of Salaried Employees (TCO) to explore the working environment for employees, especially the so-called psychosocial work environment. One year later I presented a report on my findings to their congress. One of the scariest things at the time was computers—people were very afraid of huge unemployment and afraid that the computers would take over.

In this chapter I will give you some "snap shots" from our research over the years, mainly from the most recent period. The cross-disciplinary research programs I initiated and led dealt with four main historical periods of computerization—from the mainframe period with the use of batch processing systems to the online period and use of display terminals, over to micro-computerisation with the appearance of microchips, then to the net period when online communication technologies played a dominant role at the convergence of three main technologies (ICT). The research covered companies in: mail, insurance, electronic industry, air craft industry, banking, ten high tech industries in Silicon Valley, California, and some projects on the community level.

5.2 MAIN CHANGES IN WORK LIFE

I will briefly discuss major transformation in work life during the past decades.

5.2.1   In Work Life there are Continuous and Accelerating Changes in the Net Era

We have achieved more flexible work processes regarding both the professional role itself and leadership. Furthermore the professional role, the learning role and the role of citizens are becoming more and more *integrated*. In the big industries, repetitive jobs and physically strenuous jobs, including routine work, are disappearing and a total upgrading of qualifications has occurred.

Parallel with this, the organisation has become flattened. The type of organisational structure which has become more and more common is networks. In an international perspective more work tasks are becoming similar because the same software programmes are sold worldwide and the work tasks are carried out similarly. Common work tasks also are due to global customers/clients. "Paperless offices" became "people-less offices" and "robotisation" in industry is growing. The basis is laid for a global labour market.

A crocheted lace cloth is an excellent model to show how the world is working: it represents what social systems, organisations and official authorities increasingly look like. The networks interact wirelessly. It is possible to crochet all the time: each new loop (computer) is connected to another through the same yarn (tele-technology), at present the Internet. Wisdom is needed on how to crochet to prevent becoming prisoner in one's own net.

- Power can both be centralised and decentralised. However there is indeed a tension in many countries (e.g. Russia and China) regarding interactivity and surveillance.
- The distribution of power is now possible in quite a deep sense: competence in work places is transferred to the periphery. This was started up with the introduction and use of Knowledge Based Systems (KBS systems) in the 1980s.
- The hierarchical structures of companies mirrored industrialisation during the mainframe period. The distributed computer power was a huge step in context of the PCs. And then the microchips plus high speed communication technology became a real hype. The process of "smaller, smarter, and cheaper" had begun.

5.2.2   What Characteristics does the Network Organisation Have?

Some examples are:

- New communication patterns.
- Direct communication between the various levels of the organisation. There are invisible processes, hierarchy is sometimes built into the systems.

- Barriers between ideas and execution are disappearing.
- Reallocation of power in the organisation.
- Openness to the surrounding world that is borderless.
- Complexity of the internal security situation.
- Multidimensional virtual culture.
- Network management and networking competence.
- Immediate distribution of information.
- Human competence becomes the currency.

5.2.3 How does the Workforce in the Flexible Company Function?

At the centre there is a core workforce of permanent full-time employees who enjoy a wide range of employment rights and benefits. However, the core workforce is decreasing. The other growing part is the peripheral workforce. This consists of part-time staff, self-employed consultants, sub-contracted and outsourced workers, and temporary and agency employees. Some of these "knowledge workers" are key resources, whereas others are exchangeable. Through the network organisational structure they might have very strong positions in the company through their expertise or social contacts, although this is invisible. Power is invisible in these new forms of organisations: Power has no outward manifestation and is not reflected to the same extent as before in properties and gadgets linked to leadership.

The peripheral workers are sometimes called free agents/free lancers: They take care of their own security, skills development and personal marketing. They are very loosely, if at all, tied into the welfare system. They are strong when health and good times are present, but not in a high-risk situation when health and family relations are taking away their energy and motivation.

5.2.4 Critique

Too much responsibility is laid on the individual who:

- loses permanent employment
- has to manage his/her own competence development
- has to market himself/herself
- is expected to take on "any" job and "multiple work tasks"
- is expected to be "creative"—with little compensation
- is a "unit" on a competitive world market

Is this the freedom from paid work in a traditional sense? In my perspective we all need a basic security as employees citizens. There is a need for balance between a strong society and strong individuals. Few persons are "strong" throughout life.

A situation where about 20 per cent of the population "is employed" or "within" and 80 per cent is "outside" the labour market, is a trap. I would like to see a renaissance, a strong emphasis on work that requires human unique competencies and where an important part cannot be replaced by ICTs, e.g. education and care of the elderly, children, and health care. A balance is needed between humans and machines. The industrialised world can afford this due to the rationalisation of production and the service sector that has been going on during three to four centuries.

5.2.5   Stress: With ICTs our Tempo is Increasing

Our perception of both time and space is changing. New opportunities to work and learn independently of location have changed our perception of space. What is expected from us and what we demand from ourselves is increasing all the time—the "level of aspiration" is increasing. People adapt to the machine and its tempo and become unconsciously affected by the speed of the machine with indirect effect on the perception of time. The words "slowly" and "quickly" have acquired new meanings. The same is true of the words "near" and "far away". The only thing we cannot buy is time.

There is a basic level of stress in our technological environments in large cities. It used to be entitled "techno-stress", a phenomenon at the societal level. Techno-stress is to a large extent due to effectiveness and efficiency. It may be that the use of ICTs better suits rural areas, where closeness to the environment, to nature, to the woods, lakes and the sea exists. One could talk about "overstimulation", in the big cities, and "under stimulation", both promoting stress. These two opposites could be balanced by use of ICT.

Stress can be characterised by too much or too little of various aspects. There is a clear correlation between frequent use of mobile phones and sleeping problems. There are reasons to talk about "Internet stress". We have an increased dependency on computers and networks, and an increased expectation that these technologies will function well. Stress phenomena in the Internet world are information overload, contact overload, demands for availability, a lack of organisational filters, a difficulty of separating "noise" from essentials, increasing levels of expectations and an altered perception of time and space in general.

5.2.6   Main Changes in Private Life and in the Home

Some years ago we studied the use of ICTs in homes and home environments in the USA, South East Asia (Singapore, Malaysia) and Japan. In the home many human roles and many environments are converging to one life role and one life environment.

The home is moving towards encompassing a virtual space as well as physical. The driving forces of this move are converging and embedded technologies. The home could be regarded as a communication sphere encompassing an extended family centre (online family), a care centre, a multimedia centre, a centre for democratic dialogue, a market place, a learning centre, and/or an entertainment centre.

The home is a growing market for all kinds of electronic gadgets, desirable or not. We analysed in our research the following question: What is a home? "Working from home" or "homing from work" were concepts that we explored in three subprojects in the USA, Singapore/Malaysia, and Japan.

Regarding public life and citizens' roles, there were some general observations: We are more and more doing the public service ourselves and without pay! There is a new pollution of the public environment—mobile ethics are needed. "Multitasking" is now part of daily life and a redefinition of "leisure" seems to be important. "The Political" has become a new playground, environment, sphere, landscape, whatever we call it.

5.3 THE CONVERGENCE THEORY

How do I perceive the world? The convergence model with the subtitle "ICT and the Psychosocial Life Environment" or "ICT, Society and Human Beings" illustrates on-going changes and processes in the net society, and synthesises the framework of my research on psychosocial work environment and computerisation that has its roots back in the 1970s and research programmes during various phases of the history of computerisation. Both convergence and interactions are important features in the model. Convergence here means a move towards common content.

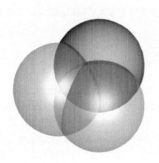

Figure 5.1 Convergence and complexity.

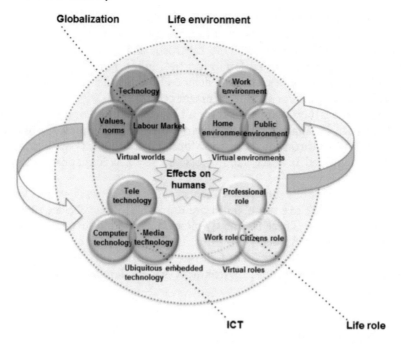

Figure 5.2   The convergence theory of ICTs, society and human beings. *Source*: Bradley 2005, 2006, 2011.

Interaction means that technology interacts with the social world's values and beliefs. There is also an on-going interaction between the "clusters of circles". There are four levels of analysis—individual, organisational, communal, and societal. Structures impact human beings but human beings also impact structures. This is valid for economic, cultural and political structures on the societal level and, for example, organisational structures and ICT infrastructure on another level. But the process of interaction differs between authoritarian and democratic societies. The main constituents of the convergence theory are represented in the circle in Figure 5.2.

5.3.1   Globalization

A convergence is occurring between technology, norms/values (economy) and the labour market and is entitled Globalization. Here technology means the overall technology that exists in society. Values related to the economic system are strong driving forces. Values related to culture and religion operate independently, supportively or oppositionaly. The geographical span is changing. The geographical space is both global and beyond—including applications of virtual reality (VR). The dotted line around the converging circles illustrates the virtual worlds (see Figure 5.3). Within the labour market we can conclude that early convergence occurred in the corporate world—multinational

1. Nature

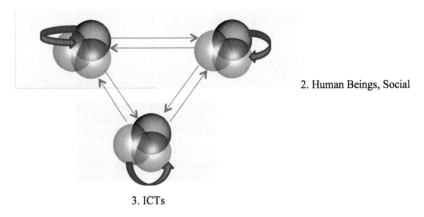

2. Human Beings, Social

3. ICTs

Figure 5.3 Societal self-production. *Based on*: Haftor and Mirjamdotter 2011

companies had their own Internet before the Internet came into public use. However, a corresponding convergence in the trade unions was late and still is not being developed to match the globalization of businesses.

5.3.2 ICTs

A convergence of computer technology, telecommunication technology and media technology occurs to become what is defined as ICTs. For a long time the borders between software and hardware have been blurred. The convergence between ICTs and bioscience and nanotechnology is contributing to the invisible convergences. The dotted line around the three circles in Figure 5.3 illustrates the embedded (pervasive, ubiquitous) technology.

5.3.3 Life Environment

Work environment, home environment and public environment are converging to a life environment, where the work and public environments move into our homes and vice versa. A new emphasis on certain dimensions and identifying new dimensions and processes in the psychosocial environment is important, e.g. the convergence between production and consumption. The dotted line around the three circles in Figure 5.3 illustrates the virtual environments.

5.3.4 Life Role

The professional role, the private role, and the citizen's role converge to become a life role. Role and role formation are central concepts in social psychology and represents a level between structures and the individual. In democracies the individual can influence and form his/her role/roles and is not solely a victim of structures. The dotted line around the three circles illustrates the virtual role (see Figure 5.3).

5.3.5   Effects on Humans

"Effects on humans" is represented by the circle in the middle, a flower or a compass card, which illustrates interactions. The individual is affected by ICTs, the life environment, life R role, and globalization, but can also influence these areas included the new VR with its subparts. Effects on the individual become more multi-faceted and complex. The way humans handle their situation can roughly be categorised as being either active or passive. Examples of active reactions are involvement, creative behaviour, and protest. Examples of passive reactions are alienation and certain psycho-physiological symptoms. The important human influence also takes place in the various roles we take on during our life time, in the professional role, privately and as citizens (see Section 5.3.4.).

5.3.6   Virtual Reality (VR)

This summarising concept is illustrated by the four circles marked with dotted lines, surrounding the four clusters of converging circles, but also by the bigger circle framing the whole model. There are various levels of participation in cyberspace that are shown in figure 5.2: There are virtual human roles: Regarding the citizen's role, VR is a strong factor that is reshaping the power balance between the present authorities and the grassroots and has a great potential to strengthen civil society. The main tools are the Internet and web technologies, mobile phones and new software applications within social media technology. New social media are transforming our roles; more time is spent on the net. In a more extreme form, VR is expressed by another person/personality that people take on, e.g. avatars in various online games.

5.3.7   Dynamics of the Model

The thin double-directed arrows in figure 5.2. in the outer part of the big circle represent interactions between the clusters of circles and the broad arrows represent the main direction for the movement in the circle model. The main direction is emphasised by an increasing change in society due to globalization and the accelerated speed within R&D in ICT. The interaction between the clusters entitled "ICT" and "globalization" gives a powerful push to the speed of the "wheel". Accelerated speed of economic transactions by robotisation puts the world economy in a high risk for crisis.

Transferring the reasoning to actions, we can in our professional role, private role and/or citizen's role influence our life environment on various levels of analyses, but an awareness of the speed of change and its causes is required, including the awareness of complexity.

5.3.8 Complexity and System Theory are "Good Friends"

A complex system is composed of interconnected parts that as a whole exhibit one or more properties (behaviour) not obvious from the properties of the individual parts. Examples of complex systems for which complexity models have been developed include human economies and social structures, nervous systems, living things (including cells), human beings, as well as modern telecommunication infrastructures. Interdisciplinary studies of complex systems include systems theory, complexity theory, systems ecology and cybernetics. Network theory is important for the study of complex system. Self-organisation in human society can explored as a form of collective intelligence, open source products and in Wikipedia.

To make the notion of complexity simpler, I have provided the illustration below that refers to societal self-production.

> Human Beings contribute to the production and reproduction of themselves, including the emergence of the Social, but also the Nature and the particular kind of artifact understood as Information and Communication Technology (ICT). Likewise, Nature is contributing to the production and re-production of itself but also of Human Beings and the ICT. Lastly but not least, ICT is contributing to the production and re-production of itself and also of Human Beings and the Nature. (Haftor and Mirijamdotter 2011, 543)

The key message of the concept of societal self-production is that everything seems to interact with everything else. In this ambivalent position towards the dialectic reproduction of physical and cultural spheres we need a compass needle.

5.4 WHAT IS THE GOOD ICT SOCIETY?

There are various questions that need to be considered for defining what the good ICT society is and how it can be achieved.

5.4.1 From Theory to Actions

When finishing various projects and books over the years, I often ended up with specifying some desirable goals and visions for the ICT society or computer society. They were sometimes formulated as research for future or policy statements. I was spending a lot of time with scholars in informatics and was increasingly becoming tired of the dominant research and conferences on system development and new strategies for information systems, etc. My visions were formed from a mixture of my theoretical perspective, empirical work and some insights from my background as a behavioural scientist and a psychologist. They mostly concerned the flower or compass needle in the middle of my model, "Effects on Human Beings", but when presenting action strategies for the ICT society, I used a picture of a tree of action that addressed changes on all levels of analysis and corresponded to all clusters of circles in the current convergence model. The oak tree of actions became a colourful book cover and was described in a special chapter (G. Bradley 2006). Since then the tree and its branches have been discussed and further developed in several conference panels with contributions from various cultures (G. Bradley and Whitehouse, 2012).

5.4.2   Effects on Humans are Multifaceted

I used to specify aspects that were very sensitive to the use of computers and later ICTs. Today many of these "hypotheses" are confirmed, but both proactive and "here and now" actions are needed. ICTs are changing our:

• identity and self-perception
• integrity
• trust/security/privacy (the terms vary)
• dependency addictiveness
• social competence (shyness)
• creativity
• involvement and alienation
• inclusion/exclusion

In the annual IADIS conference series on "ICT, Society and Human Beings", a number of "key words" have been used to stimulate research and sharing of experiences across cultures, under the headline "Effects on Humans". In parallel, the broader societal context has been stressed.

5.4.3   Focus on Some Major Psychosocial Processes as Policy Statements

In 2000, Sweden chaired the EU. I was invited to organise a workshop in Brussels and then to give a talk about the release of my edited book *Humans on the Net*, at the Malmö conference that started up Sweden's role as host country. I took the opportunity to formulate (also in the book) some positive statements of goals to be reached and the importance to activate psychosocial processes in society to reach goals such as:

• Information access for all.
• Wellbeing and quality of life for all.

- Enrichment of the social contact between people.
- Integration and respect for diversity.
- Greater autonomy for the individual.
- Prevention of various kinds of overload and stress.
- The deepening and broadening of democracy.
- E-cooperation and peace.
- Sustainability in a broad sense, including the environment, economy, and the human side.

Preparing for the unforeseen—potential catastrophes—could be added today. On a general level, a balance between emotional and rational components and a balance between female and male is more important than ever.

Internationally, the first official statements of goals for the ICT society were formulated at the first World Information Technology Forum (WITFOR 2003) in the Baltic country of Lithuania. The so-called Vilnius Declaration brought forward goals which had a great implication for the involvement of the developing countries, e.g. bridging the digital divide between the rich and poor in the world; urban and rural societies; men and women; and different generations. Another main concern was reducing poverty through the use of ICTs. Ensuring freedom of expression was a hot topic and still is. This was the first time that researchers met with and had a dialogue with politicians on the ministry level both from developed and developing countries.

WITFOR was followed up by WSIS (World Summit of the Information Society) mainly held in the developing countries where NGOs and civic society were involved. I would entitle this as an "awareness process" of the potential connected to ICTs. The Arab Spring may have got some early vitamin injections from these debates.

5.5 REFLECTIONS

I want to provide some overall reflections of the implications of the presented approach

5.5.1 Relating the Convergence Model to Marxist Concepts

There are several Marxist concepts that can be related to the convergence model:

1. Globalization cluster: ICT speeds up capital accumulation, which is met by new forms of global actions and revolts. It is possible to observe a new form of the exploitation of labour, due to an ICT related blurring of work life and private life as well as a marginalisation of labour through exclusion. The so-called playbour (the combination of

play and labour) needs a thorough analysis coupled to the economic system.

2. The ICT cluster: there is an on-going commoning of technology, for example open source, file sharing, and other new forms of co-producing and sharing of knowledge, which are driving forces in laying a base for the reconstruction of the life environment and possible seeds of a non-proprietary and more collaborative form of economy (Benkler 2006) (See 3. life environment cluster).

3. Life environment cluster (life sphere): Diversified struggles are going on at the convergence of four components (work environment, private environment, public environment, and virtual environment). Prosumption seems to be a new environment/sphere—it is neither work nor private or public, which results in a corresponding new life role of the prosumer (see 4 life role cluster).

4. Life role cluster: Humans are trying to find a balance between the converging human roles in spite of new facilitating technology. Early in our research we could report that a growing part of the labour consists of part-time staff, self-employed consultants, sub-contracted and outsourced workers, and temporary and agency employees (See Sections 5.2.3. and 5.2.4.). Some of these are key resources, whereas others are exchangeable but both are very loosely tied into the welfare system. They are sometimes called free agents/freelancers/portfolio individuals. This could be compared with Precarious workers and the precariat (originating from proletariat), expressions used within post-marxistic literature and in some current news media.

5. Effects on humans: The multifaceted effects on humans can be structured in passive reactions and active reactions (see Section 5.3.5.). Alienation, withdrawal, some psychosomatic syndromes are examples of passive reactions. Active reactions have acquired new arenas through the virtual world and the social media (see Section 5.3.6.). Social protest movements of various kinds are operating both on "the streets" and in VR and in the digital sphere.

The concept of exploitation is complex. Who is exploiting whom? What part of society forms the exploiter? What levels of analysis need to be taken into account? Can we talk about an interactive and mutual exploitation? What role do the growing amount of small entrepreneurs have in the labour market?

To be able to analyse the present trends and the future, you need to go back to basics, explore the work content, work organisation, salary policy/principles, working hours, communication patterns, reward systems, etc., and develop adequate concepts. The concept of digital labour is too broad and vague. Listening, observing, recording, structuring, refining and developing concepts are crucial processes. Social psychologists, sociologists, political scientists, computer scientists, national and global economists, micro and macro economists have to meet and listen to each other. A broad spectrum of tools is possible for modelling, collecting and analysing information of various kinds—across cultures and political systems. Research is not value free but value rich. The only way to approach this is in dialogue.

Processes like psychosocial, alienation, liberation, globalization, reification, commodification and commoning need to be analysed and described for present conditions. Research on this could also be added to a new Wikipedia entry on "ICT and Marxism".

Parts of my early empirical research were done during a time when Sweden tried to balance two political systems. The main focus in society was that computers should be a tool to rationalise work and working life, but a vision dominated that work and production life should play a smaller part of a person's life. I started my research when Sweden served as a model country for balancing capital and labour. In 1968, when the worldwide student revolt took place, I was at the department of sociology at Stockholm University. The whole university was a battlefield, comparable to other campuses in Europe and USA. The theoretical framework and concepts I developed were close to the vocabulary that workers and employees used in the working places and also mirrored the public debate and the next step in laws and agreements. I can refer in this context to my book Social and community informatics (G. Bradley 2006) and a recent article in *tripleC*, "The convergence theory on ICT, society and human beings" (G. Bradley 2010).

Within "Swedish socialism" as well as the social democracy that was in power back then, the traditional Marxist concepts were considered as being outdated. The former Soviet Union was close to the Swedish border and people were looking at Soviet socialism with disgust and fear. Countries like Cuba, Israel with its kibbutzes, and Yugoslavia with its worker-owned companies were, in contrast, at the time giving some hope for left-wing, young students. Ironically Sweden was closer than most European countries to a far reaching socialism, with preparations for introduction of economical democracy, so-called "löntagarfonder". However these plans were closed soon after the fall of the Berlin Wall and the whole economic system went global and Sweden moved "to the right", partly due to an extreme dependency on export industries.

Over the years I used to argue that "computerisation" will utmost result in a huge "allocation problem" and I listed as crucial issues the:

- Allocation of:
  - work
  - leisure time
  - citizen services (paid and unpaid)
  - production and reproduction
- Allocation between cities and rural areas
- Allocation of profits between:
  - sectors within a country
  - various industrialised countries
  - industrialised countries and the third world

Now forty years later, one can conclude:

- The accumulation of capital and a search for the cheapest and most competent labour is a fast and accelerating process.
- The algorithm for the accumulation of capital can also be used for the allocation of capital and competence and further allocation of resources with the same speed and targets.
- The danger is that investments in wisdom and in a humanising process, attending to the everyday quality of life of people, has not taken place before this "turn around".

5.5.2   Final Reflections

"ICTs should be used for the deepening of humane and societal qualities" might be the best line to sum up this chapter. In a field of research with accelerated speed of change and complexity, there is a need for a strong support for internationally, cross-disciplinary, cross-cultural and action-oriented research on the topic of "ICT for the deepening of humane and societal qualities".

With distributed computer power, strong telecommunications (e.g. the Internet) and mobile equipment, there is an inherent opportunity for the good and sustainable society. Establishing a good and sustainable information society is our responsibility for the next generation.

There is also an increasing risk of enforcing centralisation, surveillance and various misuses of power. The visions and goals for the good ICT society for human beings need a stronger recognition and action strategies on all levels of society—including the global level. There is a new kind of threat for humankind in the ICT society and this threat is particularly difficult for people and politicians to envisage. Whole societies and civilisations are so vulnerable and their infrastructures can suddenly be wiped out and/or be rendered inoperable by various forms of global risks and crises.

ICTs can and should be used to narrow the gap between subcultures. They could help us to show similarities, emphasise the synergy in the various cultural and economic realms and bring us all into a thrilling and fruitful dialogue. We need quite a different approach—a future of "unity and diversity".

ACKNOWLEDGMENT

I wish to thank Dr. Karin Bradley for her careful and constructive criticism and commentary.

REFERENCES

Benkler, Y. 2006. *The wealth of networks: How social production transforms markets and freedom.* New Haven: Yale University Press.

Bradley, Gunilla. 1977. *Datateknik, arbetsliv och kommunikation.* (*Computer technology, work life, and communication*). The Swedish delegation for long term research. FRN. Stockholm, SE: Liber (in Swedish).

———. 1989. *Computers and the psychosocial work environment.* London: Taylor & Francis.

———., ed. 2001. *Humans on the net. Information and communication technology (ICT), work organisation and human beings.* Stockholm, SE: Prevent.

———. 2003. "ICT for deepening human and societal qualities." In *Proceedings of WITFOR 2003. Humans on the net.* London: Routledge.

———. 2006. *Social and community informatics. Humans on the net.* London: Routledge.

———. 2010. "The convergence theory on ICT, society and human beings." *tripleC: Communication, Capitalism & Critique. Open Access Journal for a Global Sustainable Information Society* 10 (2): 183–192.

———. 2011. "The convergence theory on ICT, society and human beings. Towards the good ICT society." In *Information and communication technologies, society and human beings. Festschrift in honor of Gunilla Bradley,* edited by Darek Haftor and Anita Mirijamdotter, 30–46. New York: IGI Global.

Bradley, Gunilla, and Diane Whitehouse, eds. 2011. *Proceedings of the IADIS International Conferences "ICT, Society and Human Beings 201"1" and "e-Democracy, Equity and Social Justice 2011".* Part of the IADIS Multi-Conference on Computer Science and Information Systems 2011. IADIS Press.

———., eds. 2012. *Proceedings of the IADIS International Conferences "ICT, Society and Human Beings 2012" and "eCommerce 2012".* Part of the IADIS Multi-Conference on Computer Science and Information Systems 2012. IADIS Press.

Bradley, Linda. 2005. *Home of the future Japan. Information and communication technology (ICT) and changes in society and human patterns of behavior in the network era.* KTH Research report ISBN 91–7178–052–1. Stockholm: Royal Institute of Technology (KTH).

Fuchs, Christian. 2012. "New Marxian times! Reflections on the 4th ICTs and Society Conference '"Critique, Democracy and Philosophy in 21st Century Information Society. Towards Critical Theories of Social Media'"." *tripleC: Communication, Capitalism & Critique. Open Access Journal for a Global Sustainable Information Society* 10(1): 114–121.

Haftor, Darek, and Anita Mirijamdotter, eds. 2011. *Information and communication technologies, Society and human beings. Festschrift in honor of Gunilla Bradley.* New York: IGI Global.

Khakhar, Dipak, ed. 2004. *WITFOR 2003 (WORLD IT FORUM) White Book. Key note contributions and panel discussions from the 8 commissions.* Luxemburg: IFIP Press.

Part II

Critical Internet- and Social Media-Studies

6 Great Refusal or Long March
How to Think About the Internet

Andrew Feenberg

My recent co-edited book entitled *(Re)Inventing the Internet* employs an approach I call "critical constructivism" (Feenberg and Friesen 2012). In this chapter I will show that this approach is rooted in Marxist method. I also believe it has significant political implications, which I develop in concluding reflections on Marcuse, hence the title of this chapter.

6.1 MARXISM AND CONSTRUCTIVISM

Everyone is familiar with Marx, the political economist, but I want to introduce a different Marx—Marx, the social constructivist critic of technology. He is going to help us study the Internet as an unfinished technology and a terrain of struggle.

Critical constructivism differs from impact or "powerful-effects" studies we are familiar with in the writings of Adorno and McLuhan down to Castells and much postmodern theory. Recent political economy of the Internet also has a different focus (Fuchs 2010; Arvidsson and Colleoni 2012). While undoubtedly useful as partial accounts, impact studies and political economy tempt some commentators to over-generalise (Lievrouw 2012; Bakardjieva and Feenberg 2004). They then produce utopian or dystopian discourses: either we are headed toward a universal mind or a corporate dominated matrix. I cannot engage in debate with these alternatives here beyond noting that they are often associated with economic and technological determinism. Whereas Marx is often accused of these deterministic views, I would like to show that his most interesting ideas on methodology support a critical version of constructivism.

In Marx's days, most technology was deployed in factories and therefore most struggle over technology was associated with class struggle. My intention is to generalise Marx's approach beyond the factory setting to which he applied it. Today technology is everywhere including social domains remote from production. Administrative hierarchies that resemble capitalist management everywhere accompany technical mediation. Hence today's struggles over technology and its effects, which may break out far from the factory. Critical constructivism attempts to incorporate these struggles into a loosely Marxist framework. I will begin by discussing four short passages from Marx that illustrate his method.

1) All constructivist approaches, including mine, agree that technologies are products of social actors whose interests and world view influence design and use. Marx adds something that is often missing in constructivist accounts: a reference to the strategic significance of technologies in class struggle. In *Capital*, he claims that science "is the most powerful weapon for repressing strikes, those periodical revolts of the working class against the autocracy of capital". And further, that "it would be possible to write quite a history of inventions, made since 1830, for the sole purpose of supplying capital with weapons against the revolts of the working class" (1867/1906, 475–476). Marx is referring to deskilling, introduced to reduce labour costs and enhance control.

The transformation of production methods initiated in the manufacturing phase of capitalism responded to a specific concept of progress. This concept was described by Andrew Ure in 1835, at a time when it was still possible to talk honestly about class. Ure wrote: "By the infirmity of human nature it happens, that the more skillful the workman, the more self-willed and intractable he is apt to become, and, of course, the less fit a component of a mechanical system, in which, by occasional irregularities, he may do great damage to the whole. The grand object therefore of the modern manufacturer is, through the union of capital and science, to reduce the task of his work-people to the exercise of vigilance and dexterity" (1835, 18).

In the terminology of critical constructivism, Ure is here defining the "technical code" of capitalism (Feenberg 2010, chap. 4). By this I mean the rule under which a type of artefact or a whole domain of artefacts is designed. Technical codes translate worldviews and interests into technical specifications that can be implemented by engineers or other experts. The translation hides the social origin and significance of the codes behind a veil of technical necessity. This is what Lukács called "reification" in his early Marxist work (Lukács 1971; Feenberg forthcoming 2014, chap. 4). The task of critique is to reverse the process and reveal that origin and significance.

Let me give an example from *(Re)Inventing the Internet*. Online education originated in the early 1980s with a dialogic pedagogy, which was the only possible eductional application of a computer network at the time. Later, at the end of the 1990s, when the Internet was available to everyone, computer companies and university administrators imagined automating higher education on the Internet. The deskilling technical code was to be extended to the university. There were many protests from faculty and faculty associations over this attempt to make professors as obsolete as shoemakers and typesetters. Faculty protested in the name of educational traditions, which require dialogue whether online or face to face. This conflicted with the deskilling technical code derived from the Industrial Revolution. The outcome today is confused and no one is quite sure what online education is, because both codes coexist and conflict (Hamilton and Feenberg 2012).

2) The second passage I will discuss is found in the "Introduction" to *A Contribution to the Critique of Political Economy*. There Marx writes that "[t]he concrete is concrete, because it is a combination of many objects with different destinations, i.e. a unity of diverse elements. In our thought, it therefore appears as a process of synthesis, as a result, and not as a starting point, although it is the real starting point and, therefore, also the starting point of observation and conception" (1857/1904, 293).

This rather enigmatic passage anticipates the genealogical method Foucault derived from Nietzsche. The basic idea is that social "things"—artefacts, institutions, etc.—are not substances, but assemblages of various components held together by their functional role in society. They may disaggregate and combine differently as society changes. Money, for example, is differently constructed and has a different functional role in the Middle Ages as contrasted with the nineteenth century or today. It is not composed of the same "stuff" nor does it do the same sorts of things, and yet it is still called "money". The history of this artefact must trace these deep changes rather than postulating a fixed substance with a singular essence undergoing external events of one sort or another.

The genealogical approach is especially plausible in the case of technologies. The telephone, for example, retains its identity although practically every component and many usages are quite different from what they were at the time of its invention. This approach to historical study is necessary where the technical code imposed by the dominant actor is not alone in shaping design. Technologies are complicated then by the multiplicity of interests they serve. These interests show up in design as more or less coherent assemblages of structures with various and sometimes conflicting functions. Many technological artefacts thus display some of the ambiguity we associate with social institutions despite their apparently rational form.

Critical constructivism expresses this complexity through the notion of layers (Feenberg 2012). Technologies are concrete in Marx's sense because they realise in technical form multiple layers of function and meaning corresponding to the actors with influence on design. In the case of online education, to return to my earlier example, there are two principal layers combined in different ways depending on which technical code prevails. These are a communicative layer supporting online community and a data delivery layer, a broadcasting function. The communicative layer translates the traditional educational code of faculty actors whereas data delivery is compatible with the automation sought by administrative actors. One layer will dominate the future legal and technological framework, but we do not yet know which.

Unravelling the layers is complicated by the fact that technical innovation often combines multiple functions in a single structure. This process, which Gilbert Simondon called concretization (in a different sense from Marx), is an immanent criterion of progress in the evolution of artefacts (Simondon 1958, chap. 1). Simondon's examples are apolitical, such things as the air-cooled engine which combines the dissipation of heat and containment of the pistons in a single structure, the engine case. The critical constructivist version of this theory shows how technologies assemble and concretize a variety of functions to satisfy the changing demands and power relations of influential actors.

3) A third passage of interest appears in *The German Ideology*. Marx introduces the intriguing notion that capitalism produces the indi-viduals *qua* individuals by breaking their fixed lifetime relation to particular tools or circumstances. For the first time they are released from subservience to a profession or place. This "individualisation" opens democratic possibilities in contrast to pre-modern political orders based on estates with specific rights and powers.

At the same time, capitalism objectifies the totality of human capacities in machines. Thus technology is not just a means but also a reflection of the development of human nature as it transforms itself in transforming the world. Every feature of technology must therefore be traced back to the humanity it serves. Technology in a sense *represents* the corresponding aspects of its users.

This is where the problem lies: capitalism alienates the individuals in transferring their knowledge to machines and deskilling their labour. Capacities the individuals used to possess are lost to them and the new ones they acquire are trivial and inhuman. Socialism would consist in the appro-priation of the mechanical forces of production in order to transform them into instruments of human initiative. The appropriation of these forces by the individuals under socialism "is itself nothing more than the develop-ment of the individual capacities corresponding to the material instruments of production. The appropriation of a totality of instruments of production is, for this very reason, the development of a totality of capacities in the individuals themselves" (Marx 1967a, 467).

In sum, the stakes in the class struggle are not merely economic, but con-cern the form of individuality or subjectivity available in the society. The alienating effects of capitalism are felt in the industrial context, motivating struggle. Now that every aspect of social life is technically mediated, other kinds of struggle besides class struggle are engaged over the control of a wide range of technologies. Capitalism has responded to these struggles in some instances by releasing the grip of control, allowing less alienated relations to flourish, and finding innovative ways to make a profit. This is particularly true of the Internet, which is technically unsuited to the kind of control capitalism has historically exercised in production.

4) Finally, I will introduce a passage from *Wage Labour and Capital* (Marx 1978) which has a bearing on the relation of function and meaning. Marx writes: "A negro is a negro. He only becomes a slave in certain circumstances. A cotton-spinning jenny is a machine for spinning cotton. Only in certain circumstances does it become capital. Torn from these circumstances it is no more capital than gold is money or sugar the price of sugar" (1978, 207). This passage distinguishes the thing *qua* thing from the meaning it takes on through its economic function.

The meaning thus acquired is not merely subjective although it is subjectively apprehended. Economic categories are both ways of understanding the world and reflections of the practices constituting the world. The relation of function to meaning is clear at the level of everyday experience. The chair has a function as a thing on which to sit only insofar as it is recognised as a chair, that is to say, only insofar as its meaning is apprehended by potential users who interpret what they see as a chair. In the case of economic entities, the practices associated with the meaning are constitutive. In becoming capital, the spinning jenny enters a circuit that determines its usage, its location, and eventually its design as it is effected by the forces of the market. The case is of course far more serious for Marx's negro.

While Marx identifies meanings with economic functions, critical constructivism generalises his approach to social meanings of all sorts. Cultural aspects of consumption did not concern Marx, given his focus on the laws of the economy, but culture is obviously of great significance today. Nevertheless, Marx's basic insight is valid, the notion that things become what they are in society through their function in a totality, a system of meanings and associated practices.

This principle has important applications in critical constructivism because the interventions of actors in the evolution of technologies often alter their meanings and thereby introduce a different range of functions that orients their future evolution. The French Minitel system is an example. An information utility was perceived by hackers as a potential communication medium. This is a case of what is called "interpretive flexibility" in technology studies, the ability of actors to reinterpret technologies as they innovate new usages. The hackers and soon millions of ordinary users layered the Minitel with communicative functions that transformed its meaning from an instrument of social rationalisation into a sort of electronic singles bar. This change was not merely subjective, not merely in the heads of users, but was reflected in the introduction of new software on the system (Feenberg 1995, chap. 7).

This example drawn from media history begins to suggest how critical constructivism approaches the Internet. Rather than focusing directly on impacts or ownership, this approach begins with the shaping of design. The interventions of the influential actors intersect and interact with unpredictable consequences. The result may block some familiar affordances and bring out others that lay undetected until new actors discovered them. From this standpoint, we can ask the questions: What is the meaning of the Internet? What will be its primary functions? We could paraphrase Marx: "the Internet is a machine for transmitting data. Only in certain circumstances does it become capital, or alternatively, a democratic medium, a sex machine, etc".

Actors have a variety of resources they can bring to bear to further their interests through design. Ownership is of course an important resource, overwhelmingly so in the case of production technology as Marx observed, but it is not the only resource and is sometimes overshadowed by cultural and political factors in domains where the market is less central.

In sum, critical constructivism generalises from four methodological principles found in Marx. The idea of capitalist deskilling as determining a trajectory of technological development is generalised in the theory of technical codes as standardisation of actors' goals in design and technical disciplines. The idea of the concrete object as a synthesis of determinations is generalised in the genealogical notion of the layering of technological design in the course of development. The idea of the objectification of human capacities in productive forces is generalised by relating the growth of capacities to a wide variety of technologies. The interpretation of the meaning of social objects through their economic function is generalised through multiplying the contexts within which objects take on meaning and function. Together, these generalisations lay out the basis of the critical constructivist approach.

These four Marxist principles support a final generalisation. Marx shows that interests arise from technical involvements. He studied this in the case of the class interests of the proletariat in its relationship to production technology. But in a world where technology is everywhere we can generalise the notion of class interests in a concept of "participant interests" that would apply wherever individuals are involved with technologies. This enables us to reconceptualise social struggle as struggle over technology, specifically in the case of the Internet.

6.2   THE LAYERS OF THE INTERNET

I would like now to show how these principles apply to the Internet, drawing on the research documented in our new book. For the purpose of this discussion I argue that the Internet has five functional layers. These are non-hierarchical structure, anonymity, broadcasting, data storage and online community, and are some of the main affordances actors work with and incorporate into designs representing their interests. In doing so they determine the meaning of the network.

1) The non-hierarchical structure of the Internet contrasts with earlier forms of computer networking based on the X.25 protocol which centralised control in the hands of operators such as Telecoms. Centralisation had distinct advantages from a business perspective as contrasted with the Internet protocol. For example, the French Telecom could track Minitel users' online access to services to the minute and bill them accordingly on their phone bill, which they could hardly fail to pay. The Internet is quite different. In the absence of central control, online businesses at first tried to sign up subscribers and when that failed they sought revenue from advertising. A few of the big players are successful at this, but it seems a far cry from the highly efficient model implemented with Minitel. The lack of central control has had two other major consequences: the network has been able to internationalise easily and experimentation has flourished.

2) The non-hierarchical structure of the Internet has made anonymity possible not only in social interaction, but at the network level itself. Among other uses, anonymity on the network supports various forms of antisocial, stigmatised or illegal activity, such as access to pornography, coordination of criminal and terrorist activity, new forms of personal encounter, and political protest.

3) Anonymity on the Internet is not perfect. Computers store records of their own activity, including those of individuals in communicative relationships. This enables tracking individual and group behaviour to some extent. Unprecedented depth of surveillance is possible on the basis of data storage, although legal restrictions and costs place limits on the usefulness of this feature. Just as anonymity has proven particularly useful to dissenters, so surveillance has been applied primarily by dominant actors such as governments and corporations. The personalisation of advertising is one familiar application. Ocasional exceptions such as Wikileaks have turned the tables on the powers that be. Data storage can also be incorporated into the usages of individuals and online communities, where it serves to preserve their history.

4) The Internet can also broadcast to large numbers of users very cheaply and quickly. This feature can be used to mobilise people or to deliver data on a mass scale. Combining anonymity with broadcasting makes a powerful tool for political communication. But it is important to avoid exaggerating the significance of this tool so as not to provoke counter-hype. Critics all too often confuse refuting the

hype with a critique of the Internet itself (Gladwell 2010). The Internet does not make revolutions, but it is surely a more efficient means of communication than the Ayatollah Khomeini's cassette tapes or the leaflets we distributed in May 1968. Again there is an ambiguity. Both revolutionary and entertainment usages of the Internet depend on broadcasting.

These first four features illustrate the ambiguity and contingency of technological design. Various combinations of the features and corresponding usages have different social meanings and consequences. Anonymity can be appropriated to disseminate commercial pornography or revolutionary propaganda. The non-hierarchical structure of the Internet has democratic implications, but also criminal usages. And so on. In each case users layer the technology with their demands, often modifying the software running on the system accordingly. This is not to say that the Internet is a "neutral tool", but that its affordances can be combined and appropriated in a variety of ways. Each appropriation opens a distinct developmental path that may turn out to be more or less influential in the future.

5) Finally, the ability of the Internet to assemble small groups for discussion and deliberation is a fundamental innovation. This is in fact the first effective electronic mediation of small group activity. It makes possible new forms of sociability such as the online community. Because so many important human activities go on in small groups, such as education, work and political discussion, this is a major social innovation. Its uniqueness emerges clearly from a comparison with other types of mediated communication.

Regular mail links pairs of correspondents asynchronously. Each correspondent has a paper record of the communication, which must be filed locally for future use. The telephones enables pairs of individuals to communicate reciprocally in real time, but normally leaves no record. Broadcasting supports one-way communication to a passive audience. By contrast with all these earlier forms, small group communciation on computer networks is reciprocal and recorded. It concretizes the sending and filing of messages and thereby assembles groups around a virtual locus, the file to which messages are sent.

Community is the primary scene of human communication and personal development. It is in this context that people judge the world around them and discuss their judgments with others. Any technology that offers new possibilities for the formation of community is thus ethically and politically significant. But are online communities real communities, engaging their members seriously? Some impact studies cast doubt on their authenticity; there are certainly online "communities" that are no more real than Facebook "friends". It is also true that lax privacy regulation and online advertising give a consumerist bias to Facebook (Bakardjieva and Gaden 2012). But this is not the whole story. The testimony of participants as well as extensive research confirms that the Internet is the scene of new forms of sociability, some of which resemble face-to-face community in terms of loyalty and commitment (Feenberg and Barney 2004; especially Feenberg and Bakardjieva 2004).

We now have two things to bring together: a methodology for technology study and the layers of a specific technology, the Internet. The Internet can be analysed in terms of the relations of these various layers in the technical codes of actors struggling for control of its future.

The confusing mix of all these features on the Internet today results in the many layers of meaning overlapping and conflicting. This is characteristic of an immature technology. In the normal course of technological development, closure is reached around a single technical code which then orients the future evolution of the artefact. This has not yet happened with the Internet. There is no single design or model that defines the technology.

Two main alternatives are in contention, a consumption model and a community model. Each represents a technical code that may someday determine the overall design of the Internet. The consumption model follows the logic of consumer society in objectifying human capacities in commodities. By contrast the community model supports new forms of sociability through which the individuals may appropriate alienated aspects of their lives. The struggle between these models plays out in many venues that are not normally considered "political", but which do indeed have political significance. Both the meaning of the Internet and what it is to be an individual in an Internet enabled society are at stake. A critical theory of the Internet must acknowledge the struggle rather than assuming it has already ended with the victory of business or government or some ill-defined notion of "e-democracy" as do many current approaches.

First the consumption model. The layers here are non-hierarchy used for marketing, broadcasting for delivery of information, data storage for data mining, and online community as a data source. The consumption model has two main features today, both dependent on data storage. Searching the data creates a new type of market that inexpensively links up people and goods over a global territory. The most profitable Internet businesses resemble eBay in stocking little or no inventory, but instead delivering a smooth connection between supply and demand. Data mining information voluntarily supplied by users in forums such as Facebook has also revolutionised the advertising industry and supplied most of the commercial revenues of the Internet.

The consumption model has enormous potential for growth because film and television have not yet been fully adapted for broadcasting over the Internet. We can expect a huge boost in consumption usages when every sort of recorded entertainment is readily available.

To most effectively combine these layers the consumption model requires changes in the inherited structure of the Internet, which was not designed with business in mind (Abbate 1999). For example, one would need better control of the system than presently exists to insure greater security, better protection of intellectual property, and more reliable delivery of data. "Self-willed and intractable" users would be prevented thereby from "doing damage to the whole". To achieve this level of control would require the effective end of network neutrality. Predictably as more entertainment enters the Internet, it will become an enormous factor and will squeeze out or marginalise communicative usages. So in this version the word "Internet" comes to mean a mass medium like television. The "totality of capacities" represented by the Internet as an objectification of our humanity would be alienated under a technical code similar to the other mass media.

The Internet is not yet dominated by business, which co-exists online with a free space for community. The community model has layers of nonhierarchical communication, anonymity, broadcasting for mobilisation, date storage for history, and online community for community life. The two main types of personal communication are email and various forms of group communication such as social networks. The essence of the community model is reciprocity. Each participant is both reader or viewer and publisher. To maintain this structure, the community model requires the continued neutrality of the network so that non-professional, unprofitable and politically controversial communication will not be marginalised. It must be possible to introduce innovative designs for new forms of association without passing through bureaucratic or commercial gatekeepers. The involvement of open-source developers and other unpaid volunteers is essential and would not survive a commercial take-over of cyberspace. Embedding a strict regime of intellectual property in the technology of the system would be incompatible with free communicative interaction.

The conditions of community are both social and technical. Should the community model prevail, commercial, entertainment and informational applications would find their place, but they could not dominate the evolution of the system with their special technical and legal requirements. Indeed, so far business seems to be adapting to the requirements of community: the commercial operation of community sites turns them into advertising platforms without determining their communicative content. In effect, business now operates these sites as a common carrier, not so different from the telephone network. This is why the Internet continues to have political significance even as business encroaches on it more and more.

6.3   ONLINE COMMUNITY AND INTERNET POLITICS

The list of political activities on the Internet gets longer and more impressive every year, starting with the Zapatista movement in Mexico in the early 1990s and continuing with the protests against the World Trade Organization (WTO) and the International Monetary Fund (IMF), the world wide demonstrations against the War in Iraq and the Occupy movement. In China the Internet is the principal platform of dissent. It also plays an important role in electoral politics, first coming to attention with Howard Dean's campaign and finally paying off in the election of Barack Obama. The recent Arab revolts should be proof enough of the Internet's remarkable political potential. In all these cases the Internet has broken the near monopoly of the business and government dominated official press and television networks by enabling activists to organise and to speak directly to millions of online correspondents.

These examples seem to me to provide strong evidence that the Internet is politically significant, but they are not enough for Darin Barney, who argues that these alternative and resistant practices still represent a tear in a salty sea of hegemonic encounters with the broad scope of digital technology and its culture. To take the measure of the present conjuncture we need careful work that documents and even promotes tactical political uses of these technologies, but we also need to place these uses in the broader context of what remains a very powerful set of technologies configured to advance and secure what Jacques Rancière has described as the 'unlimited power of wealth". (Barney 2011)

To answer objections such as this, a theoretical framework must give substance to the political Internet. After all, as Barney suggests, political usages might be exceptional and the Internet defined by narcissistic self-advertisement and business. My main concern in what follows is to develop a coherent alternative to such critical assessments. To anticipate my conclusion, I argue that politics in the usual sense on the Internet is the tip of the iceberg, arising in the midst of a broader revival of agency in many different types of online communities, and that it deserves our full attention and, indeed, our support. These new forms of agency redefine and enlarge the public sphere. What we commonly identify as politics on the Internet is an instance of this broader phenomenon. To understand these new politics we will need to reconsider how we think about technology.

While Marx identified the objectified capacities of the individuals with production technology, today advanced technological societies assemble collectives of geographically scattered individuals around technical mediations of all sorts. Educational activities, work, entertainment, illness, even externalities such as pollution create shared worlds in which the individuals circulate just as they do in factories or local communities. These shared worlds reflect aspects of the individuals' being, as did the machines that interested Marx.

Consider, for example, a particular disease as a link between its victims and the medical institution. The patients may live far apart but they share a world through that institution. The connection may remain latent where the patients have no sense of common concerns and no means of communication. However, it can also be activated where they come together as they often do today on the Internet.

To the extent that their world is owned and/or managed by a hierarchical administration modelled on capitalist management, the hierarchical administration alienates participants as did factories in Marx's day, although generally with less dramatic consequences. Patients may be well served by the medical institution, but where they are not they are likely to come up against a rigid bureaucracy that will only yield under considerable pressure. Communication and organisation is the key to applying such pressure and so the online community can play a role (Feenberg 1996).

The most innovative aspect of the Internet is its capacity to support such collective reflection on participant interests in all domains of life. This is the central theme of Maria Bakardjieva's (2012) contribution to *(Re)Inventing the Internet*. She explains the emergence of new forms of community among Internet users in response to a wide array of civic problems and frustrations. Bakardjieva calls this "subactivism", a kind of pre-politics that involves agency in institutions such as the medical system, government agencies, and schools. She delineates the shifting boundaries between the personal and the political, the "small world" of everyday life and the larger society.

Several other chapters of *(Re)Inventing the Internet* show how online communities have begun to use the Internet to coordinate their demands for a fuller representation of participant interests. Despite discouraging developments in other domains, agency in the technical sphere is on the rise. These new forms of online politics extend activity in the public sphere to technical issues formerly considered neutral and given over to experts to decide without consultation.

I have already mentioned the case of online education, discussed in a chapter of *(Re)Inventing the Internet* by Ted Hamilton and myself. The struggle over the future of the Internet is paralleled by this controversy over how best to employ it in education, either to constitute educational communities or to distribute information and deskill the teaching corps.

The video game industry offers another example of the complex interactions that characterise the Internet today. The industry is now larger than Hollywood and engages millions of subscribers in online multi-player games. The players' gaming activities are rigidly structured by the game code, but online communities organise them in informal relationships that the industry does not control. The "ludification theory" Sara Grimes and I present explains how these communities form within and in reaction to the rationalised structures of game technology (Grimes and Feenberg 2012).

Once activated as a community, the players struggle to reconfigure aspects of the game, mobilising code and game items in new ways and contexts. Markets appear in goods won during play as players auction them off for money. Users find work-arounds to avoid restrictions on speech or activity. Games are modified by players skilled at hacking. Companies may protest these unauthorised activities, but in the end they usually give in and attempt to co-opt what they cannot control. Interaction between game designers and players and among the players themselves creates a quasi-adversarial environment unlike the typical mass audiences created by television broadcasting. Similar phenomena have been observed on other mass sites such as Facebook, with members intervening to protest or demand changes in policies.

The representation of technically mediated communities is complicated by the role of experts in the creation and operation of technical networks. Experts represent the community constituted by a technical network in the sense that they alone can implement the participant interests of its members. Kate Milberry discusses this aspect of the Internet as it has been addressed by "tech activism" (Milberry 2012). The emergence of a cohort of self-taught radical experts on the technology of the Internet opens up new possibilities. Milberry examines how and why these tech activists appropriated wiki technology, using it as a space and tool for democratic communication in cyberspace. In turn, this has enabled the realisation of new communicative practices offline, establishing a dialectical relation between experts and the social world they serve. Democratic practice online prefigures a more just society in which democratic interventions into the development and use of technology are consciously organised.

Politics is no longer the exclusive affair of traditionally constituted political groups debating the traditional issues. The range of issues and groups is constantly widening in unpredictable directions. To the extent that so much of life is now mediated by technology, more and more of it becomes available for these new forms of democratic intervention. That is, if the community model of the Internet survives. This is the ultimate challenge for online community: to preserve the conditions of community on the Internet. That depends on the capacity of ordinary users to defend its democratic potential in the coming years.

The movements to which this gives rise are still quite weak and lack an overall strategy of change. But the unfavourable comparison with earlier revolutionary movements should not blind us to subtle changes taking place in the conduct of politics and the nature of the public sphere that may yet shape a new era. At the very least these changes testify to the significance of the highly visible political movements supported by the Internet, which cannot reasonably be dismissed as exceptions to the dystopian rule. Human action, not technology, will decide the future of the

Internet. When technologies are understood as terrains of struggle rather than as fixed and finished things, they are de-reified and exposed to criticism and transformation.

I want to conclude by reflecting on Marcuse's responses to the politics of technologically advanced capitalist society as he observed it in the 1960s and '70s. Marcuse proposed two different strategies in these decades. The "Great Refusal" was an aesthetic principle he extended in the 1960s to one-dimensional society as a whole (Marcuse 1966, 160). This strategy recapitulated old debates that opposed reform to revolution. Uncompromising and absolute critique was an attractive stance in the context of a society rich enough to co-opt almost every demand. But ironically the search for the unco-optable demand led to Marcuse himself becoming an icon in the mass culture of 1968, a fact from which his reputation suffers to this day. In the contemporary context, the dystopian critique of the Internet inspires a similarly uncompromising refusal. But it overlooks the actual struggles taking place today.

Significantly, once conditions changed Marcuse did not persist in the Great Refusal. A new configuration emerged in the 1970s, which Marcuse called the "preventive counter-revolution". Co-optation continued but was supplemented by recession and repression. The New Left disintegrated, but it had created a large critical public and a sense of suppressed possibilities. Marcuse now echoed the German slogan that called for "a Long March through the Institutions" (Marcuse 1972). In a time of political eclipse, one must find a place in the institutions of society. But if it is possible to bring contestation to bear on those institutions, that is the task, accepting the likely ambiguity of the outcome. Total refusal is then no longer the touchstone of a revolutionary stance.

These two strategies exemplify two different styles of critique. The Great Refusal is a disappointed response to the failure of socialist revolution. The Long March reflects a conception of permanent struggle with neither a foreseeable horizon of victory nor a reason to give up. The obstacles capitalism places in the path of the good life are addressed piecemeal today. The system as a whole is rarely the object of resistance. Even if it could be abolished, we now know from the experience of the communist world that the reified institutions that it has established would continue to exist in other forms and continue to call for resistance. However, this is not a dystopian society, but one in which agency is exercised in ever new forms. The task of critique is to inform that agency, to, in Marx's words, "explain to the world its own acts", showing that actual struggles contain a transcending content that can be linked to the concept of a rational social life (Marx 1967b, 214).

REFERENCES

Abbate, Janet. 1999. *Inventing the Internet*. Cambridge, MIT Press.
Arvidsson, Adam, and Elanor Colleoni. 2012. "Value in Informational Capitalism and on the Internet." *The Information Society: An International Journal*, 28 (3): 135–150.

Bakardjieva, Maria. 2012. "Subactivism: Lifeworld and politics in the age of the Internet." In *(Re)Inventing the Internet*, edited by Andrew Feenberg and Norm Friesen, 85–108. Rotterdam: Sense Publishers.

Bakardjieva, Maria, and Andrew Feenberg. 2004. "Virtual Community—No 'Killer Implication'," *New Media*, 6 (1): 37–43.

Bakardjieva, Maria, and Georgia Gaden. 2012. "Web 2.0 Technologies of the Self." *Philosophy and Technology* 25 (3): 399–413.

Barney, Darin. 2011. "Darin Barney." *Figure/Ground Communication.* Interview by Laureano Ralon, April 12. Accessed November 15, 2012. http://figure-ground.ca/interviews/darin-barney/.

Feenberg, Andrew. 1995. *Alternative modernity: the technical turn in philosophy and social theory.* Los Angeles: University of California Press.

———. 1996. "The On-Line Patient Meeting, with CNS Staff." *Journal of Neurological Sciences* 139, 129–131.

———. 2010. *Between reason and experience. Essays in technology and modernity.* Cambridge, MA: MIT Press.

———. 2012. Palimpsestology: The Many Layers of Technoscience. Accessed November 15, 2012. http://www.sfu.ca/~andrewf/layers.pdf.

———. Forthcoming 2014. *The Philosophy of Praxis: Marx, Lukács and the Frankfurt School,* London: Verso.

Feenberg, Andrew, and Darin Barney, eds. 2004. *Community in the digital age.* Lanham, MD: Rowman and Littlefield.

Feenberg, Andrew, and Maria Bakardjieva. 2004. "Consumers or citizens? The online community debate." In *Community in the digital age,* edited by Andrew Feenberg and Darin Barney, 1–28. Lanham, MD: Rowman and Littlefield.

Feenberg, Andrew, and Norm Friesen, eds. 2012. *(Re)Inventing the Internet.* Rotterdam: Sense Publishers.

Fuchs, Christian. 2010. "Labor in Informational Capitalism and on the Internet." *The Information Society: An International Journal,* 26 (3), 179–196.

Gladwell, Malcolm. 2010. "Small Change: Why the Revolution Will not be Tweeted. The New Yorker," Oct. 10. Accessed February 6, 2012. http://www.newyorker.com/reporting/2010/10/04/101004fa_fact_gladwell.

Grimes, Sara, and Andrew Feenberg. 2012. "Rationalizing play. A critical theory of digital gaming." In *(Re)Inventing the Internet*, edited by Andrew Feenberg and Norm Friesen, 21–41. Rotterdam: Sense Publishers.

Hamilton, Ted, and Feenberg, Andrew. 2012. "Alternative rationalizations and ambivalent future: A critical history of online education." In *(Re)Inventing the Internet*, edited by Andrew Feenberg and Norm Friesen, 43–70. Rotterdam: Sense Publishers.

Lievrouw, Leah. 2012. "Preface: The Internet as though Agency Mattered." In *(Re)Inventing the Internet*, edited by Andrew Feenberg and Norm Friesen, vii–x. Rotterdam: Sense Publishers.

Lukács, Georg. 1971. *History and class consciousness.* Translated by Rodney Livingstone. Cambridge, MA: MIT Press.

Marcuse, Herbert. 1966. *Eros and civilization.* Boston: Beacon Press.

———. 1972. *Counter-revolution and revolt.* Boston: Beacon.

Marx, Karl. 1857/1904. *A contribution to the critique of political economy.* Translated by N. I. Stone. Chicago: Charles H. Kerr, 1904.

———. 1867/1906. *Capital. Volume 1.* Translated by Edward Aveling. New York: Modern Library.

———.1967a. "The German ideology." In *Writings of the Young Marx on philosophy and society,* edited by Lloyd Easton and Kurt Guddat. New York: Anchor.

———.1967b. "An Exchange of Letters." In *Writings of the Young Marx on philosophy and society,* edited by Lloyd Easton and Kurt Guddat. New York: Anchor.

———. 1978. "Wage labor and capital." In *The Marx-Engels reader*, edited by Robert C. Tucker. New York: Norton.

Milberry, Kate. 2012. "Hacking for social justice. The politics of prefigurative technology." In *(Re)Inventing the Internet*, edited by Andrew Feenberg and Norm Friesen, 109–130. Rotterdam: Sense Publishers.

Simondon, Gilbert. 1958. *Du mode d'existence des objets techniques.* Paris: Aubier.

Ure, Andrew. 1835. *The philosophy of manufactures.* London: Charles Knight.

7 Producing Consumerism
Commodities, Ideologies, Practices

Graham Murdock

7.1 INTRODUCTION

Marx has recently undergone a major revaluation. Dismissed as obsolete by the fall of the Berlin Wall, he is now seen as a thoroughly contemporary figure. His face has appeared in some surprising contexts. Customers of the Sparkasse bank in the former East German town of Chemnitz selected his image for a new issue of MasterCard (Jeffries 2012, 7). Given that the financial crash of 2008 was partly caused by the overextension of consumer credit, this is not without its ironies. But among critical commentators and activists it is Marx's insistence that the dynamics of capitalism are both global in scope and subject to endemic crises that has reignited interest. As Francis Wheen notes: "Marx may only now be emerging in his true significance [and] could yet become the most influential thinker of the twenty first century" (2006, 121). I want to support this claim and argue that a properly critical analysis of the cultural landscape of present-day capitalism must begin by engaging with Marx across the whole range of his writings. This is not to argue that he provides definitive answers to present problems. To look for certainties is to ignore the unfinished and provisional nature of his work. Rather he offers us essential starting points and resources that we can mobilise and build on. One of these departure points is his analysis of the social life of commodities and the culture of consumption that surrounds them.

7.2 COMMODIFICATION AND CONSUMPTION

In the two years between 1857 and 1858, Marx filled seven notebooks with ideas, drafts and comments. These notes, now known collectively as the *Grundrisse*, prepared the way for the radical critique of economic orthodoxies published a decade later in the first volume of *Capital*. But they also introduced ideas and lines of inquiry that he never developed in any detail in his later work. This unfinished business includes his brief comments on consumption.

Although he concedes that production and consumption are two "moments of one process", he is adamant that "production is the predominant moment", "the real point of departure" and the necessary starting point for any analysis (Marx 1973, 94). It is, he argues, production that "produces consumption [. . .] not only objectively but also subjectively", simultaneously manufacturing "the object of consumption, the manner of consumption and the motive of consumption" (1973, 92). By insisting that consumption under capitalism requires not only the manufacture of commodities, but also the generation of wants and desires (motive) and the construction of specific social practices (manner), Marx paves the way for an analysis that unites a political economy of production and exchange with an investigation of the social, ideological and imaginative lives of the goods and objects we surround ourselves with.

At this point it is necessary to make a clear distinction between consumption and consumerism. In any economy that has moved beyond self-sufficiency, consuming goods and services provided by other people is a social and personal necessity. The problems arise when consumption becomes wasteful, when disposability replaces durability, and when our sense of ourselves as individualised consumers squeezes out our identities as workers and citizens, dissolving the solidarities of shared conditions. This displacement is accomplished by the insistent promotion of consumerist ideology which presents the marketplace as the primary sphere of freedom, wants to persuade us that we can only be fully ourselves, and communicates this unique sense to others through our personalised inventory of purchases. This militant equation of possessive individualism with freedom of personal and social expression has come to constitute the meta-ideology of contemporary capitalism and Marx's comments on commodities are still the best place to begin an analysis that unpacks it.

At first sight it seems odd that Marx should choose to begin the opening chapter of his magnum opus, *Capital*, with a chapter on commodities because, as he notes, "a commodity appears [. . .] a very trivial thing" (1946, 41). But for him, appearances are deeply deceptive. Concealed within the commodity are the essential clues to the way capitalism operates as both a mode of social organisation and an ideological formation. The true history of commodities and the source of their value Marx argued "does not stalk about with a label describing what it is". It is written in a "social hieroglyphic" that requires decoding. Attempting "to decipher the hieroglyphic, to get behind the secret of our own social products" is a central task for critical analysis (1946, 45).

In the autumn of 1842, Marx contributed a series of five of articles to the newly launched Cologne newspaper, the *Rheinische Zeitung*, commenting on debates in the Provincial Assembly in Düsseldorf that pressed for the cancellation of customary right to gather firewood in the forests and the introduction of a new law of theft. These provisions were the latest skirmishes in a conflict that had been gathering momentum across Europe since the Middle Ages as common pool resources were progressively enclosed and converted into private property. Five years later in *The Poverty of Philosophy*, an early draft of his core ideas written 1847, Marx had come to see this "primitive accumulation" as part of the wider process of commodification propelling capitalism's expansion. Future profits, he argued, require every available resource to be converted into a good or service that can be sold for a price in the marketplace. The decisive break with the feudal past is marked by the arrival of "a time [. . .] when the very things which till then had been communicated, but never exchanged; given but, never sold; acquired, but never bought—virtue, love, conviction, knowledge, conscience, etc finally passed into commerce [. . .] when everything, moral or physical [. . .] is brought to the market" (Marx and Engels 1976, 113). For Marx, however, the main capacity "brought to the market" was labour power, and it was this process, and its consequences, that lay at the heart of his mature analysis.

Following previous political economists (including Adam Smith and DavidRicardo), Marx argues that the value of a commodity reflects the amount of labour that has gone into producing it. As workers move from the modes of self-sufficiency and barter supported by rural economies to industrial production, they become commodities themselves. They are forced to sell their labour power for a wage that will allow them to purchase the food, clothing and other goods they need to keep themselves fit for employment and able to nurture the next generation of workers. For Marx, these "socially necessary" costs of labour are met by the value produced in only part of the working day. The rest of the time generates additional or surplus value that employers can appropriate as profit. This structure of exploitation is the dirty secret buried within every commodity. Beneath the appearance of equal exchange and honest dealing in the marketplace—a fair day's wage for a fair day's work, a useful product for a reasonable price—lies the near slavery of the sweatshop and relentless regimentation of the factory clock and machine production. The promise of utility, convenience and pleasure held out by the goods displayed in shops concealed the hard realities of the everyday struggle for subsistence.

7.3 THE CONTRADICTIONS OF CAPITALIST EXPANSION

This structure was not as solid as it seemed however, and Marx saw that the very processes that ensured ever rising rates of productivity were generating contradictions that chipped away at their foundations. Firstly, the more efficient production became, the more likely it was that a crisis of overproduction would occur with goods piling up unsold, setting in motion a highly unstable cycle of boom and bust. Secondly, by bringing workers together in large industrial plants and housing them in densely packed neighbourhoods capital created social spaces in which they could recognise their shared conditions and organise to change them.

Borrowing from his favourite novel, Mary Shelley's *Frankenstein*, he argued that just as Baron von Frankenstein's desire to manufacture a perfect life form produced a monster who tuned on his creator, so capitalism's dedicated quest to maximise profits produced the conditions for its destruction. The appearance of uninterrupted progress was deceptive. The more areas of social and imaginative life capitalism invaded the more it produced the conditions for the formation of workers' movements.

Marx underestimated capitalism's resilience. In a famous phrase he hailed the working class as the "grave diggers" of capitalism forgetting that cemeteries were generally organised by public institutions and were, for many, sites of devotion. He miscalculated the extent to which the expansion of advanced capitalism required a strong state prepared to head off economic crises by increasing public expenditure on both welfare and warfare. Nor did he fully recognise the importance of populist appeals to patriotism and the imagined community of the nation in weakening class consciousness. He was however absolutely correct in seeing the fetishism of commodities as central to capitalism's efforts to cover its tracks.

7.4   DECEPTIVE SURFACES: COMMODITY CULTURE

In religious belief systems, a fetish is believed to have magical or supernatural powers. As a Jewish boy who had grown up in Trier, a mainly Catholic city that had only been reincorporated into a Protestant Prussian state three years before he was born, Marx was well aware of the power often attributed to religious relics, statues and images. He had studied the Old Testament at university, and been struck by its absolute condemnation of idol worship and the creation of graven images, and by the early 1840s he had embarked on a study of Christian art, now sadly lost (Boer 2010, 210). For him, commodities were a secular extension of religious fetishes. Once on display, they took on a life of their own and were invested with the power to change lives. The early professional advertisers, who were developing their sales techniques just as *Capital* was finally published, recognised the potency of appeals to transformation immediately. Borrowing from Christian evangelical movements they promoted the healing touch of commodities, promising that consumers could be born again and enjoy a life of comfort, peace and satisfaction. Dirt would be banished by proprietary cleaning fluids, bodily ailments addressed by patent medicines, and domestic drudgery abolished by labour saving machines. "All that was required was one single choice" (Loeb 1994, 184). This appeal to consumerism—the belief that consumption is the primary space of freedom and self-expression—proved enormously effective as an ideological system for three reasons.

Firstly, advertising and other forms of product promotion are carefully designed to project attention forwards, celebrating the pleasures of possession and use and silencing awkward questions about the organisation of production. Consumers are encouraged to think about what commodities will do for them and to forget to ask where they have come from, who produced them under what conditions, and what social and environmental costs were incurred in assembling them. This distancing of use from origins was steadily reinforced as mechanised mass production removed all marks of human labour and the growth of national road and railway systems and transnational steam ship lines steadily increased the distances commodities travelled from their point of origin to their eventual market, making it more and more difficult to recall how and where they were made. This absence was increasingly addressed by the rise of branded goods bearing the manufacturer's name. As Lord Randolf Churchill, observed at time: "We live [. . .] in the age of Holloway's Pills, of Colman's Mustard, and of Horniman's pure tea" (quoted in Richards 1991, 249). The effect was to transfer credit for their production from labour to capital.

Secondly, the proliferation of purchasable commodities operated to validate the belief in "progress" that underpinned industrial capitalism's model of modernity. Improvements to the material base of public life—street lighting, sewage systems, new transport networks—provided one highly visible index of the benefits delivered by capitalism's appropriation of invention. The domestic conveniences, comforts and consolations delivered by manufactured commodities anchored this process firmly in the intimacies of domestic life. These two modes of legitimation were welded together to spectacular effect at the Great Exhibition of 1851, held first in London's Hyde Park and later at the Crystal Palace in a southern suburb. The architects used the new technologies of steel and glass to construct the first wholly modern cathedral of capitalism and the organisers packed it with contemporary inventions and commodities of all kinds. It was "a display of [. . .] perverted ingenuity on an unprecedented scale" in which useful objects jostled for attention with commodities of dubious value, like the corset that "opened instantaneously in case of emergencies", but the overall message was clear: "the world was full of wonderful objects that you couldn't live without" (Stevenson 2006, 21) made possible by the inventiveness of scientists and engineers and the entrepreneurial spirit of the new capitalists.

Thirdly, it was no accident that the new world of goods displayed at the Great Exhibition was housed in a building that became a major destination for day trippers and tourists. There was a powerful connection between the new consumption and the new cityscapes filled with restaurants, theatres, dance halls, music venues and exhibits adapted to a variety of tastes and incomes. These new opportunities for enjoyment and relaxation lay at the heart of the pragmatic bargain struck between capital and labour. Industrialised work might be dirty, dangerous, monotonous and alienating but the wages earned provided the chance to exercise individual choices and personal expression during "free" time. In this conception the pleasures of consumption and leisure appeared as rewards for the rigours of labour.

7.5   LANDSCAPES OF DESIRE

As young man of twenty-four, Marx had ridiculed a German author who claimed that the veneration of religious fetishes raises man above his sensuous desires and saves him from being a mere animal. Far from transcending sensuous desire "Marx riposted fetishism *is* the religion of sensuous desire: 'Fantasy arising from desire deceives the fetish-worshipper into believing that an inanimate object will give up its natural character in order to comply with his desires'" (Wheen 2006, 43). Marx never returned to this argument in his later work. In *Capital* he remarks in passing that human wants may "spring [. . .] from fancy" (1946, 1), but it was left to Western Marxists, strongly influenced by Freud to explore the cultural construction of demand and desire. For Walter Benjamin, the fetishism of commodities had a strong sensuous and erotic dimension. It was a process of redirecting "desire and passion towards lifeless manufactured products [. . .] [through which] the commodity is transformed into an object of sexual desire, and to consume is to consummate this desire" (Gilloch 1996, 120). In this conception, moving through the world of commodities was no longer simply a secular form of religious devotion, it was a series of intimate encounters with objects charged with some of the same erotic intensity that devotees of sexual fetishes might derive from rubber clothing or high-heeled shoes. As with sexual fetishism, the pleasures of the new consumer landscape were as much about looking as possession.

This new landscape of desire was constructed around two major innovations: the mobilisation of mass media for advertising and promotion and the development of new retail environments. Commercialised media played a central role in the manufacture of consumer desire. New shopping environments provided spaces where desire could be enacted. Producing consumption was therefore never simply a matter of imaginative colonisation, of forging connections between goods for sale and consumers' sense of themselves. It was always also a process of integrating objects of desire ever more firmly into everyday routines of anticipation, purchase and display.

Table 7.1   The Consolidation of Commodity Culture

Medium	Retail Environment	Central Principle
Newspapers	Local shops/markets	Utility
Cinema	Department stores	Display
Commercial network television	Supermarkets	Flow
Multi-channel television	Malls	Immersion
Web 2.0	Retail destinations	Integration

As Table 7.1 shows, we can think of the production of commodity culture as a process in which developments in the organisation of retailing are accompanied by new media of popular communication and both are organised around a succession of common principles. Each stage of this process embeds consumerism ever more firmly at the centre of everyday life under capitalism both imaginatively and practically. Before we unpack these connections in more detail, however, some notes of caution. The process outlined here is emphatically not a process of cancellation. It is a process of superimposition. At any one moment particular media and retail environments may come to play a central organising role but they do not displace previous forms. They coexist alongside them generating new combinations and interactions. We are currently seeing a surge in shopping online but people are still going to markets, to thrift stores and malls. Or rather some people are. Which brings me to my second caveat. The account presented here is very much a sketch of central tendencies. A full critical history of the production of commodity culture must place the persistence of poverty, inequality and exclusion centre stage. It will also need to be more systematically comparative, exploring how developments pioneered in the United States, the most comprehensive commodity culture, have rippled out across the globe colliding with other histories.

Even so, over time we can see three general dynamics steadily gathering momentum. Firstly, commodities are increasingly promoted not for their utility or value for money but for the lifestyles and personal identities they signal. Secondly, the commodity culture constructed by commercial media and retail environments becomes increasingly enveloping and immersive. Thirdly, consumption becomes more and more an extension of labour.

7.6   UTILITY: GETTING BY AND MAKING DO

The overwhelming priority for most of the workers Marx was familiar with was making ends meet, struggling to ensure that a meagre wage or an intermittent income covered the basic necessities. The emphasis was on utility and value for money. The consumer landscape reflected these imperatives. The newspaper press carried mostly classified advertising promoting products, or second-hand items for resale, grouped into basic categories. This pattern was repeated in local shops and market stalls each of which specialised in a particular range of commodities—groceries, meat, furniture, clothing. Neither space paid much attention to visual display. Press advertisements relied wholly or mainly on printed text offering unvarnished descriptions. Traditional shops simply stacked examples of the commodities they had to sell in the window or outside on the street. There was little or no attempt to display them against enticing or glamorous backgrounds. Many of the routine goods on sale were generic rather than branded. Customers bought scoopfuls of tea or sugar or flour emptied into a plain bag.

This utilitarian and visual austerity ended with innovations in lithography that revolutionised poster design, introducing new vivid colours, the launch of new magazines dominated by display advertising, the expansion of department stores, and the popularisation of cinema

7.7 DISPLAY: LOOKING, WISHING, POSSESSING

The department stores that "emerged slowly and unevenly between 1850 and 1890" (Benson 1986, 13) were from the outset, integrated leisure environments, offering their patrons eating places and entertainment as well as opportunities to shop. Initially confined to the major metropolitan areas and catering primarily for a clientele drawn from the rising middle class of professionals and white collar workers, they gradually spread out into provincial centres. For those living in small towns and rural areas, there were the new mail-order catalogues pioneered by Richard Sears and Alvah Roebuck in the United States. First launched in 1888, by 1894 their catalogue ran to 322 pages. It was a department store in print, displaying images of goods for sale in carefully arranged sections.

Department stores took full advantage of innovations in glass technology and lighting, as electricity displaced gas, to fill the large windows that fronted onto the street with theatrical displays in which commodities featured as central characters in a variety of scenes. The key techniques in this new dramatization of goods were vigorously promoted by Frank Baum in *Shop Window*, the trade journal he launched in 1897. Three years later, in 1900, he published *The Wonderful World of Oz*, one of most successful children's books of the twentieth century. Ironically, for such an active advocate of the persuasive power of illusions, the story offered a perfect metaphor for the limits of commodity culture. It recounts the adventures of a group of incomplete figures in search of a legendary wizard who can make them whole. When they eventually find him they discover that he has no magical powers and his fabled reputation is so much hot air. It is entirely appropriate that the story was later made into one of the best known Hollywood films, because the cinema, more than anything else, animated commodities and incorporated them as actors in dramas of everyday living.

By 1920, Will Hays, the man appointed to censor the erotic excesses of Hollywood, was in no doubt that film offered a potent advertisement for American capitalism and the American way of life, carrying "to every American at home, and to millions of potential purchasers abroad, the visual, vivid perception of American manufactured products" (Eckert 1978, 5). But it was the novelist F. Scott Fitzgerald, in one of his short stories, who recognised how indelibly demand was shaped by desire. His young heroine, Yanci, sits in a movie theatre, completely immersed in images of desirable objects and sensuous styles. Watching the star "Mae Murray swirl through splendidly imagined vistas [. . .] she calculated the cost of the apartment.

She rejoiced in the beauty of Mae Murray's clothes and furs, her gorgeous hats, her short-seeming French shoes" (quoted in Fuller 1996, 162) .

The connections between looking, wishing and possessing were cemented together by a series of practical devices. Manufacturers paid to have their goods featured in films. In 1896, in the first recorded instance of product placement, crates of Lever Brothers soap were prominently displayed in front of two women filmed doing the weekly wash in a Lumiere Brothers' short. By the 1920s, promotional tie-ins were routinely transferring the aura of the screen to the stores that surrounded cinemas in town centres. As *Film Daily,* noted in 1931, it was possible to use "any feature film" to tie "the exhibition show up directly and compellingly with the nationally advertised product right in the theatre man's own home town" (quoted in Newell et al. 2006, 582). The publicity pack that accompanied the release of *Now Voyager* (1942), a film that celebrates a dull spinster's transformation into a woman of elegance and sophistication, urged local clothing outlets to devise "special windows showing travelling ensembles and accessories" under the slogan "Now Voyager, Buy Wisely. . .Now!" (quoted in La Place 1987, 142).

In 1899, the American economist, Thorstein Veblen, published the book that made his name, *The Theory of the Leisure Class.* He had grown up in a Norwegian speaking farming family in Wisconsin steeped in the Protestant insistence that consumption should meet immediate needs and reward virtuous effort. He saw the lavish displays of wealth staged by the new aristocracy of money who had made their fortunes in banking, oil and railroads, as a decisive break with this utilitarian ethos which converted consumption into a potent new medium for announcing personal achievements and tastes. The commercial democratisation of fashion, which translated styles from the silver screen and the celebrity home to the high street, generalised this new style of "conspicuous consumption" as Veblen called it. It ceased to be a language of objects spoken solely by the super-rich and became common currency. Children were increasingly incorporated into this emerging consumer complex as both apprentices in the adult workshop of desire and as a market in their own right. In 1932, Disney, seizing the moment, launched a merchandising division to promote products based on Mickey Mouse and other the characters in their successful animated films.

7.8   FLOW: CHANNELLING DESIRE

By the early 1950s, it was possible for the first time, to talk of a truly mass-consumer society in the United States. The rising affluence of the war-time boom had enabled more and more families to move from maintaining living standards to constructing lifestyles. The dictates of necessity were displaced by the pleasures of choice and the symbolic charge of brands. This new massification required a new organising principle and that principle was flow.

In 1916, the American entrepreneur, Clarence Saunders, opened his Piggly Wiggly, store in Memphis, Tennessee, reputedly named after the children's nursery rhyme, "This Little Piggy Went to Market". It was the world's first self-service store, and the blueprint for the modern supermarket. Department stores were staffed by sales assistants who advised shoppers on the qualities of the various goods available. Often they also provided a free home delivery service. Customers entering the Piggly Wiggly passed through a turnstile, walked around aisles piled high with branded goods, took their purchases to a check-out till, and then carried them away on foot, by urban transport systems or, increasingly, by car. Displays were arranged to ensure that customers wishing to reach the more desirable or inviting commodities had to first negotiate stacks of routine household goods. But it was not until later, when Michael J. Cullen opened the first of his chain of King Cullen supermarkets in the Queen's district of New York in 1930, that the principles of organising retailing around discounted prices, cash and carry, and ample car parking, became more generalised.

The carefully tracked flow system of the supermarket was replicated in the media sphere by the central organising principle of commercial network broadcasting that was being consolidated at the same time: the prime-time schedule. By arranging programmes in a carefully devised sequence designed to ensure that listeners and viewers stayed tuned to the channel, broadcasters introduced flow into the heart of domestic life. Going to the cinema or "window shopping" required effort and planning. They were events. Commercial broadcasting domesticated desire. As Frank Arnold, an early American enthusiast of commercial radio, noted in 1931: "for the first time in the history of mankind" it is possible to enter "the homes of the nation through doors and windows, no matter how tightly barred" and to deliver "the message of advertising [into] the midst of the family circle, in moments of relaxation" (quoted in Smulyan 1994, 87).

Commercial television extended this selling proposition by adding visuality to the intimacy of radio. Despite the regulators best intentions, its promotional impetus could not be confined to the designated advertising breaks. It spilled out across the entire schedule. Whatever the type of programme "the effect was a visual, visceral dazzle, an absorbing sense of pleasure in the act of perusa [. . .] Things to look at. New things. The latest things" (Marling 1994, 5). The screen became a "shop window, the box a warehouse" and "every prop" was "purchasable" (Conrad 1982, 122). Viewers were constructed as consumers twice over, as audiences for the endless parade of goods and styles on display in the programmes and as potential purchasers of the commodities promoted in the advertisements.

In Europe in contrast, terrestrial television was dominated by public service channels, funded out of taxation and carrying no advertising. But in 1955, Britain launched the first of a nation-wide network of commercial television stations. There were strict limits on the amount of advertising permitted in any one hour, but these were easily circumvented by

the introduction of "advertising magazines" which incorporated promotional plugs into programmes presented as information or entertainment
(Murdock 1992). The timing was opportune. The last vestige of post-war
rationing (for meat) had ended in 1954, and following the success of the
pioneering Premier Supermarket in South London, launched in 1951, supermarkets were reorganising shopping habits across the country.

Britain was an exception however. Elsewhere in Europe innovations in
retailing were some years ahead of the arrival of commercial television.
In France for example, the first Carrefour supermarket opened in 1958,
launching a chain that has now achieved global reach and ranks as the
world's third largest retailer by profit. But it was not until 1984 that the
public service television monopoly was broken, with the launch of Canal+.

7.9   IMMERSION: BUILDING THE GREAT MALL

The rapid growth of commercial television in 1950s America was accompanied by the rise of a new kind of retail environment, the mall.

The idea of a covered pedestrian area containing a number of separately
owned and run shops was not in itself novel. The glass covered Burlington
Arcade launched in London in 1819 provided a model adopted throughout
Europe. By the 1930s however it appeared very much as part of a vanishing
past, prompting the German critic Sigfried Kracauer to write a valedictory:
"Goodbye to the Linden Arcade", and Walter Benjamin to embark on a
massive project in cultural archaeology devoted to the Paris arcades. In
contrast, the mall was an American invention.

The Southdale Center, the first fully enclosed and covered mall, opened in
Elina, Minnesota, in 1956. But it was another Minnesota town, Blooming-
ton, which developed the mall's full potential in 1992 with the first mega mall,
the Mall of America. Alongside the myriad retail outlets it contained a theme
park, ice rink, movie theatres, restaurants, and three hotels. By combining
multiple consumption and leisure choices in one thermostatically controlled
and internally policed environment it created a classic total institution. It
promised patrons that there was no need to go anywhere else because everything one could possibly need was right there, within easy reach.

This enveloping, immersive, quality was reproduced in domestic space
by a commercial television environment irreversibly altered by the introduction of multiple cable channels and the advent of 24-hour programming. In the United Sates the major networks that had dominated television
since its introduction saw their share of the audience steadily decline. In
Europe, cable and satellite channels broke the monopoly hold of the public service broadcasters in country after country and paved the way for
the launch of new terrestrial advertising funded channels. The result was
a commodity culture more fully integrated than ever before. Mega malls
provided multiple entertainments as well as shopping opportunities. Cable

television packages offered home shopping channels alongside film, sports, and entertainment services. Increasing reliance on corporate sponsorship and product placement expanded the paid-for opportunities to integrate commodities into programming.

This multiplication of choice, with mall outlets and cable channels catering to specific market segments and taste cultures, was part of a more general response to the gathering problems facing capitalism. By the mid-1970s it was clear that "the US economy and the world economy as a whole [had] entered a full-fledged structural crisis, ending the long boom, and marking the beginning of decades of deepening stagnation" (Foster and McChesney 2012, 41). In an effort to maintain profitability, capital embarked on a sustained restructuring of both production and consumption. "The tacit guarantee that increases in workers' productivity would be met by increases in wages", that had held throughout the post-war period, was suspended (Graeber 2012, 373). Routine tasks were increasingly outsourced to the low wage economies opened up by the globalization of market dynamics while at home organised labour was undermined at every turn. These moves to drive down costs were matched by a concerted push to boost consumption by "increased product differentiation and accelerated product turnover, promoted by ever-more highly targeted marketing" (Streeck 2012, 33). This commercialised diversification shifted the locus of consumption from the satisfaction of needs to the servicing of wants. The mass production of standardised goods had allowed families to acquire a range of basic consumer durables, like cars and refrigerators, for the first time. The new ethos, based on commercialised diversification, presented consumption as an unparalleled opportunity "for the individualised expression of social identities" (Streeck 2012, 33). With real wages falling however, consumers' ability to negotiate this landscape of super abundance and intensified promotion was sustained by a significant extension of credit.

A number of companies had introduced previous schemes allowing customers to access goods and services and pay for them later, but these were confined to particular purchases or types of goods. The year 1966 saw the launch of forerunners of the two most widely used general purpose credit cards, Visa and MasterCard. For the first time it was possible to have it all, now. As Jean Braudrillard noted in *The System of Objects*, published two years later, this divorce of consumption from ability to pay was presented as a new consumer right and "restriction of any kind on the possibility of buying on credit is felt to be a retaliatory measure on the part of the state", an unwarranted attack on personal freedom (Braudrillard 2005, 169). Government endorsement of this perception later led to the deregulation of the banking sector and the profligate over lending that precipitated the financial crisis of 2008. By 2010 household debt accounted for a quarter of the total debt owed in the United States, well above the 14 per cent owed by the corporate sector and the 18 per cent owed by the federal government (Duncan 2012, 17).

The new fluidity of expenditure accelerated the eclipse of utility as a criterion of consumer choice. In a marketplace characterised by "overaccumulation, forward flight, speeded-up consumption" (Baudrillard 2005, 173), in which objects wear out as soon the credit used to buy them is paid off, and often before, their material qualities become less important than their deployment as extensions of the self and media of social communication. As a consequence, "to become an object of consumption, an object must first become a sign" (Baudrillard 2005, 218).

The System of Objects began life as Baudrillard's doctoral thesis presided over by a committee that included Roland Barthes whose 1957 monograph, *Mythologies* (Barthes 1972), suggested a new way of thinking about the operation of ideology. The book collected together a series of short pieces Barthes had written for a literary magazine, reflecting on the symbolic life of events and objects in a France slowly recovering from the ravages of war and becoming a consumer society. These fragments of empirical evidence were framed by a longer essay, "Myth Today", arguing that it is the string of associations, the connotations, that images detonate that anchor ideological systems most securely in personal experience. In this conception, consumerist ideology, to borrow Marx phrase, "does not stalk about with a label describing what it is" or broadcast directive messages through a loudspeaker. It works by weaving the multiple visual appeals, sensuous surfaces and physical pleasures, held out by everyday commodities and their promotional appeals, into a continuous master narrative based on the promise of personal fulfilment through possession.

This consumerist narrative has steadily spread to countries where broadcasting was previously strongly state directed, including China. Mainstream television services are now financed mainly from advertising revenues, multichannel television has arrived in major cities and towns, and there is sufficient disposable income among the new rich and rising the middle class to support the world's largest shopping mall, the Golden Resources, in Beijing, which opened in 2004. A similar landscape is under construction in the world's other emerging major economic power, India, and carries a powerful ideological charge. As one Indian journalist notes: "Malls have become urban India's homage to 'progress', communicating a great sense of reassurance that if the mall is large enough and has enough brands, all is well with the world" (Rao 2005). Identifying the future with increasing opportunities for consumption and lifestyle choice has steadily undermined the vision of nation building that drove post-independence "development". Personal satisfactions take priority over public investments and communal facilities.

7.10 INTEGRATION: CONSUMPTION AS WORK

One of Clarence Saunders's aims in designing his pioneering supermarket was to transfer the labour involved in comparing rival goods, transporting them, and storing them, from producers to consumers. Customers took on the tasks previously undertaken by shop assistants, delivery men, and warehouse workers. Since then leisure has involved consumers in an expanding range of work. Customers at fast food outlets are required to help themselves to salads and dispose of their leftovers when they have finished eating. Flat pack furniture requires self-assembly. Travel increasingly involves self-ticketing (see Ritzer and Jurgenson 2010).

In his seminal analysis of the "audience commodity", Dallas Smythe extended the analysis of leisure as labour to television viewing, arguing that what television advertisers are buying from commercial broadcasters is viewers' attention and receptiveness to the ads. Far from the ads interrupting the programmes, the programmes serve as a prelude and accompaniment to the ads. Like the "potato chips and peanuts given to customers of the pub bar, or cocktail lounge", they offer a "free lunch" designed to keep people relaxed and receptive (Smythe 1981, 37f). For Smythe, the pleasures of looking and the exercise of "audience power" (1981, 26) are mobilised primarily to oil the wheels of people's never-ending labour of "marketing consumer goods and services to themselves" (1981, 34). Domestic space becomes an extension of the factory assembly line (and, as we saw earlier, the supermarket), subject to the industrialised regimes of time and motion written into broadcasting schedules. This novel application of Marx's analysis of labour was taken a step further by two other North American writers, Sut Jhally and Bill Livant, who argued that in the same way that profits in production come from "surplus labour", so profits in the commercial broadcasting system come from the "surplus watching time" undertaken after the viewing time required to cover costs has been completed (1986, 127). In their hypothetical example, audiences only have to watch four of the twelve ads in a half-hour show to meet its costs. Their attention to the remaining eight is pure profit.

This analysis was presented by Smythe and his supporters, not just as a useful extension to critical political economy's analysis of commercial broadcasting, but as a necessary change of direction because in their view "mass media are not characterised primarily by what they put into audiences (messages) but by what they take out (value)" (Jhally and Livant 1986, 143). As I have argued here, realising the full potential of Marx's analysis also requires a sustained engagement with the ideological dimensions of consumption and their practical reproduction in the organisation of commercial media and retail environments. This is not an either/or choice. Recent developments have made it both/and.

Capitalism has always relied on advanced communications systems to track, collate, and co-ordinate the dispersed production and consumption activities it sets in motion. In the first phase of expansion these tasks were accomplished by the technologies of the telegraph, and later the telephone and the punched card machine. Now they depend on the convergence of computing, telecommunications and cultural production. Digitalisation has created networks of unparalleled reach and capacity. Struggles over how much of this capacity will be open to the public, how public networks will be organised, who will have access to them and for what purposes, will be major points of conflict in the coming decades.

There are two very different models of networking currently in play. On the one side we see an explosion of peer-to-peer exchange based on horizontal networks offering great potential for mobilising and coordinating oppositional activity. On the other side there is the concerted corporate push to reconstruct the Internet as a vertical, top-down, network that will install commodity culture, ever more firmly, as both an ideological formation and a set of social practices.

The stakes in this struggle are already clear. Corporate interests are devoting a great deal of energy to commandeering public networks in the service of promotion and profit. Users are tracked every time they click on a hyperlink and their progress across the Net logged and collated to provide detailed consumer profiles that can be used to personalise promotional appeals more effectively. The imaginary social spaces created by the participants in multi user online games become sites for the construction of virtual stores by real offline retail chains. These are extensions of long standing practices. More radical, and potentially far reaching in its implications, are the efforts to enlist consumers as unpaid labour, contributing their time, effort and expertise to developing and marketing products. They are no longer simply spectators and shoppers. They are invited to become "co-creators" of the products they buy, productive consumers, "prosumers". In the process, leisure and social relations become additional, and increasingly intensified, areas of exploitation (Comor 2010). Basketball enthusiast are invited to contribute ideas for modifying the sports shoes they wear. Contributors to film and music sites run by fans are enlisted as viral marketers, promoting a new release by word of mouth. Young people who join the Tremor network operated by Proctor and Gamble, one of the major manufacturers of routine household products, are urged to talk up selected items when they meet with friends online and offline. As we noted earlier, Marx saw the logic of capitalism continually bringing "things which till then had been communicated, but never exchanged; given but never sold" to the market (Marx and Engels 1976, 113). The commodification of friendship and everyday talk is a perfect instance of this process in action.

In 2012, Facebook, the most widely used of the current social networking sites, announced that it would use the photographs that users posted on their personal pages in advertisements directed at their online friends. Underpinning this move is a double exploitation. Firstly, anyone joining the site is required to sign over the intellectual property rights to anything they post for Facebook's owners to use as they wish. Secondly, every time a user creates material or follows links they are adding to the general store of digital information that maps their social location, likes and preferences. This pool of "Big Data" is then mined by multiple commodity producers to craft personalised appeals that invest promotional speech with a new intimacy. As Internet access migrates from laptop computers to tablets and smartphones which locate users geographically, promotional culture becomes ever more mobile, ubiquitous and immersive. It is always on, always there; enticing, nudging, cajoling, reminding. We are all now increasingly immersed in a promotional ocean with no islands or shores.

At one level, "Facebook's business model" clearly represents a step change in the "outsourcing/crowdsourcing of paid work to unpaid labour time" which, according to one calculation, generates 111 per cent times the monetary value of the investment the company has made in providing and servicing the site (Fuchs 2012, 715). The emergence of the "user commodity" invests Dallas Smythe's original analysis of the "audience commodity" with new salience and centrality. But as he points out, a critical, Marxist informed, political economy of culture and communications also needs to pay attention to the dialectic of consciousness, ideology, and material practices (Smythe 1981, xvi–xviii). As I have argued here, tracing the ways that consumerism, as a meta ideology, has been visualised and dramatized within promotional culture and anchored in everyday imagination and activity is central to this project.

Observers of digital technologies who argue that we are moving from living *with* media to living *in and through* them (Deuze 2012) are apt to forget that this increasing mediatisation of everyday life is not an abstract movement. It is part of a generalised, and very concrete, process of intensified integration into commodity culture

In 2008 the old slave port of Bristol, in the west of England, saw the opening of a new zoned area, Cabot Circus. Its director, Richard Belt, was adamant that it was a segment of the city, not a shopping centre. The developers behind the project set out to build a mall without walls, a "retail destination" that spreads out into the surrounding area, commandeering public spaces in the service of brand promotion. What appear, at first sight, to be ordinary streets, are privately owned and policed. As Belt notes: "These places are quite a new breed. We've applied all the usual rules that shopping centres do, but because it's a street scape, it's got customers scratching their heads a bit" (Harris 2008, 7).

7.11   NETWORKED CONTRADICTIONS

The worldwide celebration of markets and consumption has been fuelled by an increasing disillusion with state ownership and central planning. Undermined by corruption, inefficiency, and unresponsiveness to popular demand, public initiatives came to be seen as barriers rather than agents of "progress", a perception reinforced by the collapse of the Soviet Union. Some governments embraced market driven alternatives with enthusiasm and zeal, others were forced to implement "structural reajustments" as a condition of loans or membership of the World Trade Organization. As a result, there is now no major economic zone that is not incorporated into the world capitalist system and subject to its ruling ideology of consumerism. As with the first wave of capitalist expansion, however, this latest phase is simultaneously generating new contradictions and providing new means to mobilise opposition.

Marketization has been highly uneven in both its development and impacts. Firstly, there has been a rapidly growing divide between the winners and losers in this process. For every hi-tech hub and creative quarter there are continually sprawling shanty towns and slums. For every expanding town and city there is a depopulated countryside. For every corporate headquarters and research facility housing highly rewarded executives and experts, there is an "offshore" sweatshop, call centre, or factory employing workers on the minimum possible wage. For every business traveller and tourist there is a wave of migrant labourers and asylum seekers. Secondly, it is now clear that industrial expansion has imposed cumulative and irreversible environmental costs that are also unequally distributed. The strip mining and deforestation entailed in maintaining supplies of essential raw materials and foods has been located mainly in low-income countries or regions. When their "useful" life is over the pollution embedded in the standard components of washing machines, television sets, personal computers, mobile phones, and other consumer items has been transported out of city centres and suburbs and dumped in remote rural areas or on the outer edges of cities. These inequalities have created a proliferating global population of the exploited, dispossessed and humiliated. In common with many Victorian social commentators, Marx drew a sharp distinction between the labouring poor and the floating population of the "lumpen proletariat" moving from job to job. The former were the raw material for revolution, the latter a problem to be controlled. Under current conditions, this distinction no longer holds. Contemporary exploitation has multiple faces.

In response to the globalization of exploitation and destitution we see the globalization of a potential response. A new radical opposition to the empire of capital is in the process of formation, based on a philosophy of cosmopolitan citizenship and demanding the implementation of social justice on a global scale. Commodity culture has provided one key arena for mass mobilisation. The consumer boycotts of goods made by child labour or involving environmental despoliation, the rising demand for more effective recycling of discarded goods and packaging, and the growing support for Fair Trade produce, are indicators of a shift in sensibilities in capitalism's affluent centres. But the real struggle is yet to come. The gathering challenge of climate change will require not simply more ecologically informed modes of consumption but a substantial scaling down. The financial crash of 2008 and its aftermath complicates matters however. In a number of key Western capitalist economies, high rates of unemployment, particularly among the young, coupled with savage cuts in public expenditure and a sustained squeeze on personal and household finances, have forced a general curtailment of consumption. At the same time, China, faced with falling demand for its products in major overseas markets, is committed to substantially increasing domestic levels of consumption.

Governments everywhere that staked their legitimacy on the promise of increased opportunities for consumption have a vested interest in maintaining or restoring "business as usual". The challenge for radical critics is to devise workable alternative models of consumption underpinned by principles of sustainability, mutuality and social justice. In the battle for popular consent to a post-consumerist social order, the struggle for control of the new global networks of communication will play a pivotal role.

It is tempting to see the main business of radical political economy as demolishing the facile utopianism of the more naïve Internet enthusiasts and developing a comprehensive inventory and critique of the formidable weapons the Internet is adding to capitalism's armoury. This is certainly necessary, but it is not sufficient. We also need to work towards an alternative grounded in practical principles of cosmopolitan citizenship and workable proposals for creating the institutional anchors that will secure a global network of popular communication capable of delivering the basic resources for understanding and action that will implement these principles across the full range of everyday experience.

REFERENCES

Barthes, Rolandes. 1972. *Mythologies*. London: Paladin.

Baudrillard, Jean. 2005. *The system of objects*. London. Verso.

Benson, Susan P. 1986. *Counter cultures: Saleswomen, managers and customers in American department stores, 1890–1940*. Urbana, IL: University of Illinois Press.

Boer, Roland. 2010. "That hideous pagan idol: Marx, fetishism, and graven images." *Critique: Journal of Socialist Theory* 31 (1): 93–116.

Comor, Edward. 2010. Contextualising and critiquing the fantastic prosumer: power, alienation and hegenomy. *Critical Sociology* 37 (1): 309–327.

Conrad, Peter. 1982. *Television: The medium and its manners*. London: Routledge and Kegan Paul.

Deuze, Mark. 2012. *Media life*. Cambridge: Polity Press.

Duncan, Richard. 2012. "Interview: A new global depression?" *New Left Review* 77: 5–33

Eckert, Charles. 1978. The Carole Lombard in Macy's window. *Quarterly Review of Film Studies* 3 (1): 1–21.

Foster, John Bellamy, and Robert W. McChesney. 2012. *The endless crisis. How monopoly-finance capital produces stagnation and upheaval from the USA to China*. New York: Monthly Review Press.

Fuchs, Christian. 2012. "Dallas Smythe today. The audience commodity, the digital labour debate, Marxist political economy and critical theory. Prolegomena to a digital labour theory of value." *tripleC: Communication, Capitalism & Critique. Open Access Journal for a Global Sustainable Information Society* 10 (2): 692–740.

Fuller, Kathryn H. 1996. *At the picture show. Small-town audiences and the creation of movie fan culture.* Washington, DC: Smithsonian Institute Press.

Gilloch, Graeme. 1996. *Myth and metropolis: Walter Benjamin and the city.* Cambridge, MA: Polity Press.

Graeber, David. 2012. *Debt: The first 5,000 years.* New York: Melville House.

Harris, John. 2008. "Hard Sell." *The Guardian*, G2, October 24: 4–7.

Jeffries, Stuart. 2012. "Top Marx." *The Guardian*, G2, July 5: 6–9.

Jhally Sut and Bill Livant. 1986. "Watching as working. The valorization of audience consciousness." *Journal of Communication* 36 (3): 124–143.

La Place, M. 1987. Producing and consuming the woman's film: discursive struggle in Now Voyager. In *Home is where the heart is: Studies in melodrama and the woman's film*, ed. Christine Gledhill, 138–166. London: British Film Institute.

Loeb, Lorri A. 1994. *Consuming angles. Advertising and Victorian women.* Oxford: Oxford University Press.

Marling, Karal A. 1994. *As seen on TV. The visual culture of everyday life in the 1950s.* Cambridge, MA: Harvard University Press.

Marx, Karl. 1946. *Capital. A critical analysis of capitalist production. Volume 1.* London: George Allen and Unwin.

———. 1973. *Grundrisee: Foundations of the critique of political economy.* Harmondsworth: Penguin Books

Marx, Karl, and Friedrich Engels. 1976. *Collected works. Volume 6.* New York: International Publishers.

Murdock, Graham. 1992. "Embedded persuasions. The fall and rise of integrated advertising." In *Come on down. Popular media culture in post-war Britain*, edited by Dominic Strinati and Stephen Wagg, 202–231. London: Routledge.

Newell, Jay, Charles T. Salmon, and Susan Chang. 2006. "The hidden history of product placement." *Journal of Broadcasting and Electronic Media* 50 (4): 575–594.

Rao, Geeta. 2005. *Mall and supermalls.* Accessed December 21, 2012. http://www.hindu.com/mp/2005/06/11/stories/2005061103190300.htm.

Richards, Thomas. 1991. *The commodity culture of Victorian England. Advertising and spectacle, 1851–1914.* London: Verso.

Ritzer, George, and Nathan Jurgenson. 2010. "Production, consumption, prosumption. The nature of capitalism in the age of the digital 'prosumer'." *Journal of Consumer Culture* 10 (1): 13–36.

Smulyan, Susan 1994. *Selling radio: The commercialization of American broadcasting 1920–1934.* Washington, DC: Smithsonian Institution Press.

Smythe, Dallas W. 1981. *Dependency road. Communications, capitalism, consciousness and Canada.* Norwood, NJ : Ablex.

Stevenson, Jane. 2006. Power to the people. *The Observer*, Review, August 13: 21.

Streeck, Wolfgang. 2012. "Citizens as customers. Considerations on the new politics of consumption." *New Left Review* 76: 27–47.

Veblen, Thorstein. 1899. *The theory of the leisure class.* New York: Macmillan.

Wheen, Francis. 2006. *Marx's Das Kapital. A biography.* London: Atlantic Books.

8 Social Media?
The Unsocial Character of Capitalist Media

Marisol Sandoval

8.1 INTRODUCTION

Social media are commonly understood as media that foster social interaction, collaboration, sharing and participation. Clay Shirky argues that social media "increase our ability to share, to cooperate, with one another, and to take collective action, all outside the framework of traditional institutional institutions and organizations" (Shirky 2008, 20f). Van Dijk stresses that "The very word 'social' associated with media implies that platforms are user centered and that they facilitate communal activities, just as the term 'participatory' emphasises human collaboration. Indeed, social media can be seen as online facilitators or enhancers of *human* networks—webs of people that promote connectedness as a social value" (van Dijck 2013, 11). According to boyd the term social media "is often used to describe the collection of software that enables individuals and communities to gather, communicate, share, and in some cases collaborate or play" (boyd 2009).

These definitions show that qualities such as sharing, collaborating and participating are often considered to be essential characteristics of what academics and the public now tend to term social media—Facebook, YouTube, Twitter, Wikipedia, etc. The current debate about social media however solely focuses on the level of productive forces. Following this rhetoric, new technologies increase the degree of social interaction and thus make certain media social. Media and media technologies however not only are productive forces but are also embedded into certain relations of production.[1] Private companies dominate the contemporary media system. Today's media not only satisfy certain needs, but also are a profitable business. By neglecting the level of the relations of production, accounts of social media do not capture the entirety of the social and/or unsocial character of the media today.

This paper aims at extending the debate about social media to the level of the relations of production that shape media production, distribution and consumption. I will therefore look at the social impacts of the practices of media companies and discuss whether these contribute to a social or unsocial media system.

8.2   UNSOCIAL MEDIA

Looking at the activities of the most successful media and communication companies reveals that their practices often have a negative impact on individuals, society and the environment. I will in the following consider some concrete examples:

8.2.1   Apple's Exploitation of iSlaves

Apple is one of the most successful computer hardware producers in the world. In 2011 *Forbes* ranked Apple as the biggest computer hardware company and the second most profitable company in the world.[2] Between 2000 and 2012 Apple's profits grew 39.2 per cent each year and reached 41.7 billion USD in 2012 (Apple SEC-Filings).

This economic success comes at a price—a price that is paid mainly by workers in Apple's supply chain. In May and June 2010 many major Western media reported about a series of suicides at factory campuses in China. The factories, at which seventeen young workers jumped to death,[3] belonged to the Taiwan-based company Hon Hai Precision Industry Co. Ltd, better known as Foxconn, which is a major supplier for computer giants such as Apple, Hewlett-Packard, Nokia and Sony Ericsson (FinnWatch et al. 2011, 8). For some weeks public attention was directed at Apple's supply chain and was shown a glimpse of the working reality behind the bright and shiny surface of computer products.

However, these suicides only are the tip of the iceberg. For several years NGOs have stressed that computers, mp3 players, game consoles, etc. are often produced under miserable working conditions. Far away from shopping centres and department stores, workers in developing countries are producing these products during ten to twelve hour shifts, a minimum of six days a week for at best a minimum wage. Apple's suppliers are no exception.

Among the main critics of Apple's supply chain business practices are China Labour Watch and Students and Scholars against Corporate Misbehaviour (SACOM), as well as member organisations of the European project makeITfair, which have investigated and criticised working conditions in Apple's supplier factories. Based on interviews with workers outside factory premises these organisation detected:

- Compulsory and excessive overtime (SOMO 2007, 22; FinnWatch et al. 2009, 37; SACOM 2011b, 5f).
- Low wages that are barely enough to cover basic living expenses such as food and housing (Wong 2005, 27; SOMO 2007, 21; FinnWatch et al. 2009, 44; SACOM 2011b, 4).
- Major restrictions of the freedom of association (Finnwatch et al. 2009, 2011).

- Lack of health protection equipment (SOMO 2007, 23; SACOM 2011a, 14), exposure of workers to hazardous substances that resulted in poisoning (SACOM 2010, 2; 2011a, 14; 2011b, 7), as well as insufficient information of workers about the chemicals they were using (SACOM 2011a, 14).
- Harsh management style, strict disciplinary measures and harassment of workers (FinnWatch et al. 2009, 38).
- High work pressure (FinnWatch et al. 2011, 30) and social isolation (FinnWatch et al. 2011, 30; SACOM 2011a, 12f).

After the suicide tragedies Apple put renewed emphasis on its commitment to meeting its supply chain responsibility. In its 2013 Supplier Responsibility Report, Apple states: "Workers everywhere should have the right to safe and ethical working conditions. They should also have access to educational opportunities to improve their lives. Through a continual cycle of inspections, improvement plans, and verification, we work with our suppliers to make sure they comply with our Code of Conduct and live up to these ideals" (2013, 3). In order to demonstrate this commitment Apple in early 2012 published a list of its suppliers and was the first electronics company to join the Fair Labour Association (FLA) (Fair Labour Association 2012).

In February 2012, the FLA audited three Foxconn factories in Guanlan, Longhu, and Chengdu in China. This audit shows that major violations of labour rights at Foxconn campuses still persist (FLA 2012). The results of the audit were summarised as follows: "FLA found excessive overtime and problems with overtime compensation; several health and safety risks; and crucial communication gaps that have led to a widespread sense of unsafe working conditions among workers"(FLA 2012).

Doubts need to be raised whether any fundamental changes of working conditions in Apple's supply chain will occur in the near future. According to the 2013 Supplier Responsibility Report the steps Apple is taking in order to improve the situation focus on worker training, monitoring working hours in order to ensure that they do not exceed sixty hours per week, strict policies against child labour and conducting worker safety assessments (Apple 2013). These steps leave one of the most fundamental and most structural problems untouched: the extremely low wage level. Watchdogs have argued workers often depend on overtime work in order to increase their income because their wages are too low to cover their basic living expenses (SACOM 2011a, 10). Apart from the fact that a sixty-hour work week is still very long, the measures Apple is proposing do not include any wage raises. Higher wages would have a direct negative impact on Apple's profit margins. However, as the second most profitable company in the world,[4] Apple certainly could afford ensuring higher wage levels.

MacBooks, iPhones, iPads and iPods are a symbol for modern twenty-first century lifestyle and progress. The conditions under which these products are produced however resemble the early days of industrial capitalism. The fact that, for example, an iPhone costs at least twice or even three times as much as the average monthly salary of a worker in the electronics supply chain reveals a deep separation between workers and the fruits of their labour.

Low wages and long working hours in manufacturing factories on the one hand, enable high profit margins on the other hand. Such business practices are unsocial as they conflict general social well-being and the common good—economic success requires the misery of workers and thus hampers the emergence of decent work and self-determined labour in the media and communication sector.

8.2.2 Google's Exploitation of Digital Labour

Google controls 84.77 per cent of the global search engine market.[5] According to the Alexa Top Sites Ranking, Google.com is the most frequently accessed website on the Internet.[6] The company's profits between 2001 and 2010 on average grew by 103 per cent each year and reached 8.5 billion USD in 2010 (Google SEC-Filings). This value is almost entirely based on advertising: In 2010 Google's revenues were 29.3 billion USD, 96 per cent of which was generated through advertisements (Google SEC-Filings).

Users can access all of Google's services free of charge. However, while using these services users produce a huge amount of information. This data ranges from demographic user information, to technical data and usage statistics, to search queries and even the content of emails. Google turns this data into a commodity in order to generate profit: Instead of selling its services as a commodity to users, its business model consists in selling user data as a commodity to advertisers.

Google considers this business model as socially responsible. Its famous corporate credo is "You can make money without being evil".[7] The company describes its business model as beneficial for both advertisers and users. Advertisers would benefit from personalized marketing opportunities while users would receive relevant ads: "We give advertisers the opportunity to place clearly marked ads alongside our search results. We strive to help people find ads that are relevant and useful, just like our results."[8]

However, critics highlight that Google's business model is more problematic than this description suggests. Scholars (e.g. Fuchs 2010; Fuchs 2011; Vaidhyanathan 2011; Tene 2008; Tatil 2008; Zimmer 208; Blackman 2008) as well as corporate watchdogs (GoogleWatch.com[9]; Privacy International 2007; Privacy Rights Clearinghouse 2004; Corporate Watch 2008; Google Monitor 2011) highlight that Google's business model of selling user data to advertisers for creating personalized advertisements constitutes a fundamental invasion of user privacy. Google Monitor for example stressed: "Google's targeted advertising business model is no 'privacy by design' and no 'privacy by default'" (Google Monitor 2011). Likewise Vaidhyanathan argues that Google's privacy policy is "pretty much a lack-of-privacy policy" (Vaidhyanathan 2011, 84). Zimmer points out that the model of "search 2.0" which combines search infrastructure with web 2.0 applications leads to "the concentrated surveillance, capture, and aggregation of one's online intellectual and social activities by a single provider" (Zimmer 2008). Maurer et al. stress that "Google is massively invading privacy" (Maurer et al. 2007, 5).

These critics show that the commodification of user data entails the threat of surveillance and invades of the rights of Internet users. The use of user data for advertising purposes requires the creation of databases that contain huge amounts of information about each Google user and make that information available to private companies. The information stored in databases can be combined in different ways in order to identify different consumer groups that might be susceptible to certain products. For Internet users it becomes impossible to determine, which of their data is stored in which database and to whom it is accessible. The fact that this information is available could at some point in the future have negative effects for an individual user. The available data could for example support discriminatory practices (Gandy 1993, 2) by allowing to identify which individuals have a certain sexual orientation or political opinion or suffer from a certain disease.

Furthermore extensive advertising contributes to the commercialization of the Internet. As a consequence of an advertising-based business model, which characterises not only Google but most web 2.0 companies (Sandoval 2012), users are permanently confronted and annoyed with ads for consumer goods and services.

Google's philosophy is based on the principle of not being evil. The inventor of this famous motto, Paul Buchheit stressed in an interview that this slogan was intended to demarcate Google from its competitors which "were kind of exploiting the users to some extent" (Buchheit 2008, 170). However, Google's business model is also based on the exploitation of users (Fuchs 2010, 2011) as it turns data, which Google users produce while using their services, into its property that is then sold as a commodity to advertisers.

Google, like many other online media companies such as Facebook or Yahoo, provides services that are highly valued by most Internet users. However, if they want to use these services they have no other choice than to consent to Google's terms of services and the usage of their data for advertising purposes. This gives Google a high amount of power over deciding how user data are used and to whom they are made available. The free accessibility of Google's services thus comes at high costs: the renunciation of the right to determine the use of personal information. Despite the fact that Google's products and services enhance social interaction, collaboration and sharing, at the level of corporate practices the company remains unsocial as its business interests contradict the possibility of a freely shared and socially controlled online infrastructure.

8.2.3 News Corporation's Destructive Ideology

News Corporation owns TV channels and newspapers around the world that supply millions of people with their daily news. Arsenault and Castells estimate that News Corp today reaches around 75 per cent of the global population (Arsenault and Castells 2008, 491). At the same time News Corp ranks among the most economically successful companies in the world. In 2011 the company's founder Rupert Murdoch was the 24th most powerful and the 108th richest person in the world.[10] His power and money are based on the operations of News Corp, the worldwide 158th biggest public company and the 3rd largest media content company.[11]

For News Corp the production of news is a profitable business. News Corp's media empire extends through North and South America, Europe, Australia and Asia. The company's extensive reach does not only guarantee high profits, but at the same time gives it the power to influence the knowledge, beliefs, and worldviews of its recipients around the globe.

The bigger the economic success of a media company the more capital it can invest for employing journalists, purchasing production technology, advertising, etc. This again increases the likelihood of further expansion. Those media that are unsuccessful in attracting recipients and advertisers run danger to remain marginal. In order to be attractive to as many recipients and advertisers as possible, media content needs to be oriented at the interest of the majority and create an advertising-friendly climate. Media that touch oppositional topics or topics that are of interest to political, cultural or other minorities, are critical of consumerism and corporations, or provide alternative, critical content are less likely to generate enough income to fund high quality production and to advertise their products. A commercial media system thus privileges media that provide mainstream media content and advocate corporate capitalism and consumerism.

In the media content sector, economic power is inherently connected to cultural power. Economically successful media companies can distribute their content to a large number of people. As critics highlight, News Corp uses this power to promote a specific political agenda, while arguing that its journalism is neutral and objective. Critical studies show that News Corp's media content:

- Pushes a specific ideology while at the same time claiming to be fair and balanced—studies found biased reporting practices, particularly in regard to the US war on terror (Greenslade 2003; Project for Excellence in Journalism 2005; Arsenault and Castells 2008, 501) and climate change (McKnight 2010b; Goodell 2011; Media Matters 2010; Toffel and Schendler 2012, 1). Furthermore critics argue that

News Corp is promoting a neoliberal and market populist worldview (Thussu 2007; McKnight 2003, 2010a).

• Diminishes diversity through enforcing a uniform editorial line throughout its media outlets around the world (Manne 2005, 75f; Greenslade 2003).

• Creates misperception among its audience regarding important issues such as climate change or the US war in Iraq (Goodell 2011; PIPA and Knowledge Networks 2003), and leaves its audience uninformed about current political events (Morris 2005, 68; Fairleigh Dickinson University 2011, 1).

Media content companies have the power to act as public watchdogs, to hold the powerful accountable, to provide information and to spur public debate. News Corp exploits this power to promote a destructive world-view: War, the destruction of nature, economic crises and social inequality pose a threat to individuals and society and are socially undesirable. When arguing for the necessity of war, downplaying the threats of climate change, and advocating neoliberal policies News Corp is presenting the particular interest of some individuals who benefit from war, environmental destruction, and neoliberalism as the general interest of society. News Corp instrumentalizes its media power for distributing ideologies. Furthermore News Corp's reporting creates disinformation and ignorance in society: studies show that its audience often is less informed than people who do not consume any news at all (Fairleigh Dickinson University 2011, 1; Morris 2005, 68). News Corp's practices contradict the potential of media to provide information, to foster education, enlightenment, critical thinking, and debate in society. Quite on the contrary the company instrumentalizes its power for promoting destructive and anti-humanist ideologies that present the particular interests of privileged groups as the general interest of society.

8.2.4   Microsoft's Knowledge Monopoly

Microsoft is the largest software company in the world. People around the globe use Microsoft's proprietary software: In September 2011 the operating system MS Windows had a worldwide market share of 86.57 per cent.[12] Given this dominant market position, it is not surprising that Microsoft is economically highly successful: In 2011 it was the largest software company and the forty-second largest company in the world.[13] In the financial year 2012 Microsoft's net profits were almost 17 billion USD, its revenues amounted to 73.7 billion USD and its total assets were 121.2 billion USD (Microsoft SEC-Filings). The business practices that made Microsoft such a successful company have been strongly criticised. In the late 1990s the company was criminally convicted both in the United States and in Europe,[14] for maintaining "its monopoly power by anti-competitive means".[15]

Apart from these violations of anti-trust law, critics highlight that even on a more basic level Microsoft's business model is socially irresponsible. Microsoft's business success is based on proprietary software and thus on software patents. As of September 28, 2011, Microsoft had registered 22,501 patents at the U.S. Patent and Trademark Office.[16] Further 26,398 patent requests were currently pending.[17]

Civil society initiatives such as the Free Software Foundation's "End Software Patents in the United States" and "No Software Patents in Europe" highlight that software patents are problematic in several respects. Their main arguments against software patents include that software patents create advantages for large corporations and lead to monopolization; hinder innovation; threaten the freedom of information; create artificial scarcity and that software consists of mathematical formulas and abstract ideas, which are not patentable.[18] Open Source Watch stresses: "For many in the open source community, the company [Microsoft] represents all that is troubling about closed source software development" (OSS Watch 2011).

Software is a form of knowledge—its development requires certain skills and previous knowledge ranging from mathematical rules to specific programming languages. Microsoft's software thus contains previous knowledge and through patenting software Microsoft exploits the common stock of knowledge of society for creating private property. Based on this privatization, Microsoft is able to prevent others from accessing this knowledge.

Microsoft is aware of the fact that patents are a fetter to creativity and innovation. Bill Gates in 1991 stressed that patents hamper technological innovation: "If people had understood how patents would be granted when most of today's ideas were invented, and had taken out patents, the industry would be at a complete standstill today" (1991).

Microsoft's business practices thus deprive society from the best possible software. Making all software source codes publicly available would allow other programmers to further adapt, develop, and improve software. Collectively, the chances are higher that software that matches the various needs of individuals and society would be developed.

Microsoft's business interests conflict with the common good. Instead of allowing the collective capacities of the human intellect to develop the best possible software for society and making it universally accessible, Microsoft patents software and monopolizes access to knowledge in order to create the highest possible profits for the company.

8.2.5 HP's Hazardous Products

HP, according to the market analyst International Data Corporation (IDC), in September 2011 controlled 41 per cent of the worldwide hardcopy peripherals market (IDC 2011). In 2011 its profits amounted to 5.9 billion USD and *Forbes* ranked HP as the second biggest computer hardware company worldwide.[19]

HP generates profit through the sale of computer hardware. Computer products often contain various toxic substances that threaten human health and the environment. HP is no exception. The company has been criticized for:

- High concentrations of toxic substances in HP products (Greenpeace 2005a, 2006a, 109; 2009, 32).
- False claims about the elimination of certain flame-retardant PDBE chemicals (Greenpeace 2006b).
- Insufficient take back programs, especially in developing countries (Greenpeace 2011, 1).
- HP products found at waste dumps in developing countries (BAN 2005, 37; Greenpeace 2005b, 2007).

Insufficient take back programs increase the likelihood of used HP products being inadequately disposed and ending up as part of (illegal) e-waste exports to developing countries. The recycling of e-waste without proper protection equipment, as it takes place in many developing countries, can have devastating effects on human health and the environment.

One important measure to reduce these dangers is to avoid the production of waste. HP is one of the largest hardware companies in the world. Generating profit requires the continuous sales of computer hardware. Short life spans and high obsolescence of computer products allow increasing sales numbers. Most computers today are built in a way that makes the exchange of individual parts difficult. The difficulty to exchange individual computer parts, combined with high prices for repair services, force many computer users to replace their computer device as soon as one part of it breaks. Advertising and the rapid introduction of new product versions and follow up-products that promise increased functionality and improved optical design, albeit often containing little technological innovation, further contribute to the creation of a throw-away culture. In financial terms HP benefits from this fast-paced waste culture. The design of HP's ink cartridges for example directly fosters the production of waste. HP's inkjet printers are sold at relatively cheap prices. The corresponding ink cartridges are not refillable. This means that after having printed some hundred pages the ink cartridge needs to be disposed and a new cartridge needs to be bought. AlterNet therefore called HP's printer cartridges an "e-waste disaster".[20]

For example, HP's most popular printer on Amazon.com is the HP Deskjet 1000 Printer. It is the #5 bestseller in the category "printers" and the #1 bestseller in the category "inkjet printers".[21] The printer costs 29 USD. The black ink cartridge is sold at 14.5 USD and the tri-colour ink cartridge at 16.65 USD. According to HP the black cartridge allows printing up to 190 pages and the tri-colour cartridge prints up to 165 pages.[22] The price of the printer seems low compared to the price of ink cartridges, which need to be repurchased regularly. Based on this business model it seems obvious that HP has no interest in selling fewer cartridges. As the above example shows, one ink cartridge allows for printing less than two hundred pages. If the cartridge is empty consumers have no other option than disposing and replacing it by a new one. HP does not remanufacture ink cartridges or provide refilling options. On its website HP states that this policy is due to the circumstance that refilled cartridges lower the printing quality.[23] A refilling model however could contribute to avoiding waste and therefore be more sustainable than a model based one-way cartridges that have to be replaced frequently.

HP has the power to decide how computer products should be designed. They could be built in an environmentally friendly way. In this regard important measures would be to foster innovation that allows reducing the amount of hazardous products to an absolute minimum, to construct robust products with long life spans and exchangeable parts, to build refillable ink cartridges, etc.

In its CSR communication HP commits itself to environmental protection: "Environmental protection is a complex undertaking, but the laws of nature are simple. We will provide leadership on the journey to an environmentally sustainable future, with efficient products and creative recycling systems" (HP 2001,1). HP's goal regarding waste is to increase the total amount of recycled products (HP 2010, 119). However, an absolute increase of the amount of recycled products does not necessarily indicate an improvement. An absolute increase of the amount of recycled products would only mean an improvement if the total number of sold products remained the same or was reduced. HP however does not aim to increase product-life spans or reduce the amount of products sold to users. At a certain point, every computer product will need to be disposed. The shorter the product's lifespan, the more products can HP sell, and the more waste will be produced. Short product lifecycles thus benefit the profit interests of HP, but increase the amount of e-waste which threatens the environment and human health, particularly in developing countries in which HP's take back programs are insufficient, and to which e-waste continues to be (illegally) exported.

The practices of the media companies discussed above are unsocial as they privilege private profit interests over general social well-being. Rather than fostering self-determined work, developing sustainable IT products, creating a shared and safe online infrastructure, an open, accessible culture and collective knowledge resources or encouraging critical thinking, the practices of these companies rest on the exploitation of workers, threaten human health and the environment, push the commodification of user data, create cultural enclosures and monopolize knowledge or promote destructive ideologies.

Based on these examples that evidence the unsocial character of corporate media, in the next section I will move on to a more theoretical level in order to further explore why capitalist relations of media production have implications that are unsocial.

8.3   PRIVATE MEDIA VS. COMMON MEDIA

The unsocial media I discussed above are all private companies that produce media for a profit. In order to do so they need to sell commodities. For that purpose, either media products themselves such as hardware, software, movies or books, or data about, as well as the attention of, audiences are transformed into commodities. While the former are sold to media consumers, the latter are sold to advertisers. Private media companies therefore adhere to the logic of property that is based on private ownership of means of production and individual property holders that engage in the purchase and sale of commodities. The exchange of commodities is grounded in the logic of property. The logic of property is opposed to the logic of the common. Nick Dyer-Witheford argues that the common, contrary to the commodity, is not sold, but shared: "A commodity is a good produced for sale, a common is a good produced, or conserved, to be shared" (2010a, 82). Similarly, David Harvey points out that the common is collective and non-commodified: "At the heart of the practice of communing lies the principle that the relation between the social group and that aspect of the environment being treated as common shall be both collective and non-commodified—off limits to the logic of market exchange an market valuations" (2012, 73). According to Hardt and Negri commons on the one hand are "the common wealth of the material world" and on the other hand are the "results of social production that are necessary for social interaction and further production such as knowledge, languages, codes, information, affects, and so forth" (2009, viii). Slavoj Žižek distinguishes between the commons of culture such as language and education as well as important social infrastructure, and the commons of internal and external nature (Žižek 2009, 91). Nick Dyer-Witheford identifies different moments in the circuit of the common: eco-social commons as collective planning institutions for internal and external health; labour commons as the "democratized organization of productive and reproductive work" (2010b); and networked commons referring to networks as collective infrastructure. In the circulation of the common these different moments reinforce each other and enable the production of common goods and services, a "commonwealth" (2010b).

In order to better understand the logic of property and the logic of the common and how they relate to (un)social media, it is necessary to describe both in a more systematic way: Hofkirchner and Fuchs (2003) argue that society consists of an economic, a political and a cultural system. The economy is the system that organises the production, distribution, and consumption of resources. The central power in this area thus is the possession of ownership rights (2003, 5). The system of politics is concerned with making collective decisions regarding all aspects of social life. Power in this system is related to the ability to participate in decision-making processes (2003, 6). The system of culture deals with the rules of society. Power in this system means the power to define rules, norms, values, and morals (2003, 6). The three sub-systems of society, in summary, regulate ownership rights, decision power, and the rules and norms of society.

The logic of the common and the logic of property differ regarding each of these three aspects:

- *The logic of property*: Following the logic of property, the means of production belongs to individual property holders. Production is privately organised and individual property holders exchange commodities among each other. Decision power in the logic of property is concentrated in the hands of political and economic elites. Elected representatives decide on the rules of society. Economic life is largely excluded from democratic decision-making. Within a certain legal framework the owners of means of production have the right to decide how to employ them to produce which goods in which way. Following the cultural logic of property the common good can be realised based on particularistic values that support economic and political elitism such as self-interest, profit maximization and competition.
- *The logic of the common*: In the logic of the common the economy is organised based on the principle of common ownership of means of production. Production is collectively organised. The commons are shared among collectivities. The main principle that guides the sphere of politics is participatory democracy. Every member of society has the power to participate in decisions concerning the important areas of social life, including the economy. According to the cultural logic of the common, achieving the common good requires universal values that support economic and political participation such as solidarity, equality, inclusion, sharing and cooperation.

To sum up: The logic of the common is based on common ownership, participatory decision power and universal values. It is economically, politically and culturally inclusive and solidary and can therefore be described as a social logic. The logic of private property is based on private ownership, elitist decision power and particularistic values. It is economically, politically and culturally exclusive and self-interested and can therefore be described as an unsocial logic.

At these three levels—(a) economy, (b) politics, and (c) culture—the business practices of the companies I discussed in Section 8.1. exhibit the logic of private property:

(a) *Economy*: The studied companies are privately owned corporations that produce commodities that are exchanged on the market. Their business practices require the commodification and appropriation of commons, i.e. the transformation of social and collective goods into private and individual property. This commodification process affects all moments of the circuit of the common: eco-social commons, labour commons, networked commons (Dyer-Witheford 2010b):

- Commodification of the eco-social commons: HP is an example for the appropriation of eco-social commons. Products with short lifespans increase HP's sales numbers and at the same time increase the amount of e-waste that can potentially destroy the environment and that threatens human health. High quality sustainable IT products with long lifespans would reduce profit margins because they are more expensive to produce and at the same time would reduce sales numbers, as sustainable products can be used for longer periods of time. HP's business model on the contrary generates high profits while threatening internal and external nature.
- Commodification of the labour commons: The Apple example illustrates that the logic of property depends on the commodification of labour power. Millions of workers, especially in developing economies, who do not have anything else to sell but their labour power, are forced to work in factories in order to make a living. The conditions under which workers in China and other low-cost production countries are working today resemble nineteenth century capitalism. Low wages combined with excessive working hours allow companies such as Apple to lower production costs and increase profit margins, while threatening the physical and mental health of workers. These companies exploit the human propensity to work in order to maximize private profit.
- Commodification of the networked commons: The examples of Microsoft, News Corp and Google illustrate the appropriation of the networked commons. In order to realize profit, companies such as Microsoft depend on intellectual property rights that turn cultural and knowledge products into scarce commodities. Instead of allowing an open and accessible culture to flourish, they introduce access restrictions that hamper creativity and knowledge production while fostering cultural inequality.

Google provides free access to its services for all Internet users. This universal access contradicts the logic of property. In order to generate profit, Google depends on the sale of a different commodity: user data. In the logic of property, free access on the one hand comes with further commodification on the other hand. Google's services make the Internet searchable and online content accessible and thus form an important infrastructure of the web. However, Google's business interests prevent this infrastructure from becoming common and collective as its usage comes at the cost of the commodification of personal information, which enforces the logic of property.

News Corporation generates profit by selling space for advertisements as well as restricting access to media content. For News Corp, media content is a means for generating profit. Either it is sold as a commodity to consumers or it is used for attracting an audience whose attention can be sold to advertisers. News Corp has been successful in generating profit through producing media content. This allowed the company to expand its reach and to gain high symbolic power, which News Corp uses for promoting the values of the logic of property. Instead of being a collective knowledge and information resource, News Corp turns media content into a means for both generating profit and promoting particularistic values that ideologically support the imperative of profit maximization.

(b) *Politics*: Also at the political level the studied companies illustrate the logic of property. As they are private companies the decision power over the companies' activities is concentrated in the hands of their owners. Other actors who are either directly or indirectly affected by a private company's activities, such as workers or local communities, have no influence on the company's decisions. The only way society can influence the activities of corporations is indirectly via government regulation. Their economic power gives the owners of the studied companies the power over decisions that affect all members of society. The private organisation of the media and communication system empowers companies to decide which hardware products are produced and how, how they are designed, which music is "worth" producing, how software is designed, which topics are worth reporting about, who receives access to the Internet at which speed, and which user data is stored and who can access it, etc. In a commercial media system, owners individually control the media. They deprive the members of society of the opportunity for democratic control of the media because democracy is a collective endeavour, not an individual one.

(c) *Culture*: All discussed companies are economically highly successful. Generating profit is their main purpose of existence. At the same time these companies commit to certain values that go beyond the mere pursuit of profit. They highlight that they do not exclusively focus on the particularistic value of individual profit maximization, but care about how business practices affect the common good. Apple for examples stresses that "Workers everywhere should have the right to safe and ethical working conditions" (Apple 2013, 3). Microsoft repeatedly made a "comprehensive commitment to digital inclusion, and to help address inequities" (Microsoft 2004, 48).

News Corp claims to be a "fair and balanced company".[24] Google stresses that "You can make money without being evil".[25] HP highlights that it is "pursuing a vision of corporate success that goes beyond just creating value for shareholders—we are helping to create a better world" (HP 2010, 4).

These statements taken from the companies' corporate communication draw on values of the logic of the common in order to provide greater legitimacy to corporate behaviour. However, research conducted by corporate watchdogs reveals that despite commitments to social values, corporate practices in many respects are unsocial. During the past ten years the studied companies increased their profits, while at the same time created miserable working conditions, exploited human labour power, threatened human health and the environment, promoted destructive ideologies and restricted access to culture, knowledge, and important technological infrastructure of society. Unsocial media make use of universal values, which characterize the logic of the common, while actual corporate practices privilege profit maximization over the common good. They instrumentalize the cultural logic of the common as they strategically refer to universal values for generating legitimacy for corporate practices that follow the logic of property and the particularistic value of profit maximization.

To sum up: The business activities of the studied media and communication companies are based on the unsocial logic of property. They commodify the commons of society, rely on undemocratic decision-making, and are guided by the particular value of profit maximization.

8.4 SOCIAL MEDIA AS COMMONS-BASED MEDIA

In principle, private media and communication companies such as the ones presented in Section 8.1. produce goods and provide services that are beneficial for society: computer hardware, software, news and entertainment, music, movies, online search infrastructure, telecommunication infrastructure, etc. Even though some of them are social at the level of productive forces as they enable social interaction and cooperation, they remain unsocial at the level of relations of production as they are privately owned (economy), privately controlled (politics) and based on socially exclusive values (culture).

By subordinating the production and distribution of media and communication products to the logic of property, commercial media support the profit interests of shareholders but cannot unfold their full benefits for society. The ways hardware, software, music, news and entertainment, Internet and telecommunication infrastructure are produced under the logic of property, have negative side effects for individuals, society and the environment. Capitalist media thus remain unsocial in a very profound way.

Truly social media on the contrary are media that are socially owned (economy), socially controlled (politics) and are based on socially inclusive values (culture). They benefit all members of society rather than serving private profit interests. Creating a media and communication system that is truly social requires looking at alternatives that are based on the logic of the common.

The commodification of the common through private media is not unchallenged. Commercial media not only commodify and appropriate the commons but also depend on them (in this context see Hardt and Negri 2009, 153). Massimo de Angelis therefore calls the relationship between capitalism and the commons schizophrenic: "On the one hand, capital is a social force that requires continuous enclosures; that is, the destruction and commodification of non-commodified common spaces and resources. However, there is also an extent to which capital has to accept the non-commodified and *contribute to its constitution*" (2009, 33). Hardt and Negri argue that "contemporary forms of capitalist production and accumulation in fact, despite their continuing drive to privatize resources and wealth, paradoxically make possible and even require expansion of the common" (2009, ix). By following the "social media" trend and increasingly providing products and services that enable social connections, sharing, cooperation and the production of media commons, private media companies at the same time accelerate the antagonism between the social character of productive forces and the unsocial character of relations of production.

However, until today media companies have been quite successful in capturing the social usage of media that produces media commons and transforming it into a means for generating private profit. Sublating this contradiction thus requires resistance against the capture of social media within unsocial relation of production. It requires a political movement that takes up this contradiction and struggles for the expansion of the social logic from productive forces to relations of production in order to establish a commons-based media system that allows the media to become truly social.

NOTES

1. In Marxist theory the notion of productive forces describes labour power, raw materials, and means of production (technologies, etc.), whereas the concept of relations of production refers to the social relations through which production, distribution, and consumption are organized. Marx described the unfolding of an antagonism between productive forces and relations of production: "At a certain stage of development, the material productive forces of society come into conflict with the existing relations of production or—this merely expresses the same thing in legal terms—with the property

relations within the framework of which they have operated hitherto" (Marx 1859/1994, 211).

2. *Forbes*, "The World's Biggest Public Companies," accessed February 15, 2013, http://www.forbes.com/global2000/list/.
3. Joel Johnson, 2011, "1 Million Workers. 90 Million iPhones. 17 Suicides. Who's to Blame?" *Wired*, February 28. accessed October 23, 2011, http://www.wired.com/magazine/2011/02/ff_joelinchina/all/1
4. *Forbes*, "The World's Biggest Public Companies," accessed February 15, 2013.
5. NetMarketshare, "Search Engine Market Share," accessed January 19, 2012, http://netmarketshare.com/report.aspx?qprid=4&qptimeframe=M&qpsp=145.
6. Among the top one hundred websites are nineteen Google websites: Google.com (#1), YouTube.com (#3), Blogger.com (#7), Google.de (#19), Google.com.hk (#20), Google.uk (#23), Google.co.jp (#24), Google.fr (#25), Google.com.br (#33), Google.it (#35), Google.es (#41), Google.ru (#46), googleusercontent.com (#50), Google.com.mx (#55), Google.ca (#58), google.co.id (#69), google.com.tr (#80), google.com.au (#81), google.pl (#92). Alexa.com, "Top 500 Global Sites," accessed November 17, 2011, http://www.alexa.com/topsites.
7. Google, "Ten Things We Know to be True," accessed February 15, 2013, http://www.google.cn/intl/en/about/company/philosophy/.
8. Google, "Facts about Google and Competition," accessed November 18, 2011, http://www.google.com/competition/howgoogleadswork.html.
9. GoogleWatch.com, "And then we were four," accessed January 21, 2012, http://www.google-watch.org/bigbro.html.
10. *Forbes*, "Rupert Murdoch," accessed April 22, 2012, http://www.forbes.com/profile/rupert-murdoch/.
11. *Forbes*, "The World's Biggest Public Companies," accessed March 26, 2013.
12. NetMarketshare, "Top Operating System Share Trend," accessed October 14, 2011, http://www.netmarketshare.com/os-market-share.aspx?qprid=9.
13. *Forbes*, "The World's Biggest Public Companies," accessed February 15, 2013.
14. Mark Tran, 2006, "EU Hits Microsoft 280.5m Antitrust Fine,". *The Guardian*, July 12, accessed October 3, 2011, http://www.guardian.co.uk/business/2006/jul/12/europeanunion.digitalmedia.
15. United States of America vs. Microsoft Corporation, 2000, "Conclusions of Law," CNET News.com, accessed October 3, 2011, http://news.cnet.com/html/ne/Special/Microsoft/conclusions_of_law_and_order.html
16. U.S. Patent and Trademark Office, "List of Microsoft Patents," accessed September 28, 2011, http://patft.uspto.gov/netacgi/nph-Parser?Sect1=PTO2&Sect2=HITOFF&p=1&u=%2Fnetahtml%2FPTO%2Fsearch-bool.html&r=0&f=S&l=50&TERM1=microsoft&FIELD1=ASNM&co1=AND&TERM2=&FIELD2=&d=PTXT..
17. U.S. Patent and Trademark Office, "List of Microsoft Patent Applications," accessed September 28, 2011, http://appft1.uspto.gov/netacgi/nph-Parser?Sect1=PTO2&Sect2=HITOFF&u=%2Fnetahtml%2Fsearch-adv.html&r=0&p=1&f=S&l=50&d=PG01&Query=an%2Fmicrosoft%24.
18. End Software Patents, "Why Abolish Software Patents," accessed October 6, 2011, http://en.swpat.org/wiki/Software_patents_wiki:_home_page on.; No Software Patents.com, "The Dangers," accessed October 6, 2011, http://www.nosoftwarepatents.com/en/m/dangers/index.html.
19. Forbes, "The Biggest Public Companies," accessed March 26, 2013.
20. ZP Heller, 2007, "HP's Printer Cartridges Are and E-Waste Disaster—Does the Company Really Care?" AlterNet, October 28, accessed November 15, 2011, http://www.alternet.org/environment/65945/hp%27s_printer_cartridges_are_an_e-waste_disaster_—_does_the_company_really_care/? page=2.

21. Amazon.com, "Bestsellers in Computer Printers," accessed November 15, 2011, http://www.amazon.com/Best-Sellers-Electronics-Computer-Printers/zgbs/electronics/172635/ref=zg_bs_unv_e_3_3071697011_2.
22. HP Home & Home Office Store, "HP 61 Black Ink Cartridge" and "HP 61 Tri-Color Ink Cartridge," accessed November 15, 2011, http://www.shopping.hp.com/en_US/home-office/-/products/Ink_Toner_Paper/HP%20Ink.
23. HP, "The Truth About Remanufactured Ink and Toner Cartridges," accessed November 15, 2011, http://www.hp.com/sbso/product/supplies/remanufactured-ink-toner.html?jumpid=ex_R295_go/suppliesreliability.
24. Rupert Murdoch quoted in Claire Cozens, 2004, "Murdoch: Fox News Does Not Favour Bush," *The Guardian*, October 26, accessed February 12, 2012, http://www.guardian.co.uk/media/2004/oct/26/newscorporation.uselections2004.
25. Google, "Ten Things We Know to be True."

REFERENCES

Apple SEC-Filings. "10-k forms 1994–2010." *Edgar database.* Accessed October 23, 2011. http://www.sec.gov.
Apple 2013. "Supplier responsibility report." Accessed February 14, 2013. http://images.apple.com/supplierresponsibility/pdf/Apple_SR_2013_Progress_Report.pdf.
Arsenault, Amelia, and Manuel Castells. 2008. "Switching power: Rupert Murdoch and the global business of media politics: A sociological analysis." *International Sociology* 23 (4): 488–513.
BAN. 2005. *The digital dump. Exporting re-use and abuse to Africa.* Accessed November 6, 2011. http://www.ban.org/BANreports/10–24–05/documents/TheDigitalDump.pdf.
Blackman, Josh. 2008. "Omniveillance, Google, privacy in public and the right to your digital identity." *Santa Clara Law Review* 49: 313–392.
boyd, danah. 2009. "Social media is here to stay . . . Now what?" *Microsoft Research Tech Fest*, Redmond, Washington, February 26. Accessed July 23, 2013. http://www.danah.org/papers/talks/MSRTechFest2009.html.
Buchheit, Paul. 2008. "Interview" (interviewed by Jessica Livingston). In *Founders at work: stories of startups' early days*, edited by Jessica Livingston, 181–172. New York: Springer.
Corporate Watch. 2008. "Google's new spy." Accessed January 21, 2012. http://www.corporatewatch.org/?lid=3134.
de Angelis, Massimo. 2009. "The tragedy of capitalist commons." *Turbulence* 5: 32–33. Accessed June 4, 2012. http://turbulence.org.uk/wp-content/uploads/2009/11/turbulence_05.pdf.
Dyer-Witheford, Nick. 2010a. "Commonism." *Turbulence* 1: 81–87. Accessed June 28, 2012. http://turbulence.org.uk/wp-content/uploads/2008/07/turbulence_jrnl.pdf.
———. 2010b. "The circulation of the common" (lecture, University of Minnesota, March 5). Accessed June 4, 2012. http://www.globalproject.info/it/in_movimento/nick-dyer-witheford-the-circulation-of-the-common/4797.
Fair Labor Association. 2012. *Independent investigation of Apple supplier, Foxconn.* Accessed April 10, 2012. http://www.fairlabor.org/sites/default/files/documents/reports/foxconn_investigation_report.pdf.
Fairlaigh Dickinson University. 2011. "Public mind poll: Some news leaves people knowing less." November 21. Accessed February 23, 2012. http://publicmind.fdu.edu/2011/knowless/final.pdf.

FinnWatch, SACOM, and SOMO. 2009. "Playing with labour rights." Accessed October 19, 2011. http://makeitfair.org/en/the-facts/reports/2007–2009/reports-from-2009/playing-with-labour-rights/at_download/file.

———. 2011. "Game console and music player production in China." Accessed October 18, 2011. http://somo.nl/publications-en/Publication_3627/at_download/fullfile.

Fuchs, Christian. 2010. "Labor in informational capitalism and on the Internet." *The Information Society* 26 (3): 179–196.

———. 2011. "A contribution to the critique of the political economy of Google." *Fast Capitalism* 8 (1).

Gandy, Oscar. 1993. *The panoptic sort. A political economy of personal information.* Boulder: Westview Press.

Gates, Bill. 1991. *Challenges and strategy.* May 16. Accessed September 28, 2011. http://www.std.com/obi/Bill.Gates/Challenges.and.Strategy.

Goodell, Jeff. 2011. "Who's to blame. 12 politicians and excess blocking progress on global warming." *The Rolling Stone*, February 2. Accessed February 2, 2012. http://www.rollingstone.com/politics/lists/whos-to-blame-12-politicians-and-execs-blocking-progress-on-global-warming-20110119.

Google SEC-Filings. "10-k forms 2004–2010." In *Edgar database.* Accessed January 16, 2011. http://www.sec.gov..

Google Monitor. 2011. "Google's no privacy by design business model." Accessed January 21, 2012. http://googlemonitor.com/2011/googles-no-privacy-by-design-business-model/.

Greenpeace. 2005a. *Hewlett Packard in global toxic trouble.* Accessed November 12, 2011. http://www.greenpeace.org/international/en/news/features/hewlett-packard-toxic-trouble-111/.

———. 2005b. *E-waste wave sweeps the globe.* Accessed November 13, 2011. http://www.greenpeace.org/eastasia/news/stories/toxics/2005/20050523-e-waste-wave/.

———. 2006a. *Toxic chemicals in computers exposed.* Accessed November 3, 2011. http://www.greenpeace.org/international/Global/international/planet- 2/report/2006/9/toxic-chemicals-in-computers.pdf..

———. 2006b. *Toxic substances in laptops: Greenpeace study exposes HP's lie.* Accessed November 3, 2011. http://www.greenpeace.org/international/en/press/releases/toxic- substances-in-laptops-g/.

———. 2007. *Toxic tea party.* Accessed November 4, 2011. http://www.greenpeace.org/international/en/news/features/e-waste-china-toxic- pollution-230707/.

———. 2009. *Guide to greener electronics.* Version 11. Accessed November 3, 2011. http://www.greenpeace.org/usa/Global/usa/report/2009/3/guide-to-greener-electronics-11.pdf.

———. 2011. *Guide to greener electronics.* HP. Accessed November 13, 2011. http://www.greenpeace.org/international/Global/international/publications/climate/2011/Cool%20IT/greener-guide-nov-2011/hp.pdf.

Greenslade, Roy. 2003. "Their master's voice." *The Guardian*, February 17. Accessed February 6, 2012. http://www.guardian.co.uk/media/2003/feb/17/mondaymediasection.iraq.

Hardt, Michael, and Antonio Negri. 2009. *Commonwealth.* Cambridge, London: Belknap Press.

Harvey, David. 2012. *Rebel cities.* London: Verso.

Hofkirchner, Wolfgang, and Christian Fuchs. 2003. "The architecture of the information society." In *Proceedings of the 47th Annual Conference of the International Society for the Systems Sciences (ISSS)*, edited by Jennifter Wilby and Jenet K. Allen. Accessed June 14, 2012. http://fuchs.uti.at/wp-content/uploads/ArchitectureInformationSociety.pdf.

HP. 2001. *Social and environmental responsibility report.* Accessed October 18, 2011.http://www.hp.com/hpinfo/globalcitizenship/08gcreport/pdf/hp_csr_full_hi.pdf.

———. 2010. *A connected world—The impact of HP global citizenship in 2010 and beyond.* Accessed October 18, 2011. http://www.hp.com/hpinfo/globalcitizenship/pdf/hp_fy10_gcr.pdf.

International Data Corporation (IDC). 2011. *Growth in worldwide hardcopy peripherals market slows in second quarter despite strong results in emerging markets.* Accessed November 13, 2011. http://www.businesswire.com/news/home/20110907006815/en/Growth-Worldwide-Hardcopy-Peripherals-Market-Slows-Quarter.

Manne, Robert. 2005. "Murdoch and the war on Iraq." In *Do not disturb: Is the media failing Australia?*, edited by Robert Manne, 76–97. Melbourne: Black Inc.

Marx, Karl. 1859/1994. A contribution to the critique of political Economy. Preface. Karl Marx. Selected Writings edited by Lawrence H. Simon, 209–113. Indianapolis: Hackett Publishing.

Maurer, Hermann, Tilo Balke, Frank Kappe, Narayanan Kulathuramaiyer, Stefan Weber, and Bilal Zaka. 2007. *Report on dangers and opportunities posed by large search engines, particularly Google.* Accessed January 21, 2012. http://www.iicm.tugraz.at:8080/Ressourcen/Papers/dangers_google.pdf.

McKnight, David. 2003. "A world hungry for a new philosophy: Rupert Murdoch and the rise of neoliberalism." *Journalism Studies* 4 (3): 347–358.

———. 2010a. "Rupert Murdoch's News Corporation: A media institution with a mission." *Historical Journal of Film, Radio and Television* 30 (3): 303–316.

———. 2010b. "A change in climate? The journalism of opinion at News Corporation." *Journalism* 11 (6): 693–706.

Media Matters. 2010. "News Corp's support for combating climate change undermined by deniers at Fox News, *WSJ.*" Accessed February 10, 2012. http://mediamatters.org/research/201001220027.

Microsoft SEC-Filings. "10-k forms 1994–2012." *Edgar Database.* Accessed October 5, 2011. http://www.sec.gov/cgi-bin/browse-edgar?action=getcompany&CIK=0000789019&owner=exclude&count=40.

Microsoft. 2004. *Global citizenship report.* Accessed September 26, 2011. http://www.microsoft.com/about/corporatecitizenship/en-us/reporting/.

Morris, Jonathan S. 2005. "The Fox News factor." *The Harvard International Journal of Press/Politics* 10 (3): 56–79.

OSS Watch 2011. *Microsoft: An end to open hostility.* Accessed September 27, 2011. http://www.oss-watch.ac.uk/resources/microsoft.xml.

PIPA and Knowledge Networks. 2003. *Misperceptions, the media and the Iraq war.* Accessed February 24, 2012. http://www.worldpublicopinion.org/pipa/pdf/oct03/IraqMedia_Oct03_rpt.pdf.

Privacy International. 2007. *Consultation report. Race to the bottom?* Accessed January 21, 2012. http://www.privacyinternational.org/issues/internet/interim-rankings.pdf.

Privacy Rights Clearinghouse. 2004. *Google's new email service, Gmail, under fire for privacy concerns.* Accessed January 21, 2012. https://www.privacyrights.org/ar/GmailAGadvisory.htm.

Project for Excellence in Journalism. 2005. *The state of news media.* Accessed February 23, 2012. http://stateofthemedia.org/2005/cable-tv-intro/content-analysis/.

SACOM. 2010. *Apple owes workers and public a response over the poisoning.* Accessed October 16, 2011. http://sacom.hk/wp-content/uploads/2010/05/apple-owes-workers-and-public-a-response-over- the-poisonings.pdf.

———. 2011a. *Foxconn and Apple fail to fulfil promises: Predicaments of workers after the suicides.* Accessed October 20, 2011. http://sacom.hk/wp-content/uploads/2011/05/2011–05–06_foxconn-and-apple-fail-to-fulfill-promises1.pdf.

———. 2011b. *iSlave behind the iPhone. Foxconn workers in central China.* Accessed October 20, 2011. http://sacom.hk/wp-content/uploads/2011/09/20110924-islave-behind-the-iphone.pdf.

Sandoval, Marisol. 2012. "Consumer surveillance on web 2.0." In *Internet and surveillance,* edited by Christian Fuchs, Kees Bursma, Anders Albrechtslund, and Marisol Sandoval, 147–169. New York: Routledge.

Shirky, Clay. 2008. *Here comes everybody.* London: Penguin.

SOMO. 2007. *Apple. CSR company profile.* Accessed October 17, 2011. http://somo.nl/publications-en/Publication_1963/at_download/fullfile.

Tatli, Emin Islam. 2008. "Privacy in danger. Let's Google your privacy." In *The future of identity in the information society.* Vol. 262 of *IFIP International Federation for Information Processing,* edited by Simone Fischer-Hübner, Penny Duquenoy, Albin Zuccato, and Leonardo Martucci, 51–59. Boston: Springer.

Tene, Omar. 2008. "What Google knows: Privacy and Internet search engines." Accessed January 21, 2012. http://works.bepress.com/omer_tene/2.

Thussu, Daya Kishan. 2007. "The 'Murdochization' of news? The case of Star TV in India." *Media Culture and Society* 29 (49): 593–611.

Toffel, Michael, and Auden Schendler. 2012. *Where green corporate ratings fail. Harward Business School Working Knowledge.* Accessed March 5, 2012. http://hbswk.hbs.edu/pdf/item/6906.pdf.

Vaidhyanathan, Siva. 2011. *The Googlization of Everything (And Why We Should Worry).* Berkeley: University of California Press.

van Dijck, José. 2013. *The culture of connectivity. A critical history of social media.* Oxford: Oxford University Press.

Wong, Monina. 2005. *ICT hardware sector in China and corporate social responsibility issues.* SOMO. Accessed October 16, 2011. http://somo.nl/publications-en/Publication_624/at_download/fullfile.

Zimmer, Michael. 2008. "The externalities of search 2.0. The emerging privacy threats when the drive for the perfect search engine meets web 2.0." *First Monday* 13 (3).

Žižek, Slavoj. 2009. *First as tragedy then as farce.* London: Verso.

9 The Global Worker and the Digital Front

Nick Dyer-Witheford

9.1 THE GLOBAL WORKER

That the working class is changed in cycles of struggle which alter both its technical and political composition—the use of machinery and division of labour that shapes the class, and the degree and forms of challenge it makes to capital—was the thesis of *operaismo* (workerism). This school of composition traced how the resistances of skilled workers in early capital were in the Taylorist and Fordist factory transformed into the powerful organisations of the mass industrial worker. At the end of the twentieth century, however, capital halted and rolled back the wage and welfare state gains of the mass worker in North America and Europe in a campaign that conjoined corporate, state, and, crucially, techno-scientific power. The computers and networks of the cybernetic revolution developed in the Cold War, which would in 1989 drive the USSR to death by military competition, were also deployed at home.

Over some forty years, capital decomposed the factory bases of the classic working class, the mainly male, eventually relatively well-waged mass worker of the planetary North-West by automation, container transportation and electronic networks, relocating industrial production to the former periphery of the world system, and, in the core, shifting to service and technical work. With this transformation, an entire culture of class struggle was swept away. What recomposition can follow such apparently decisive defeat? Post-operaismo thinkers make several answers. Antonio Negri and Michael Hardt (2009) propose a "multitude" led by "immaterial labour"; George Caffentzis (2013) and Karl Heinz Roth (2010) see a planetary proletarianization. Drawing on, but also departing from, their accounts, this paper posits the emergence the "global worker".

"Global worker" is an occasional translation of Marx's *Gesamtarbeiter*, more commonly rendered as "collective worker" or "total worker", designating the combination of labourers whose cooperative powers—manual, intellectual, technical, supervisory—are mobilised by capital (1973, 643, 709). Marx based his *Gesamtarbeiter* on the nineteenth century factory, where he saw workers individually reduced and fragmented, "appropriated and annexed for life by a limited function" (Marx 1977, 469), but collectively powerful and multi-competent. Under capitalist command, this workforce was divided into a "hierarchy of labour powers, to which there corresponds a scale of wages" (1977, 469), and confronted with the force of science and technology, "the general intellectual product of the social process" that now appear as "the direct offshoot of capital" (Marx 1977, 1053). Nonetheless the *Gesamtarbeiter* was the potential form of a free association of common producers.

The thesis of this chapter is that at the start of the twenty-first century, when the unit of operations is no longer the factory, or even social-factory, but rather a planet-factory, we see a new, exploded-view of *Gesamtarbeiter*, *Weltgesamtarbeiter* (Haug 2009), "world-total worker". Of course, capital has always depended on worldwide work: slaves, coolies, and the peasantry of the periphery all attest to this usually brutal truth. What differs today is the degree to which such labours are systemically integrated and connected.

Today's global worker is collective labour that is:

i) trans-nationalized by the movement of industrial capital beyond its traditional heartlands;
ii) variegated by an increasingly complex division of labour, with the fastest growth neither in industry nor agriculture but in the circulation and social reproduction (a.k.a. "the service sector");
iii) feminized by the inclusion of women who both work for a wage and perform the unpaid domestic labour that is the basis of the formal economy;
iv) mobile and migrant both within and across borders;
v) precarious, rendered chronically insecure by a vast reserve army of the un- or under-employed vi) earth-changing in the effects of labours that, while historically cumulative, are only now becoming visible in an anthropogenic crisis of the natural environment; and finally—the focus of this essay—
vii) connected by 2 billion Internet accounts and 6 billion cell phones.

Capital's shattering "cybernetic offensive" (Tiqqun 2001), pursued across the theatres of production, circulation and finance, decomposed the mass worker, but also collaterally constituted a global worker whose strengths and weaknesses, including possibilities and limits for network re-appropriation, were glimpsed in the economic crisis of 2008 and the uprisings of 2011.

9.2   VALUE CHAINS

The global worker is not just an aggregate, the sum of all labours directly and indirectly mobilized by capital, a reckoning that could have been made any time in the last three hundred years: what gives this abstraction a contemporary concreteness is its organisational form, that of the "value chain". This term, with its close synonyms, "supply chains" and "commodity chains", identifies how a dominant capitalist enterprise organises subordinate aspects of the commodification process, dispersing each value adding activity to geographic locations that optimize labour costs, access to raw materials, or proximity to markets, and then links the chain in a continuous, integrated sequence. The value chain, with digital links, became the primary instrument for the elimination or intimidation of the mass worker in a process that connected two other manifestations of the cybernetic revolution, the robot and the genetically modified seed.

Robots played a role in the dismantling of the mass worker factory. But the speed of automation was tempered by what was in many ways a more cost-attractive alternative to yet more fixed capital investments—off-shoring to cheap labour areas. In this process, the deindustrialization of the north matched, both as cause and effect, the other ever more momentous dynamic—the rural depopulation in the global south. There subsistence farming that had for millennia provided the means of survival for the largest part of the world's people was undermined by mechanized large-scale farming, assisted by waves of genetic modification of plant crops, the consequences of climate change, and the expropriations of land for urbanization or extractive industries (Roth 2010; Cleaver 1981).

Increasingly able to sustain itself by subsistence farming alone, the global peasantry was disintegrating as it became dependent on periodic or permanent wage labour, setting in motion massive movements of continental and transcontinental migration (Wildcat 2008). In a repetition of primitive accumulation's release of the landless labour that provided capital's early proletariat, these migrants streamed into the vast new metropolitan slums of Asia, Africa and Latin America (Davis 2007). To eke out a living, the self-employed in so called informal economies, attempted further perilous journeys towards service labour in the global north, or entered the factory dormitories of *maquiladoras* and housing in special export zones that are sites of relocated industries.

As capital broke through its former partition of the globe into first, second and third worlds, or core and periphery, and sent itself snaking across a series of zonal arrangements, the value chain became to the global worker as the assembly line was to the mass worker—the technical basis for a new class composition. In its ur-form the value-chain headquartered research, design, and marketing in the high-wage areas of the global economy, subcontracted manufacturing, assembly, and back-end office functions in new industrialized territories, where they could be rapidly scaled up or down with market fluctuations, and sent mining and waste disposal to abyssal sacrifice zones. During the 1980s old industrial centres began to drain toward export zones. In two decades major parts of key sectors—cars, shipyards, textiles, electronics and chemicals—had been moved, and the former periphery attained new status as China became the "workshop of the world".

Value chains depend on cybernetic systems, telecommunications to coordinate dispersed operations, software for modular production and routinized interfaces, and Universal Product Codes for the logistics revolution that tracks commodities in motion round the world. These functions are integrated in packaged Enterprise Resource Planning systems from vendors such as Microsoft, Oracle, Epicor and SAP, offering automated alerts as markets fluctuate, and simulated scenarios to assess the impact of replacing suppliers, switching transportation modes, establishing new routes, increasing product prices and sudden labour troubles.

But cybernetic technologies are also themselves enabled by value chains. From the 1980s on Silicon Valley companies were dispatching hardware manufacture and the toxic processes of chip manufacture to the nimble fingers of female proletarians in Asia and Central America. By the 2000s, laptops, mobiles and consoles had become the convergence point for a transnational network of labours, with electronic assembly work concentrated in Southern China's new mass worker factories, of which Foxconn would become notoriously emblematic, key minerals flowing in from the coltan mines of the eastern Congo or the rare earth deposits of Borneo (Mezzadra and Neilson 2013), and e-waste disposal going to waste dumps of West Africa or India, in processes whose bleakly physical exploitation undermined all characterization of cybernetics as a sphere of "immateriality".

The computer revolution was thus both a producer and product of a new class composition. The networked links of the value chain exploded the spatial concentration and cultural solidarity of the mass worker, and then sliced, diced and dispersed it across a planet striated by the legacy of uneven and combined development, in shards subject to savage labour arbitrage which fractioned manufacturing costs. In the process, it massively expanded capital's waged labour force, which grew to some 3.1 billion workers, over 70 per cent in what was once called the developing world, 40 per cent in India and China alone (ILO 2012). In this process, it drew on a "global reserve army of producers for whom low-wage labour represents a significant step upward in terms of their ability to meet their needs" (Lebowitz 2011, 254).

To a far greater extent than the left likes to admit this has raised standards of living. The global worker is wealth producing. Capital can boast it has lifted millions out of poverty, even if this elevation is measured by a grotesquely low standard, and leaves millions in gratuitous abjection. This wealth is distributed with dizzying differentials that separate workers not only from capital but from one another. The "hierarchy of labour powers, to which there corresponds a scale of wages" is now exaggerated on a world scale, giving sectors of the global worker, particularly in the global north investment, metaphorically and literally, in the current system, but by the very extremity of its inequalities also creating potential crises for capital itself.

9.3 UNIVERSAL INTERCOURSE

If the dirty secret of the digital revolution is the supply chain, its happy face is a vast expansion of communication. Marx (1977, 90) described the commodity as the "cell form" of capitalism. Today a bad pun and an inversion give us the *cell-phone* as the genotypic commodity of the world market. Six billion mobiles, one for almost every person on the planet, are to-hand techno-science for a system that requires people in perpetual motion, in touch, up to speed, always on, constantly annihilating space through time, and circulating commodities. Cell phones inscribe in their production massive global inequalities, but seem to negate these by offering in communication plenitude refused in other dimensions of life, permitting a shanty dweller without clean water, adequate food, or education to call half around the world.

The networks for this traffic are connected to the creation of a new level of scientific labour, originating in the imperial centres of US military power, outside the formations of the mass worker, growing from the early computer hackers of the 1970s into professionalized strata of programmers, software engineers, application developers, network experts, web designers, systems administrators, security specialists and telecommunications workers. From this core, digital competencies have spread through the entertainment, advertising, administrative and financial sectors, and, as computers and network access became consumer goods in the 1980s and '90s, across broader populations, first in capital's core regions, then globally.

From the moment this scientific labour took the Internet on a line of flight out of the Pentagon, two different models of its organisation have contended and coexisted. The first, the hacker model, discovered in the networks an autonomous zone, separated from impure industrial materiality, for the cooperative production and sharing of non-rivalrous virtual goods. Its slogan is "information wants to be free", its paradigmatic practices are open source and peer to peer. The second, the model of capital, comprehends networks solely as a way of accelerating the circulation of commodities, either directly by virtual sale, or indirectly, through advertising, conducting commerce "at the speed of light".

Whereas the growth of the Internet was part of the overarching cycle of struggle leading from the mass worker to the global worker, it also manifested its own, internal sub-cycles, moving at net speed, in which these models both conflict and intertwine. Early turns in this spiral included the hacker separation of the Net from its military-academic incubator, the creation of an experimental digital counter-culture in the 1980s, its capture by libertarian entrepreneurialism in the dot.com boom of the 1990s; and the implosion of that boom in the meltdown of 2001, parallel with a surge of *altermondialiste* hacktivism, indie media, free software and creative commons.

Subsequently, however, re-appropriation has run the other way. After the 2001 crash, networked capital resurrected itself in a search-engine and social-media driven web 2.0, with Google and Facebook as flagships, resting largely on the absorption of earlier commons experiments, including user-generated content as a major source of "free labour" (Terranova 2010); commercial absorption of open-source software; give-aways of services and content backing reliance on networked advertising; and, in tandem with this, massive accumulation of data about the identity and preferences of networked subjects. This is the apparatus now extended globally by mobile media, rapidly adding 24/7, omni-locational envelopment and "mobile wallet" integration with credit and finance.

The role of networks in accelerating the horizontal, circulatory movement of commodities complements its vertical, surplus value-extraction via global value chains. As capital revoked the wage and welfare gains of the mass worker for a trans-nationally stratified low-wage economy, so identification and targeting of specific planetary bands of consumption capacity grew in importance. The "ubiquitous marketing" and "big data" aggregation of social media surveils the fragmented segments of the collective worker and addresses them, as their spending power warrants, in the language of commodity exchange.

Internet industries not only identify but also constitute these new consuming segments, as creating an intermediate stratum of high-tech jobs on the borders between labour and capital, supplanting the declining middle class of the welfare state. The developmental path of "shining India" is paradigmatic. In a process that typified the dual processes of migration and off-shoring and that recomposed the global worker, Silicon Valley software capital attracted programmers and engineers from India, then relocated this work to the high tech centres in Bangalore and Hyderabad, where software production co-existed with call centres answering complaints about digital malfunctions. Not only the toil of hardware manufacture but also "cybertariat" (Huws 2003) work and even higher echelons of scientific labour followed the low wage logic of the value chain, and subverted the neo-imperial assumption that knowledge work would remain in the global north while the south suffered through industrialization.

This does not, however, mean a smoothly unified class composition, in which the commonalities of immaterial labour generate spontaneous solidarities. The "universal intercourse" of global capital is superimposed on, without superseding, the hierarchical divisions of class (Marx and Engels 1970). As Jack Qiu (2009) suggests in his study of a Chinese "networked working class" permeated by cheap cell phones, messaging services and cyber-cafés, the international division of digital haves and have nots is giving way to divisions between gradations of digital "haves" and "have lesses". The falling cost of computing power and capital's drive to integrate virtual labour and consumer markets tend towards the absorption of global populations into the networks, yet huge gulfs remain. Broadband access in particular is a division line.

In this context the networks grow their shadow side. The Internet offers virtual entertainment and sociality to the professional-managerial sectors, credit-affluent workers of the global north and the emergent middle classes of the south. But for other sections of the global worker, connecting via cheap cell phones and Internet cafés, the online world is yet another arena for proletarian survival by the sale of cheap labour power, receipt of remittances from immigrant diasporas and grey-, black- and red- market activities. In these contexts the property-disruptive potentials of networks first explored by hacker elites re-appeared on a mass scale as globalized digital crime (Glenny 2012): Nigerian 419 scams, Chinese gold-farming, Russian hacking, and, above all, omnipresent digital piracy, now accounting for the majority of digital music, games, film and other software distributed Asia, Africa, Latin America and Eastern Europe.

Entering the new millennia the oppositional capacities of so-called "immaterial labour" therefore appeared largely subsumed within "communicative capital" (Dean 2009), or manifesting transgressively as its criminalized mirror image. Anti-commodifying projects persisted in the networks, but as subordinated tendencies, just as an un-romantic view of the traditional commons of medieval Europe reveals them as supplements to a brutal and dominant feudal order. Or, to put it more hopefully, the networked socialization of the means of communication remained "within the shell of the old". A crack in that shell would open, but one made, in the first instance not by labour's militancy, but by the very severity of its defeat.

9.4   MONEY GRIDS

The rift came in the great crash of 2008. Some *operaismo* theorists see this as an event purely internal to capital (Tronti 2008). Others claim fatal debt as backhanded class resistance (Midnight Notes Collective 2009). But the financial implosion was the paradoxical result of capital's class-war victory over the mass worker. Wages and social costs in the centre could be held in check by global outsourcing to the margins, but this brought lack of global purchasing power, and a shortage of investment opportunities, which finance capital addressed through debt and speculation. Debt, via credit cards, housing mortgages or micro-finance, created consumption power the global worker lacked (with interest). Derivatives and other speculative instruments enabled capital to make money without actually producing and selling commodities by betting on the risks of its own circuit, as if autonomous from labour. However this flight from the actual sources of value could only go on so long: capital's contradictory need for low wages and high consumption collided in the sub-prime mortgage collapse that destroyed the US housing sector and disrupted the entire world market.

Cybernetic systems of exceptional scope and speed created the conditions for this runaway breakdown. Banks and stock markets had been amongst the first sectors of capital to realize the civilian potential of the Internet, creating transnational electronic networks second in sophistication only to the Pentagon's: it was across this "money grid" (Patterson 2010, 218) that US finance companies distributed esoterically packaged toxic subprime mortgages, designed by the best and brightest of graduates in mathematics, physics, and computing science—the quants—primed to explode like time bombs. Once these started to go off, financial markets responded at speeds dictated by algorithmic trading programmes sensitive to millisecond time-arbitrage possibilities. Thus the house of cards fell fast and hard, as defaults on sub-prime mortgages spread to a general credit crisis, paralysis of industrial capital, government bailouts, and fiscal crises of the state.

The meltdown set off world scale economic waves, though moving in complex and contrary directions. The US, Britain and Southern Europe were almost immediately plunged into austerity; parts of the developing world less integrated with financial hubs suffered more delayed currency effects that sent food prices skyrocketing, and other sectors actually did well: the BRIC (Brasil, Russia, India, China) complex, after temporary setbacks, maintained or even accelerated its growth, taking up the slack from stalled core economies. This unevenness produced a de-synchronization of capitalist accumulation zones; but it also resulted in a strange synchronization of diverse struggles moving simultaneously within a tightly meshed global space. The crisis that arose from the defeat of the mass worker also became a moment that disclosed, if only momentarily, the class power of the global worker in the widespread insurrections of 2011.

These are now indexed to a handful of iconic sites—Tahrir Square, Zuccoti Park, Puerta del Sol, Syntagma Square—but were far more widespread. Very schematically, we can speak of four main wheels or hubs of struggle. One, centred in the de-industrialized North America and Europe, was composed of defensive resistances against austerity by students, public sector workers, and the poor. A second, that of the Arab Spring, unleashed alliances of students, intelligentsia, slum dwellers and workers against despotic regimes presiding over stagnant, often oil distorted, economies. A third wheel, already rolling for several years, was that of Chinese migrant proletariat workers, whose militancy, set back by economic contraction in 2008, revived in strikes in car and electronic plants round the Pearl River. A fourth emerged in Latin America around peasant and indigenous battles against extractive and energy sector capital. There was definitely no central committee orchestrating this. The wheels seemed to spin independently, sometimes in opposite directions. But there were contagions, resonances, and amplifications. The simultaneous revolts of precarious workers in the decadent zones of capital on the way down the global wage hierarchy and Chinese proletarians in emerging zones pushing their way up convulsed an increasingly unified global labour market (Colatrella 2011).

9.5   STRUGGLE CASCADES

The role of digital networks in these events is difficult to discuss because liberal commentators have so fetishized it—as if, for example social media, not unemployment, rising food prices and authoritarianism caused uprisings in Egypt. This "Facebook revolution" trope vindicates high-tech capitalism, locking attention on the digitally well-connected strata of the global worker at the expense of manual labourers and the unemployed. Nonetheless the revolts did occur within populations, and generations for whom the virtual was increasingly commonplace: ubiquitous in the developed world, still concentrated amongst students and professionals in the former periphery, but not simply an elite phenomenon, network use became one of several factors that transformed isolated outbursts into a struggle cascade.

In the mid-1990s the Zapatista's digital call for resistance to neoliberalism had galvanized an alter-globalization movement whose summit-busting manifestations from Seattle to Genoa wove "an electronic fabric of struggle" (Cleaver 1994). But as the tide of alter-globalization ebbed in the wake of 9/11, so too did a cyber-activism whose apparently subversive possibilities were often incorporated into a commodified web 2.0. The "global slump" (McNally 2010), however, offered another turn of the screw in the helical story of network counter-power.

In the global north, resistance was slow to emerge, but when it did it had a very different tone from alter-globalization. Confronting, not to the possibility of "another world", but the bleakness of "no future", a logic of occupation spread from the streets of Greece to US university blockades, French factory seizures and British student occupations, leapt from the Mediterranean into Tunisia, spiked momentously in Tahrir Square, and then spread back to the movement of Spanish *indignados*, returning across the Atlantic to Occupy Wall Street (**OWS**). Occupations are bodies filling space. But they involve communication in two aspects—general assembly decision-making and networked social media.

As we saw, the social media of web 2.0 captured the communal aspects of the net, demonstrating what Paolo Virno (2004) terms "the communism of capital". But this proved a double game. Web 2.0 is a commodification apparatus that paradoxically depends on collectivism and association. Safe for capital in a US intoxicated by debt-driven consumerism, in other contexts, and in other times, it carried risk. The events of 2011 showed that, in the digital arena, the digital communism of capital could, at least briefly, become the social media capitalism of the commune. Transposed to situations of heightened political struggle, such as those of the Arab Spring, the anti-austerity struggles of Europe, and then the sudden North American mobilization of OWS, network forms, always alongside the more traditional radical word-of-mouth and photocopied pamphlet, constituted one of the "spaces of dissent" (Aouragh and Alexander 2011).

As Paolo Gerbaudo (2012) shows in his scrupulous study of the "tweets and the streets" of Egypt, Spain and North America, in 2011, the digital did not constitute a distinct autonomous zone of struggle but was tied to physical action. The square went virtual. The virtual came down to the square. Net and square, net and factory, net and barricade were super-imposed, and the viral images were of the beaten, imprisoned, tortured, and protest suicides. Mobile devices, in particular, played a special role in the sudden self-organised revolts, in the coordination of demonstrations and riots. These efforts were countered by security forces' monitoring, surveillance, censorship and shutdowns. However, these interventions did not always succeed, and sometimes backfired badly. Mubarak's attempted Internet shutdown was technologically circumvented *and* provoked and intensified street demonstrations.

Alongside the strongly terrestrial nature of the struggles, there were also links to specific highly technical hacker groups such as Wikipedia and Anonymous. In North America, Anonymous both provided iconography and actively mobilized street participation in OWS. Moreover both hacker projects like WikiLeaks and militant street-level social media were linked to mainstream broadcast media increasingly dependent for newsgathering on digital sources. The interactions of Tunisian and Egyptian protesters with Al-Jazeera, and OWS with the New York media showed that if protest could even briefly occupy not just street space but also digital space there was a possibility of reversing the well-known vicious media spiral of silencing dissent, generating instead a virtuous spiral of amplification. The arena of net activism was national, regional, and urban, but also transnational, sometimes as a transmission of tactics, as when Spanish indignado's manual for general assemblies was distributed in the initial calls for Occupy Wall Street, more generally, as a diffuse relay of rebel news, sometimes from sites very far away. Not only images of Tahrir Square but photos from Foxconn factories were familiar to OWS protesters, passing from worker cell phones to Chinese news organisations then circulated by international media. All contributed to a generalized sense of global revolt.

Yet this moment of convergent outbreak was brief. As Mike Davis (2011) observes, since 2011 "spring" has met "winter"; the Egyptian revolution yielding victory not for progressive workers movements, but religious fundamentalists; Libya and Syria descending into civil wars stoked by foreign intervention; southern Europe sealed off in a slow-motion agony of austerity; US Occupy, gone up like a rocket, coming down like a stick; and in China, strikes driving up wages, but, perhaps because of this, not dislodging the pro-market, technocratic wing of the party. If the meltdown of 2008 demonstrated capital's continuing vulnerability to major crisis, subsequent events have, so far, demonstrated its robust survival capacities.

This subsidence of the 2011 revolt can no more be solely attributed to digital media than can its outburst. But speed of mobilization was not necessarily matched by long-term strength. Sectors familiar with social media, prominent in early phases of outbreaks, did not necessarily connect with other groups used to more traditional forms of organisation (as the students and precarious workers of OWS never truly spliced with US unions and community organisations) or were defeated by reactionary elements with better on the ground organisation (as in Egypt where post-Mubarak's elections saw liberal-left groupings lose to the religious parties' stronger presence in communal spaces). In some cases—such as OWS—the hyper-horizontality that linked consensus-based assemblies and social media conversations sustained an amorphous populism but became a barrier to the articulation of goals and objectives. And in the aftermath of risings, the immense panoptic potential of digital networks was revealed, as security forces, having recaptured the streets, followed up with arrests based on cell-phone and video records. Thus if the revolts of 2011 hinted that a planetary working class might be reaching for forms of political recomposition in which the networks were an important ingredient, on every front including the digital, this remained a global-worker-in-process.

9.6   THE DIGITAL FRONT

The economic crisis that started in 2008 is, however, taking a very long goodbye, and even more severe tumults may combine with it: geo-political enmity crises catalysed by the decline of the global imperial hegemon; ecological crises, of which global warming is the most serious; and entity crises, arising from capital's breakneck technological alteration of previous biological givens. The problem of the global worker confronting capital is that of a technical division of labour so complex, and a hierarchy of labour powers and wages so steep, as to apparently disable political composition. Indeed these issues are so extreme that it might be considered not just a problem of the global worker but with the concept itself, precluding the putative recomposition it implies. However, as Beverley Silver (2003) has observed, in previous cycles of struggle workers have recaptured the most apparently inimical technical features of capital: the Fordist factory appeared at its origins as the death-knell to the skilled worker before it became the fortress of the mass worker. To name the global worker is to make a map; and a map is also a weapon.

Mario Tronti, reviewing the history of the operaismo tendency from which he eventually diverged, writes: "Workers' struggles determine the course of capitalist development; but capitalist development will use those struggles for its own ends if no organized revolutionary process opens up, capable of changing that balance of forces" (Tronti 2012). The mixed outcomes of 2011 have contributed to renewed discussion of the "communist horizon" (Dean 2012)—and a revived advocacy for the Leninist party. Yet the strongly horizontal tendency of contemporary struggles, strongly associated with peer-to-peer network practices, makes it unlikely any vanguard group will hegemonize their myriad molecular components under some molar organisation. What may be more feasible however, is a "becoming party" of multiplicitous movements which learn in the course of struggle an increasing self-discipline of prioritizing objectives, formulating demands, and coordinating operations around a gradually developed common program. In this sense, and in this sense only, we might say that whereas in the era of the mass worker the party constructed the cells, in that of the global worker the cells must create the party, an organisation as far from Leninism as contemporary military organisation, with its all-round battle-spaces and mobile fronts, is from vanguards.

Along these lines, Karl Heinz Roth (2010) has suggested forms of trade union—and social movement—association that, as short term goal would "impose and sharpen" reformist programmes to overcome the crisis, pushing "anti-cyclical" Keynesianism beyond its intended limits, promoting workers control in recovered industries, and through progressive taxation and re-appropriation effecting a "massive top down redistribution of wealth" (Roth 2010, 229). Longer-term goals would include radical reductions in working time, and the democratization of municipal governance, with local and regional socialization of resources gradually connecting in federated structures. Emphasizing "mass co-ordinated action" linked with a "world-wide information campaign" and "mass learning processes", and noting the critical role of new scientific-technological labour in such activity, Roth calls for a "globally linked association" that would not be a "cadre organization claiming to be a vanguard" but a "free and democratic association of people who have criticized, corrected, revised, expanded and subsequently appropriated this concept to test its usefulness in dialogue with the proletarian multiverse" (Roth 2010, 230).

Going further, and specifically invoking the figure of the "global collective worker" Mike Lebowitz has observed that today the "challenge to socialist theorists" is to envision "a producer composed of differing limbs and organs from around the world, who produces the necessary inputs for that collective worker" (2011, 254), as Marx put it, "in full self-awareness as one single social labour force" (1977, 171). Lebowitz sketches a "socialist globalization" based on collective ownership of the means of production, democratization of workplaces, and development for communal needs, and a new international division of labour to overcome disparities, and competition between workers in different zones. This, he writes, should have at its core "maximizing the productive capability of the least well off in the global society" with "local producers [. . .] providing for many local needs" not on a primitive basis but "using the most advanced productive forces", a process that "in making unnecessary much energy-intensive shipping and transport over long distances" has ecological as well as class dimensions (Lebowitz 2011, 255).

In the dialogues and proposals envisaged by Roth, Lebowitz, and others today conceiving a society beyond capital, four capacities of cybernetic networks deserve particular consideration. The first is free reproduction and circulation of socially-created products and knowledge: open-source software, even though now largely co-opted in corporate systems, remains pre-figurative. Second is the potential for the planned linking of socially-owned enterprises, public works and worker cooperatives along the lines envisaged by some theorists of solidarity economics. Third is the role of large-scale "knowledge infrastructures" of the type now critically important to climate science, to determine the dimensions of ecological and social problems. Fourth is the use of networks as elements in democratic, distributed social planning processes. Struggles for such cybernetic re-appropriations, as well as for the circulation of news, analysis and support of struggles in other areas, will constitute the global worker's digital front.

REFERENCES

Aouragh, Miryam and Anne Alexander 2011. "The Egyptian experience: Sense and nonsense of the Internet revolution." *International Journal of Communication* 5: 1344–1358.

Caffentzis, George. 2013. *In letters of blood and fire: Work, machines, and value in the bad infinity of capitalism*. New York: PM Press.

Colatrella, Steven. 2011. "A worldwide strike wave, austerity and the political crisis of global governance." *lib.com*. Accessed July 23, 2013, http://libcom.org/library/worldwide-strike-wave-austerity-political-crisis-global-governance-steven-colatrella.

Cleaver, Harry. 1981. "Technology as political weaponry." In *Science, politics and the agricultural revolution in Asia*, edited by Robert S. Anderson, 261–276. Boulder, CO: Westview.

———. 1994. "The Chiapas uprising and the future of class struggle in the new world order." *Studies in Political Economy* 44: 141–157.

Davis, Mike. 2007. *Planet of the slums*. New York: Verso.

———. 2011. "Spring confronts Winter." *New Left Review* 72: 5–15.

Dean, Jodi. 2009. *Democracy and other neoliberal fantasies: Communicative capitalism & left politics*. Durham: Duke University Press.

———. 2012. *The communist horizon*. London: Verso.

Gerbaudo, Paolo. 2012. *Tweets and the streets: Social media and contemporary activism*. London: Pluto.

Glenny, Misha. 2012. *DarkMarket: How hackers became the new mafia*. New York: Vintage.

Hardt, Michael, and Antonio Negri. 2000. *Empire*. Boston: Harvard University Press.

Hardt, Michael and Antonio Negri. 2009. *Commonwealth*. Cambridge, London: Belknap Press.

Haug, Wolfgang Fritz. 2009. "Immaterial labour: Entry for Historical-Critical Dictionary of Marxism." *Historical Materialism* 17 (4): 177–185.

Huws, Ursula. 2003. *The making of a cybertariat: Virtual work in a real world*. London: Merlin.

International Labour Office (ILO). 2012. *Global employment trends: The challenge of global of jobs recovery*. Geneva: ILO.

Karaganis, Joe, ed. 2011. *Media piracy in emerging economies*. New York: Social Science Research Council.

Lebowitz, Michael. 2011. "Socialism for the twenty-first century and the need for socialist globalization." *International Critical Thought* 1(3): 249–256

Marx, Karl. 1973. *Grundrisse.* New York: Penguin.

———. 1977. *Capital: Volume 1.* New York: Penguin.

Marx, Karl, and Friedrich Engels. 1970. *The German ideology.* New York: International Publishers.

Mason, Paul. 2012. *Why it's kicking off everywhere: The new global revolutions.* London: Verso.

McNally, David. 2010. *Global slump: The economics and politics of crisis and resistance.* Oakland, CA: PM Press.

Mezzadra, Sandra, and Brett Neilson. 2013. "Extraction, logistics, finance." *Radical Philosophy* 178: 8–17.

Midnight Notes Collective, 2009. *Promissory notes: From crisis to commons.* Accessed July 23, 2013, http://www.midnightnotes.org/Promissory%20Notes.pdf.

Patterson, Scott. 2010. *The quants: How a new breed of math whizzes conquered Wall Street and nearly destroyed it.* New York: Crown Business.

Qiu, Jack Linchuan. 2009. *Working-class network society: Communication technology and the information have-less in Urban China.* Cambridge, MA: MIT Press.

Roth, Karl Heinz. 2010. "Global crisis-global proletarianization-counter-perspectives." In *Crisis in the global economy: Financial markets, social struggles, and new political scenarios,* edited by Andrea Fumagalli and Sandro Mezzadra, 197–236. Los Angeles: Semiotext(e).

Silver, Beverly J. 2003. *Forces of labor: Workers' movements and globalization since 1870.* Cambridge, MA: Cambridge University Press.

Terranova, Tiziana. 2010. "New economy, financialization and social production in the web 2.0." In *Crisis in the global economy: Financial markets, social struggles and new political scenarios,* edited by Andrea Fumagalli and Sandro Mezzadra, 153–170. Los Angeles: Semiotext(e).

Tiqqun. 2001. "L'hypothese cybernetique." *Tiqqun* 2: 40–83.

Tronti, Mario. 2008. "The old guard on the new crisis, pt. 2: Mario Tronti, Politics at Work." *Institute for Conjunctural Research.* Accessed July 23, 2013, http://conjunctural.blogspot.ca/2008/10/old-guard-on-new-crisis-pt-2-mario.html.

———. 2012. "Our operaismo." *New Left Review* 73: 119–130.

Virno, Paolo. 2004. *A grammar of the multitude.* New York: Semiotext(e).

Wildcat. 2008. "Beyond the peasant international." *Wildcat* 82: 5–6. Accessed July 23, 2013, http://www.wildcat-www.de/en/wildcat/82/w82_bauern_en.html.

10 Alienation's Returns

Mark Andrejevic

10.1 UTOPIAS AND DYSTOPIAS

The promise of the information economy has a split personality: on the one hand, it promises an era of unprecedented access to the means of communication, information, and self-expression. We can develop our understanding of the world, our relationship with others, our own creative and communicative skills in new, exciting and powerful ways. On the other hand it foreshadows an era of unprecedented monitoring and sorting in which our every action and communication is captured, stored, and mined with an eye to anticipating and influencing our future behaviour. The utopian aspect of the promise is a familiar one—everyone (with the access, the skills, and the time) can have his or her own TV show, podcast, or blog. Anyone can find out as much information as they need to know about areas of interest or concern. We will have unprecedented opportunities for conversing with one another, for sharing our thoughts, ideas, and expressions—for expanding our social and professional lives in new, exciting and efficient ways. And in so doing, we will be encouraged to develop the skills once thwarted, suppressed, overlooked, or otherwise devalued and underemphasized by the top-down forms of elite-controlled mass media that dominated the twentieth century.

The dystopian threat is becoming equally familiar: A world in which our job prospects, our educational opportunities, perhaps even our health care is shaped by databases and algorithms beyond our comprehension and control. Does the algorithm say that people who share certain seemingly random traits with me do not do well at a particular type of job? Then I'm out of luck, perhaps without even knowing why. In the era of big data, correlation threatens to eclipse explanation: even if I had the right to question why a particular decision has been made there may be no ready explanation available. One of the beauties or horrors of data mining, depending on how you look at it, is that it is designed to discover unanticipated and indiscernible patterns—that is, patterns that may not have any clear or ready explanation but that emerge when enough different variables are taken into consideration in a large enough pool of data. Perhaps some combination of my tastes in food, my birthplace and the climate in the city where I currently live, groups me with others who are proven susceptible to a particular type of illness. The database can determine this long before anyone figures out why. For many of those involved, the why will be irrelevant—what will be important is the probability of the prediction. By now, anyone who has been paying attention understands that the big data economy is about a lot more than ad targeting, or as it is framed by marketers and their allies, the "benefit" of being exposed exclusively to ads that we're interested in instead of ones that are irrelevant.

Targeted advertising is little more than the alibi for the much greater designs of the big data era: the ability to mine giant troves of data to develop useful patterns for law enforcement, health care, employers, educators, realtors, investors, landlords, and just about anyone who has any interest in anticipating, pre-empting, or otherwise influencing human behaviour. There are many potentially benevolent uses of such information in a wide range of fields. MIT's big data guru Alex Pentland, who has coined the term "reality mining" to describe the breadth and depth of new forms of data capture, anticipates a world in which the insights gleaned from the database will assist in creating a more healthy, secure, and efficient world: "For instance, the correlation of behavior data with medication data from millions of people could make drug therapies more effective and help medical professionals detect drug interactions more quickly. If behavior data were correlated with medical conditions, the data could illuminate the etiology and preconditions of disease far more powerfully than is possible today and, further, serve as an early warning system for epidemic diseases such as SARS" (Pentland 2009, 75). Just as the data collected covers the entire realm of human behaviour (and much more), so it can be used to help rationalise all dimensions of social, political and economic life:

> For society, the hope is that we can use this new in-depth understanding of individual behaviour to increase the efficiency and responsiveness of industries and governments. For individuals, the attraction is the possibility of a world where everything is arranged for your convenience—your health checkup is magically scheduled just as you begin to get sick, the bus comes just as you get to the bus stop, and there is never a line of waiting people at city hall. (Pentland 2009, 79)

As always, the shadow of perfect rationalisation is that of total control: a world in which we are sorted at important life moments according to genetic, demographic, geo-locational, and previously unanticipated types of data in ways that remain opaque and out of our control.

In reality, we face neither simple utopia nor unvarnished dystopia. The point of juxtaposing these two views of the digital promise is to suggest the need for thinking of both the potential benefits and drawbacks together, in the hopes of starting to imagine the type of world we might want to create out of the raw materials of the information age and to craft the guiding principles that might help realize it. One important starting point, I would argue, is to counter the ideological conflation between the claim that new forms of un-alienated activity are fostered by the emergence of the online economy and the celebration of the potential benefits of the big data economy. One is about greater transparency and control on the part of users, the other is not. These are both potential benefits, but they operate in very different registers. One relies on de-centralization and distribution of access to the means of sense making. The other proposes just the opposite: the centralization, or at least the aggregation of the database and the development of techniques for sense-making that are limited to those with control over the costly resources for data collection, storage and processing. That anyone who wishes (and who has a computer and an Internet connection) can use Twitter to express him- or herself is something very different from anyone being able to access and mine Twitter's "firehose". In the first instance we are talking about widespread access to communicative resources, in the other about concentrated control over the ownership and related uses of the communication infrastructure and the data it generates.

This distinction is frequently lost in discussions of "immaterial labour" and the information economy. The explanation for the loss of this distinction is, amongst other things an unwillingness to focus on infrastructure embodied by the ideology of post-materiality. Its symptom is the dismissal of the critique of alienation. We live—and not for the first time—in an era of the ostensible overcoming of alienation, to hear the various theorists of the era of immaterial labour put it: "in the digital economy, the worker achieves fulfilment through work and finds in her brain her own, un-alienated means of production" (Don Tapscott, as quoted in Rey 2012, 405). Even those who seek to preserve the critique of exploitation seek to sever it from that of alienation—at least when it comes to forms of so-called "prosumption", in which consumers generate value for others through their use of available communication resources for networking, interacting, and expressing themselves. "The voluntary nature of social media use seems to indicate that users are not alienated by it. However, both social media and the factory are products of capitalism and are, ultimately, adapted to its purposes [. . .] Most notably, both institutions are oriented toward enriching owners by expropriating value created by others" (Rey 2012, 401). The picture painted here is one of exploitation (in the form of value capture) without alienation: when people go on Facebook they do so voluntarily, not under the threat of coercion. Moreover, they do not surrender control over their productive activity—that is, overseers from Facebook, Google, or Twitter do not tell them what to talk about, what materials to upload and so on (although they do, of course, impose some constraints).

Nevertheless these companies find ways of extracting value from the un-managed activities that their sites facilitate. As Rey puts it in an apparent epitaph for alienation: "Capitalism in the digital age does not merely diminish the need for mindless, coerced labour but actually reconfigures itself to promote and benefit from intentional, spontaneous activity (i.e., unalienated labour)" (2012, 410). Here again, a form of conflation is at work: in this case between the intentional activity of creating blog or twitter posts, of updating one's Facebook status, etc., and the largely unintentional activity of generating troves of data about one's activities, one's time-space path, one's tastes and preferences, and so on.

10.2   ALIENATION IS DEAD! LONG LIVE ALIENATION!

The thesis of this chapter is that claims of the death of alienation are premature in a world in which our own activity generates data that others can aggregate, mine, sort, and analyse in order to generate ways to more effectively manipulate us, to include or exclude us from access to jobs or educational opportunities, to access to health care or other forms of insurance or benefit. One of the more compelling formulations of alienation provided by Marx recurs in the repeated image of the products of our own activity turned back upon us. Thus, in the classic formulation of alienation in the *Economic and Philosophical Manuscripts*, Marx observes that, "the object which labour produces—labour's product—confronts it as something alien, as a power independent of the producer" (1974, 324). The greater one's labour, the greater the sense of alienation: "the more the worker spends himself, the more powerful becomes the alien world of objects which he creates over and against himself" (1974, 325). And this independent power comes to be seen not simply as beyond the control of the producer, but as turned back upon him or her: "The alienation of the worker in his product means not only that his labour becomes an object, an *external* existence, but that it exists *outside him*, independently, as something alien to him, and that it becomes a power on its own confronting him [. . .] the life which he has conferred on the object confronts him as something hostile and alien" (1974, 325).

This formulation takes on renewed salience in the era of the "data double" or the "digital shadow": the creation of highly detailed personal profiles over which we have little or no control but which are increasingly being used to determine our life chances, our access to resources and benefits, even our mobility, in the digital era. The data shadow is a figure of the alienated self—one whose actions are largely invisible to us but who intervenes in our daily lives in ways that embody the imperatives of others turned back upon us. Reporter and author Charles Duhigg describes a relatively simple example—with the suggestion that this is little more than a foretaste of things to come—in his discussion of how credit card companies track purchases that might auger life events with implications for people's creditworthiness. Lenders worry, for example, when their clients get divorced, Duhigg said, "because divorce is expensive and they are paranoid that you might stop paying your credit card bill. For example, if you use your card to pay for a marriage counsellor, they might decrease your credit line" (as quoted in Nolan, 2012). This example relies upon a pre-big-data model—that is, it relies upon a ready explanation of causation that does not need to be "run through the data" to be understood. A life-changing event is in the offing—one that has the potential to affect a borrower's finances adversely. In the big data world, such simple and transparent explanations will likely be eclipsed by complex interactions of variables that may have no ready explanation. The whole point of big data mining is to discover unpredictable and even potentially inexplicable patterns. The goal, in other words, is to use the fruit of our own activity—the data it generates—in ways that are impossible to anticipate, difficult to discern and hard to explain or justify, but that nevertheless have an important impact on our lives. Far from figuring the end of alienation, the increasingly comprehensive surrender of control over personal information and the uses to which it is put, augers its redoubling.

Suggestively Rey's analysis of "immaterial" labour opens up an avenue for re-considering the role of alienation in the online economy. One of the characteristics of the products of this labour, at least in its informational form, is that it is, as economists put it, "non-rival" in consumption. Whereas I cannot have my cake (or give it to someone else) and eat it too, I *can* have my status update even while Facebook collects it, sorts it and puts it to use. Information, in short, is not destroyed because someone uses it. I can share an idea with you without losing it—and, legal restrictions aside, I can copy and share data at minimal cost to myself and without any damage to my original version of that data. What this means for Rey is that, "The fact that it is possible for both the users and site owners to access, use, and possess the *immaterial* information that exists on social media sites makes it possible for each party to derive a distinct type of value from the site. The fact that the site owner benefits from the exchange value of the information on the site in no way impinges on the user's ability to enjoy the use value of that site" (Rey 2012, 413). From a glass-half-full perspective, that means that users can engage in voluntary, uncoerced activity while simultaneously generating value for companies that collect and use their information. From the half-empty perspective, however, such redoubling opens up the possibility that even seemingly voluntary activity can be captured and turned back upon users. Even Rey's article, which sets out by positing the unalienated character of immaterial labour concedes that, "the remaining forms of alienation have simply been hidden from the prosumer [. . .] In the paradigm of digital information, users are often unaware of the full extent of the information that they are producing. In fact, even the knowledge of what information is being gathered on a particular site is often proprietary" (2012, 410). This point bears repeating—it is not simply that users are unaware of the ways in which their contributions are collected and used, but that they are largely incognizant of the breadth and the depth of the contextual information being collected about them, and of the increasingly sophisticated ways in which this data is being put to use. Drawing on the insight that user-generated content is not simply what users post, but also the huge amounts of data about their activities that they generate unintentionally and often unknowingly, we might say that their activity has both an unalienated and an alienated dimension—and that the latter is shaped by the relations of ownership and control over the infrastructure of interaction: the *means* of the new forms of information production, sharing and retrieval enabled by the social web.

The danger of the notion of "immaterial labour" is that it backgrounds the expensive, all-too-material infrastructure upon which the activities it designates rely. There are many challenges to creating a non-commercial, independent, not-for-profit social web, but one of them is surely the cost of building out the network's physical infrastructure, buying and maintaining the routers and servers. Storing the huge amounts of data required for, say, indexing and searching the Internet is a costly endeavour that requires expensive hardware and huge amounts of power. Server farms can consume as much energy as a small town. Yes, immaterial labour can produce a "social relation" (in Lazzarato's [1996] formulation)—in the form of, say, a status update, an influential blog post, a "like", or an attention grabbing "tweet" (among other things), but none of these are solely the result of the user's labour, any more than an auto-worker can build a car without the factory, the parts, the power source, and so on. Surely we can perform "immaterial" labour without such an infrastructure—but there is nothing new about that, people have been producing and maintaining social relations since the dawn of society. The forms of so-called immaterial labour that have captured so much attention in the Internet era are treated as distinct or unique to the development of the technology, and thus reliant upon it—in this regard they are necessarily dependent upon what has become an increasingly privately owned and operated material infrastructure. Matter still matters profoundly, even for the seemingly immaterial productions of the social web. It is precisely the attempt to profit from control over this physical infrastructure that has led to the creation of a commercial model based on the capture, storage, and sorting of the huge amounts of information that come to be turned back against their users in forms unrecognizable to them. This infrastructure matters because it is being mobilised as an infrastructure of alienation.

10.3   GENERAL INTELLECT AND "RESKILLING"

With this in mind it might be helpful to sort out some conceptual muddles. Perhaps the most important regards the status of so-called "general intellect" that has played such an important role in the formulation of arguments about immaterial labour. The recent gesture of autonomist Marxism has been to reclaim and revise Marx's original formulation in the *Grundrisse*—a formulation meant to describe the creation of machines that incorporate human knowledge in the form of fixed capital, transferring expertise and knowledge from the worker to the device:

> it is the machine which possesses skill and strength in the place of the worker, is itself the virtuoso, with a soul of its own in the mechanical laws acting through it [. . .] The appropriation of living labour by objectified labour [. . .] which lies in the concept of capital, is posited, in production resting on machinery, as the character of the production process itself. (Marx 1973, 693)

With a few tweaks and upgrades this formulation could provide a compelling description of the forms of automated decision-making envisioned by data mining techniques that avail themselves of the rhetoric of a humanly impossible collectivity: the ability to make sense of more information than any one individual or even collection of individuals might be able to handle—indeed to transform this information using algorithms that generate decisions for us. Even without such changes, this formulation of the general intellect is one of alienation, and some work must be done to recuperate through the claim that, in the current state of affairs, "productive activity is no longer separated from the intentions of the intellect" (Rey 2012, 406). The claim of autonomy is related to a reframing of the notion of "general intellect" so as to focus not on the way in which social knowledge takes the form of fixed capital (embodied by increasingly sophisticated, and flexible machines) but on the important role played by the reskilling of the workforce, what Paolo Virno has described as "mass intellectuality": "the depository of cognitive competences that cannot be objectified in machinery" (as quoted in Smith 2008, 6). The "general intellect," in other words, invokes the productivity increases associated with automation (enabled by "smart" machines), whereas "mass intellectuality" refers to the productivity of the mental or creative labour of the networked workforce. The underlying claim is one of re-skilling: the information economy no longer relies on the Fordist-era logic of reducing the mental labour of the worker to next to nothing, but rather on the enhanced productivity of an increasingly educated and creative workforce: the "collective reappropriation of knowledges" (Smith 2008, 6). As Smith points out, the impetus for deskilling is not a structural component of capitalist value extraction so much as a means to an end: "Everything else being equal, the owners and controllers of capital do indeed desire to limit wage costs, limit training costs, and control labour. Deskilling is often an effective manner of attaining these objectives" (Smith 2000, 37). However, under changed circumstances, it is possible to imagine ways in which "the 'logic of capital' points away from deskilling, and toward a management strategy of developing workers' skills in the labour process" (Smith 2000, 37). Those circumstances presumably include contexts in which new skills do not give workers greater control vis-à-vis employers, do not command a wage premium, and do not entail new expenses for employers.

We might put this somewhat differently: the notion of "skill" is not an absolute abstract one, but a relational, socially determined one. Once upon a time, basic literacy was a rare skill that could, in certain contexts, command a premium. As literacy spread, as its cultivation was socialized by public educational systems, it lost its relative standing (at least in some locales) as a skill that might command a premium, increase costs to an employer, or give a worker a greater degree of control or autonomy. We might then take the "upskilling" of labour associated with the information economy and the widening scope of so-called "immaterial labour" as the very opposite of a new form of empowerment: an indication, rather, that the development of these skills no longer poses a threat to capital. That is, that they do not challenge the underlying power relations that structure the extraction of value. Shifts in the education sector toward an embrace of industry's imperatives facilitate the socialization of training costs and the simultaneous generalization of higher-level skills (or, to put it in somewhat differently, the deskilling of skill, that is the undermining of its ability to command a premium in the form of either wages or job security). The recent reflexive trend toward concern over new forms of "precarity" in the various culture and creative "industries", bears out the hypothesis that skill no longer commands the forms of security or compensation once expected for it, and the concern on the part of highly trained professionals that they have become subject to forms of insecurity and exploitation hitherto largely relegated to the realm of unskilled and untrained labour. Indeed, this might be one of the less savoury aspects of so-called "convergence": the erosion or reconfiguration of some of the practical distinctions between skilled and unskilled labour in ways that work to disempower rather than empower workers. The newfound concern with "precarity" in the academic realm is in no small part a result of the fact that academics are increasingly subject to it—but this does not make it a new condition of labour, merely one that is working its way up the professional ladder and threatening the hard-won gains of organised labour in some nations.

There is a disconcerting tendency in the literature on immaterial labour and digital media to lump together waged and unwaged forms of activity, as if that distinction has dissolved along with reliance upon fixed capital and the forms of alienation that accompany it. In contrast to Rey's assertion that "in the digital economy, labour itself is no longer coerced by the threat of deprivation of biological needs" (Rey 2012, 409), in actuality waged labour continues to take place under the compulsion of necessity. Online activities are not severed from the broader economic logics in which they are embedded. For many of those involved, such activities may take place in a context distinct from that in which they earn their livelihood, but for many professions an online presence has become an important part of earning a living. By the same token, the "immaterial" activity of providing content, expressing and sharing sentiment, and so on takes place against the background of the commercial processes that support it. There is no way other than the sales of goods and services as commodities in the marketplace to valorize so-called immaterial labour. As Tony Smith puts it, even in the context of post-Fordism, the expressions of

general intellect [. . .] are still expressed within the social forms of dissociated sociality [commodities]. Privately undertaken labour must still be validated as socially necessary through the sale of commodities for money, no matter how highly developed the general intellect manifested in that labour might be and this privately undertaken labour is validated as socially necessary only insofar as surplus value is produced and appropriated" (2008, x).

Producers' ability to capture and benefit from employee participation in the planning and production process heralded not the increasing power of workers, but the fact that such forms of participation increased productivity without surrendering meaningful forms of control. Indeed, techniques of interactive management and employee participation *anticipated* the widespread embrace of strategies for crowd-sourcing and otherwise putting the "immaterial" labour of audiences and consumers to work. It is not a coincidence that the embrace of these forms of "up-skilling" coincided with the development of the interactive capability of digital technologies and with the weakening of organised labour in the wake of the breakdown of the post-war settlement and rise of global competition between labour markets. As the structural position of labour weakened, up-skilling posed less a threat to exploitation than a boon: increasingly productive workers were not positioned to capture the new forms of surplus they generated.[1] Moreover, the development of interactive technologies for monitoring, tracking, and otherwise supervising forms of flexible, "immaterial" labour contributed to its domestication. Rather than treating the forms of up-skilling associated with post-Fordism or "cognitive capitalism" as a rising force challenging the control of capitalists over the production process, we might frame them as productive skills that can be folded into the valorisation process without necessarily threatening it, thanks to changing historical conditions.

In the realm of unwaged labour, the development of new forms of information retrieval, sharing, and production have coincided with an increasing reliance upon a privately owned and operated commercial infrastructure. The story of the social web, in this regard, is a story of the migration of broad swathes of social, professional, and personal life onto an infrastructure whose owners set the terms of access. It would be strange to figure this as a form of autonomy: subtract the various networks—cable, cellular, wireless, along with applications that run on them—and the new forms of interaction, networking, communication, and information retrieval evaporate. Thus, the notion of "mass intellectuality" is a misleading one if it is meant to suggest activity that takes place free from reliance upon fixed capital in either the realms of labour or consumption. A blogger may have well-developed skills in the manipulation of symbols, the creation of particular types of social relations, but without an Internet the blogger has much in common with a worker without a factory or a farmer without a field: skills, but no access to the material infrastructure for putting these to work.

10.4   ALGORITHMIC ALIENATION

The notion of mass intellectuality may well signal a general up-skilling of labour in the era of informational capitalism, but this ought not to be equated with empowerment simply on the basis that deskilling served, once upon a time, as a strategy for disempowerment. There are, perhaps, deeper arguments in play: that fostering an ethos of participation and more developed forms of social networking and social interaction might have political consequences and tendencies of their own, even if these remain dependent on private, commercial, infrastructures. Much the same might be said of the ongoing development of creative skills associated with participatory elements of digital media—that these work to foster a sense of autonomy and engagement that fosters dissatisfaction with alienating social structures. Such arguments are compelling, and may well be correct, but they require further elaboration regarding how to distinguish between progressive participation and simply staging the scene of one's own submission. There is no clear indication that up-skilling leads inevitably to socialism or the overthrow of capitalism. The recent fascination with the way in which power functions in neoliberal capitalist regimes has focused precisely on the ways in which forms of up-skilling and participation intensify and channel subordination to capitalist priorities. It is no coincidence that the critical literature on neoliberalism has coincided with the somewhat more optimistic literature on the political potential of the new forms of autonomy associated with some sectors in the digital information economy.

It is precisely at this level of infrastructure that the issue of exploitation remains salient. The alibi for the large-scale forms of commercial monitoring that take place online is that they are necessary not simply to recompense new media entrepreneurs, but also, and relatedly, to support the sprawling infrastructure that provides us with our miraculous new information and communication services and applications. The infrastructural complement of the "immaterial labour" that takes place online is comprised of largely privately-owned networks and server farms that cost billions of dollars to build, operate, and power. As if to thwart the recognition of the costly, brute, materiality of these structures, they are collectively described in popular parlance as "the cloud"—an airy metaphor in keeping with the rhetoric of "immateriality". Yet, I would argue, they serve as the foundation of informational alienation: the separation of users from their data, and thus of some part of the fruit of their online activity.

But are we really separated from our data if we can access it any time we want (barring server, network, or power failure)? And perhaps more pointedly, why would or should we care? We remain "connected" to our data, in the sense suggested by Rey insofar as our blog posts, our tweets, and so on are seen as deliberate intentional products of our consciously directed activity. In physical terms, however, we are disconnected from it insofar as the actual data is hosted externally. Yes, we may have backed it up, but we don't independently of the hosting organisation have the means for sharing and distributing it—that is, for endowing it with its social-relational life. This separation provides the basis for dictating the terms of access and therefore for the collection and use of increasingly detailed forms of personal information in ways that are becoming increasingly opaque to users. The loss of control over the use of such information and the inability to predict how it will be used represents one aspect of what Fuchs (2008) has described as the dialectic of cyberculture between socialization and alienation (see in particular, 300ff). More specifically, this chapter claims that we are facing a digital future that will be increasingly characterized by what might be described as "algorithmic alienation" in which automated decisions based on huge databases and complex forms of data mining will shape institutional decisions that influence the life chances of a growing number of people in a growing range of contexts. It is time to move beyond the question of whether or not we want targeted advertising—the real issue is whether or not we want to create a world in which every detail of our behaviour and communications with one another feeds into giant databases that are used to sort and evaluate us in ways that remain completely opaque to us, by a range of institutions whose imperatives are not necessarily our own. In such a context, to deny the existence of alienation recalls the Situationist International's rejoinder to the leftist Catholic thinker Jean-Marie Domenach's dismissal of the concept: "Domenach wants people to stop talking about alienation so that they will become resigned to it" (Situationist International 1966).

NOTES

1. The Economic Policy in the United States, for example, reported that in the three decades starting in 1979, productivity increased by 80 per cent, whereas the hourly wage of the median worker has increased only 10.1 per cent (Bradford 2011).

REFERENCES

Bradford, Harry. 2011. "U.S. Wages aren't keeping up with U.S. productivity, EPI says." *The Huffington Post*, March 19. Accessed July, 23, 2013, http://www.huffingtonpost.com/2011/03/18/wages-productivity-report_n_837814.html.
Fuchs, Christian. 2008. *Internet and society: Social theory in the information age.* New York: Routledge.

Lazzarato, Maurizio.1996. "Immaterial labor." In *Radical thought in Italy: A potential politics* edited by Paolo Virno and Michael Hardt, 133–149. Minneapolis: University of Minnesota Press.

Marx, Karl. 1973. *Grundrisse.* London: Penguin.

———. 1974. *Early writings.* London: Penguin.

Nolan, Rachel. 2012. "Behind the cover story: How much does target know?" *The New York Times*, February 12. Accessed Accessed July, 23, 2013, http://6thfloor.blogs.nytimes.com/2012/02/21/behind-the-cover-story-how-much-does-target-know/.

Pentland, Alex. 2009. "Reality mining of mobile communications: Toward a new deal on data." In *The global information technology information report 2008–2009: Mobility in a networked world*, edited by Soumitra Dutta and Irene Mia, 75–80. Basingstoke: Palgrave Macmillan.

Rey, P. J. 2012. "Alienation, exploitation, and social media." *American Behavioral Scientist* 56 (4): 399–420.

Situationist International. 1966. "Domenach versus alienation." *Bureau of Public Secrets.* Accessed July, 23, 2013, http://www.bopsecrets.org/SI/10.domenach.htm.

Smith, Tony. 2000. *Technology and capital in the age of lean production: a Marxian critique of the "New Economy".* Albany: SUNY Press.

———. 2008. "The 'General Intellect' in the *Grundrisse* and beyond." Accessed July, 23, 2013, http://www.public.iastate.edu/~tonys/10%20The%20General%20Intellect.pdf.

11 Social Media and Political Participation
Discourse and Deflection

Peter Dahlgren

11.1 INTRODUCTION: SOCIAL MEDIA AND DEMOCRATIC HOPES

At the national, regional/EU, and global levels, the political economic and social crises are intensifying. There has been a marked decline in both trust and participation in the formal electoral politics in much of the Western world, which often serves to intensify the crises. Yet we witness at the same time a resurgence of participation in the realm of alternative politics. Much of this can be seen as responses to the specific devastations that derive from the crises and ensuing austerity measures, but it also represents a general world-wide confrontation—on many fronts—with neoliberal policies and their vision for societal development. The broad array of alter-globalization movements in particular gives witness to this. In other parts of the world, people have been challenging authoritarian regimes with varying degrees of success. In all of these contexts, media are a central feature; traditional mass media still play an important role, but increasingly citizens are making use of the web generally, and social media in particular, for their political purposes.

Since the mid-1990s a good deal of debate and research has been aimed at the role of the Internet in democracy, often framed in terms of the public sphere. With advent of web 2.0, this has continued, with the focus shifting to emphasise social media in particular. Enthusiasts laud the democratic potential of social media (Benkler 2006; Sunstein 2008; and Castells 2010, 2012 are, from different angles, among the more optimistic). Sceptics, or those with a more critical analysis, underscore the constraints of these media in the face of other factors that shape political realities (Fuchs 2011; Hindamn 2009) and even how they may be deployed for anti-democratic measures (Morozov 2011). Others position themselves in more nuanced ways (Van Djik 2013; Gerbaudo 2012; Lievrouw 2011) or offer a mix of voices (Loader and Mercea, 2012; see also *Journal of Communication*, 2012).

I am wary of cheery prognoses about what the web can do for democracy, especially if they build on techno-determinism or -essentialism, and yet I am also convinced that the new communication technologies do offer unprecedented possibilities for democratic (as well as undemocratic) intervention into the political arena. As with all other facets of modern life, the political realm has been altered by these media. My aim in this chapter, however, is not to come up with the ultimate verdict on this issue, not least because I hold the view that there cannot be any simplistic assessment of this kind. Whereas there are some basic features about these media that have general significance in this regard, it is also the case that their potential and their limitations vary to some extent with their circumstances. That is to say, they are subject to different sets of contingencies in different settings.

Rather, what I intend to do here is explore a particular aspect of the democratic role often assigned to social media, namely participation. My approach is to a great extent conceptual: I want to illuminate what we mean by political participation, and how we might perceive this in relation the affordances and attributes of social media and the web environment. The impact of political economy is of course crucial in shaping the contingencies of social media, but my focus is their discursive environment, understood as ensemble of various discourses in these settings. I probe the links between discourses and subjectivity, and examine how discourses can serve to impede the democratic potential of these media, particularly through the various ways by which they tend to deflect participation.

11.2   PARTICIPATION AND POWER RELATIONS

Deriving from several different fields in the social sciences, the notion of participation remains somewhat fluid. It often varies with the contexts of its use, not least within media and communication studies (see Carpentier 2011 for an extensive treatment). I will not attempt a once-and-for-all definition, nor offer an inventory of possible usages, but rather will simply highlight what I take to be the key features of participation as it pertains to political agency and media. A starting point is the notion of the political, which refers to the ever-present potential for collective antagonisms, conflicts of interest, in all social relations and settings (see for example Mouffe 2005). This is a broader notion than that of politics, which is often restricted to the formalised institutional contexts. Thus, we can say that participation means involvement with the political, regardless of the character or scope of the context. It therefore always in some way involves struggle. Certainly some instances of the political will be a part of electoral politics and involve decision-making and/or elections, but it is imperative that we keep the broader vista of the political in view as the terrain of political agency and participation.

By extension, democracy refers to something beyond formal structures and procedures; it has to do with a way of life and is ultimately anchored in the cultural patterns of society, in its values, assumptions, ways of dealing with other people, and so on. Without this cultural anchoring, without some degree of taken-for-granted democratic impulses it is hard for the formal system to function as it should. Of course in the real world of Western democracies we are mostly dealing with situations of more-or-less and uneven fulfilment of such ideals rather than their total absence, and even under authoritarian regimes one can find submerged traces of such thinking—which can nourish resistance.

Drawing boundaries in the modern world between the political and the non-political has become increasingly difficult, especially given the understanding that the political is always something concrete that can arise dynamically, and is not something pre-existing. Participation in broader social and cultural activities, including consumption, can always take a turn towards the political. What becomes decisive is not the particular terrain as such, but the character of the engagement: it always has to do in some way, however remote (or mediated), with power relations. It may involve civil agonism, confrontational conflict, invective, or any of a wide array of modes and practices. Carpentier argues that ultimately participation is all about co-decision-making within democratic norms and rules.

This perspective is a normative one and must of course be tempered by sociological realism that takes into account the prevailing circumstances. In considering the possibilities for participation it makes a big difference if we are talking about a group of committed activists or a group of individuals who only occasionally attend to political matters. Also, the specific political context must be considered. Access to social media per se usually will not turn people into engaged citizens, yet, to the extent that the political can arise, and indeed go viral, social media can play an important function in facilitating participation. As a manifestation of political agency, participation is embodied in concrete. These usually take the form of some kind of communicative activity, that is, discursive involvement. The affordances of the web and the specific platforms of social media permit not only a wide array of practices, but also allow people to develop new ones, to appropriate the technologies for ever new purposes and strategies.

It is worth noting that in contemporary democratic theory of political participation, there is often a strong emphasis on rational deliberation as a normative ideal of how it should proceed. Such a communicative mode is of course important, especially as one begins approaching formal decision-making. However, to insist on it as the overall model of participatory practices can become constrictive of expression and even excluding in terms of participation—especially when we keep in mind the extensive multimedia possibilities that social media encompass. Also, genuine deliberation assumes a degree of power equality that is often absent—and not likely to be attained merely by deliberation (I address this in more detail in Dahlgren 2009).

11.3 DISCOURSE AND SUBJECTIVITY

At the most fundamental level, the political emerges through talk. It need not necessarily be formalised deliberation, but the political becomes manifested through communication. This can empirically vary enormously with the specific circumstances, local cultures, existing political traditions, historical experience and organisational situations. We can treat the process as akin to a continuum, whereby talk may move from the pre-political to the para-political (which manifests traces and potential) and then to the full-blown political itself. From there it may enter the arena of formal politics. In more formalised methodological terms, one can say that the political emerges within discourses, understood as fairly stable patterns of language use and meaning that occur in—as well as shape—social contexts. They of course shape our subjective realities and our identities as well (here I am loosely following the discourse theory of Laclau and Mouffe, 2001).

Political participation requires some self-understanding as a political agent, an identity whose subjective elements can nourish such agency. There is of course an array of factors that come into play in shaping such identity (I discuss this at length in Dahlgren 2009), but one important aspect is the discursive environment in which such agency (forms of participation) might take place. The analysis of discourses provides a way to elucidate major currents of meaning that are in circulation in society. These, often in tension with each other, inscribe themselves in subjectivity, in our inner reality. And because discourses are social, subjectivity is never merely a "private" reality, even if it will always comprise individual, personal elements (moreover, in the context of politics, our emphasis is on collective, social side of subjectivity).

This inner space is on the one hand a source of agency. We develop our identities, make decisions, and take action based on the coordinates we have with us in our subjective realities. On the other hand, this space is also a terrain in which society and culture is discursively inscribed in us, making us not just human in general, but also providing us with specific influences. Thus discourses can be seen as the way society and culture, not least in the form of power relations, shape us, yet they also function as enabling resources. We use discourses, and they use us, while the entanglements with power relations are always present. From this rendering of subjectivity, we can understand that political participation will always be conditional, shaped by shifting contingencies in the social world, not least discursive currents.

In addition, from the standpoint of psychoanalytic theory, our subjectivity is never fully unitary and centred, and we are never fully transparent to ourselves, because the unconscious always intervenes to some degree, operating, as it were, behind our back. Subjectivity straddles the rational-affective distinction. Thus political participation builds upon the interplay of both of these aspects of our mental dynamics. Rationality can offer reasons, good or bad, for engagement and participation, but affect provides the psychic energy. Politics is entwined with people's desires, anxieties, visions, and hopes, and all such subjective elements feed affective charges into their engagement, mingling with rational, analytic elements.

11.4 THE MEDIA CONNECTION

In examining the role of the media for participation, some researchers distinguish between participation *in* the media and participation *via* the media. The two strands are of course interwoven and have a long history (see Carpentier et al. 2013). Participation in the media has to do with using the media, but also with being involved in the production of content. Understandably, in the context of mass media such opportunities were few and quite constricted, while with the web possibilities for participation in media production have expanded enormously. While this is an important democratic step, we must still bear in mind the distinctions in scale and impact between the productions of major corporate actors and those of small organisations, groups and individuals. Indeed, the corporate colonisation of communicative space in social media and the growing domination of market logic on the web has major implications for power relations online.

Participation *via* the media by definition links users to social domains beyond the media. Participation in these domains is facilitated by the media, but the analytic focus lies with the contexts and issues that media connect us to. Increasingly in the modern world our relation to the social takes this route, captured by the concept of mediatisation. A crucial point concerning mediatisation, of course, is that media can never simply provide a "neutral" link or "mirror" of the social, but through varying media logics and contingencies always impact on the relationship in particular ways. Thus, in the case of social media, there are a number of significant features to take into account in this regard, which I will get to shortly. First, however, let us consider the character of *political* participation via media.

With our schematic view of the political as a discursively emergent and constructed reality, access to and interaction with media content obviously becomes not only helpful but also often absolutely necessary. However, as Carpentier (2011) argues, access and interaction are seldom sufficient by themselves to embody political participation. In everyday terms, we can think for example of following the news on a website and participating in a political discussion online. These are important steps but would not automatically constitute political participation. When does participation in the media and via the media become political participation? The answer must be: when these activities in some way connect with the political—when online networking and involvement through media in larger societal contexts articulates with the terrain of power relations and when those using the media position themselves in relation to issues, that is, when these activities become situated in agonistic fields of conflicting interests.

Political participation can take place *in* the media: there can be disputes about content, about access and any number of possible issues that can emerge within, say the context of given online networks in which one is involved. However, ultimately the media as a terrain of themselves becomes a rather confined space and their politics circumscribed. The real significance of the media in terms of political participation is their capacity to link us to the greater social world, where we encounter the political *via* the media. The political takes shape in discursive contexts, whether face to face or mediated; the media are often required to encounter the political, but participation *in* the media does not guarantee political participation *via* the media—more is required. We should be aware that these distinctions are conceptual, and applying them in the empirical world may at times require analytic effort, but they remain significant.

11.5. THE ENVIRONMENTS OF SOCIAL MEDIA

Turning specifically to social media, we should note that the term encompasses a variety of forms, including *blogs, microblogs* (e.g. Twitter) and *social networks* like Facebook, which are built on sites that allow people to generate personal web pages and to connect with others to share content and communication. There are also *content networks* that organise and share particular kinds of content (legal as well as and illegal)—the largest is of course YouTube. *Wikis* are websites where people add and modify content collectively, generating a communal database, whereas *forums* are areas for online discussion, usually focused on specific topics and interests. *Podcasts* make audio and video files available by subscription, through different commercial services. This non-exhaustive list at least conveys a sense of the diversity involved, which means that talking about "social media" in general always risks missing important distinctions.

That said, there is of course also much that unites various forms and people switch readily between them for different purposes: to send written and spoken words, to upload, remix, link and share, in increasingly complex and developed ways. The overall ubiquity of social media means that they are not just something people "visit" on occasion in order to seek something special, they form increasingly a central terrain of our daily lives. They offer possibilities that are harnessed and mobilised in varying ways, and thus impact on the strategies and tactics of everyday life and the frames of reference that provide them with meaning. Their discursive character thus has major significance.

Social media are of course a part of the larger social and cultural world, intertwined with the offline lives of individuals as well as with the functioning of groups, organisations, institutions and societal power relations.

There are significant contingencies of political economy and technical architecture (not least centred on Google and Facebook) that impact on the character, use, and consequences of social media and the web generally (for some helpful texts, see Dwyer 2010; Feenberg and Freisen 2012; Fuchs 2011; Goldberg 2010; MacKinnon 2012; McChesney 2013; Pariser 2012; Schiller 2010; articles published in the journal *tripleC*; Turow 2011; Vaidhyanathan 2011). My focus here, however, will lean more towards the discursive and socio-cultural aspects of social media.

It is important to underscore the social character of social media practices. Baym (2010) offers a detailed analysis of how the reach and capacities of social media for interaction, their modes of social cues, their temporal structures, their mobility, and other features serve to facilitate social connections. While this is of sociological interest in itself, I would highlight that this digital lubrication of the social is also essential for the emergence of the political. Such networking can be enabling for political participation in that it can help promote a subjective sense of empowerment through the mastery of and development of new practices in using them. Moreover, social media can provide an enhanced sense of agency based in horizontal communication—participation *in* social media can be a cogent experience.

However, when we turn to participation *via* social media, the limitations become visible, certainly, when we see social media through the analytic lens of critical political economy, but also—which is my main focus here—when viewed from the standpoint of the discursive and socio-cultural attributes on what we might call, using the Bourdieuian term, the habitus of social media (see also Papacharissi and Easton 2013). In contrast to the experience of mass media, with social media the discourses are to a great extent anchored in the mediated social communication we directly have with others, and become all the more compelling; there may still be offline two-step flows we find in the mass media, but here the discourses are often embedded in initial mediated social experience.

11.6 DISCURSIVE ATTRIBUTES

To begin with, the discursive density of the web environment in the contemporary media landscape results in an intense and incessant competition for attention. This means generally that the web environment is structured to facilitate various actors to continually vie for the attention of users, engendering a discursive environment that is characterised by flux, fragmentation and the ever-present promise of the new and tantalizing. While this may in fact at times give rise to the political, more often than not it may impede the sustained concentration needed for doing the "work" of political participation.

Further, the entire media sphere, including the web environment, is strongly dominated by entertainment, popular culture, consumption and massive amounts of information that largely have no apparent bearing on the dynamics of democracy. We are much more strongly offered subject positions as consumers and spectators than as political agents. There is, concomitantly, a strong dimension of pleasure associated with social media in that they can be experienced as a spaces of freedom that one (seemingly) has considerable control over. There are many choices and few demands. Social media can offer intense experiential immersions with strong affective valences, putting the question of political participation at a competitive disadvantage.

Of course political participation is by no means an exclusively rational enterprise—it engages emotional dimensions as well. The point here simply boils down to the potential for distraction and the fragmentation of thought. It has been the case that throughout the history of democracy most people's engagement most of the time is not with politics. With the web the competition for attention reaches a new level of intensity.

There are also darker tones to this development. Authors such as Dean (2010) and Papacharissi (2010) argue that it is not just a question of people choosing politics or consumption/popular culture, but that the web environment in its present form promotes a transformation of political practices and social relations whereby the political becomes altered and embodied precisely in the practices and discourses of privatised consumption. If it is the case—as many scholars suggest—that the boundaries between the political and popular culture/consumption have become more porous, we may still need to reflect on analytic and normative limits to such fluidity, where it at some point undermines the vitality of democratic political agency.

While it is only human to be drawn to people who are like oneself and think in the same way, this is not necessarily a healthy pattern for democracy or for the enhancement of political participation. The trend towards withdrawing to enclaves of like-mindedness is enhanced with social media, most notably Facebook, where the definitive logic is "to like": you click on people that you "like", i.e. that are "like" yourself. Differences tend to get filtered out. The encounter with difference, indeed, the capacity to meet others with coherent arguments, seems on the wane in some corners of the web, which erodes the basic idea of dynamic public spheres.

A final attribute emerging in social media that seems detrimental to political participation is a form of what we can call personalised visibility, which includes self-promotion and self-revelation. When (especially) younger people do turn to politics, it seems that the patterns of digital social interaction increasingly carry over into the digital. Papacharissi (2010) argues that whereas digitally enabled citizens may be skilled and reflexive in many ways, they are also generally removed from civic habits of the past. She suggests that this is engendering a new "civic vernacular". I call it the solo sphere, and it can be seen as a historically new habitus for online political participation, a new platform for political agency.

From the networked and often mobile enclosures of this personalised space, the individual engages with a vast variety of contexts in the outside world, which at some point will have to be seen as a retreat into an environment that many people feel they have more control over. A networked yet privatised sociality emerges. We need not occupy ourselves with essentialist distinctions between on- and offline realities. It suffices to simply indicate that they have to some extent different affordances, cue some different kinds of social skills, and most importantly offer differing spaces of social interaction, with often differing implications. These contrasts can be significant for political participation. It may well be that the online setting, with its powerful technical affordances, discourages engagement beyond itself. To the extent that this is true, it is understandable, yet it also introduces, rather problematically, a historically new set of contingencies for political participation.

11.7 THE HEGEMONY OF POLITICAL DEFLECTION

Prevailing, or hegemonic discourses are not airtight. They can be challenged, but to the extent that they reflect structural power relations they tend to have a relative stability that is routinely reproduced. The overarching collective meanings embedded in such discourses are anchored in repetitive representations that become not so much a series of messages but rather pervasive templates for thought and experience. Discourses mobilise cognitive thoughts but also affect. They can promote and articulate intentions as well as resonate in the unconscious. They provide frameworks for making sense of the world and one's place in it, serving thus to adjust not only our perceptions of external reality but also our inner subjective dispositions. They must also be seen as resources for agency, but set in the context of the power relations that they are a part of, one could argue that the degree of freedom accorded to agency has fairly well-functioning boundaries. Discourses, operating via our subjectivity, have political import.

In a compelling analysis of prevailing ideational vistas, Straume (2011) maps the various elements that comprise the key elements of the neoliberal global economic system from the standpoint of the social world. She pinpoints such themes as a sense of never-ending economic growth, freedom, rationality, an absence of serious environmental concern, consumerism, a sense of privatised fulfilment, and a stance of non-interference in market mechanisms. An upshot of this analysis is that a basic feature of the relationship of the individual to economic society is one of de-politicisation: citizens are disinvited from engaging with economic issues in ways that would situate them within the realm of the political (Dean 2010 makes a similar argument). We can call this mechanism the deflection of political participation—recalling Carpentier's understanding of participation precisely as a democratic "invitation".

These discursive currents seemingly hover at a rather high level of abstraction, but are visible in concrete circumstances. We should be wary of reducing today's wide range of political expression (at times positively cacophonic) to just positions that support or criticise the dominant economic arrangements, but how the political character of the economic system is perceived—that is, if it viewed as one of several possible alternatives, the only "realistic" alternative, or simply as "natural"—is of fundamental significance for capitalism and its legitimacy. Beyond that, however, the question of participation—how, where, when, if at all—is crucial for the life of democracy. Thus, it is of great consequence that the discursive currents that characterise the habitus of social media resonate rather harmoniously with the themes that Straume (2011) delineates. They are by no means unique for the web, in that they generally reflect the prevailing discursive milieu of contemporary politics and society, but their online manifestations take particular forms of expression, guiding the routine practices of social media use. It is important to keep in mind that these discursive currents do not only operate as formal ideas, but also in the realm of affect, not least at the unconscious level. Fears, desires, anxieties, conflicts, denials, repressions—all these mechanisms can be present in the practices we enact in social media.

11.8   CONCLUSION

There is no doubt that social media can and have been used with great efficacy for political participation and they will be creatively adapted in the future for such purposes. Yet, such use is largely the domain of activists, who remain, in sociological terms, deviants in relation to the majority of citizens. Activists do not grow on trees, obviously enough, they are socially and discursively produced, and as noted at the outset, the realm of alternative politics at present is experiencing an upsurge in the face of the growing crises. However, the argument I have been pursuing is that if we understand participation as deriving from a sense of agency embedded in our subjective reality, in our identity, social media on their own will not do much to promote it. Rather, for those without an already existing political sense of self, the discursive contribution of social media will tend to deflect political participation—and offer instead an array of tantalizing privatised alternatives. These may have many social benefits, but the promotion of democratic political life is largely not among them.

REFERENCES

Baym, Nancy K. 2010. *Personal connections in the digital age.* Cambridge: Polity Press.
Benkler, Yochai. 2006. *The wealth of networks: How social production transforms markets and freedom.* New Haven, CT: Yale University Press.

Carpentier, Nico. 2011. *Media and participation: A site of ideological-democratic struggle*. Bristol: Intellect.

Carpentier, Nico, Peter Dahlgren and Francesca Pasquali. 2013. Waves of media democratization: A brief history of contemporary participatory practices in the media sphere. *Convergence*. First published on May 16, 2013: *doi:10.1177/1354856513486529*

Castells, Manuel. 2010. *Communication power*. Oxford: Oxford University Press.

———. 2012. *Networks of outrage and hope: Social movements in the Internet age*. Cambridge: Polity Press.

Dahlgren, Peter. 2009. *Media and political engagement*. New York: Cambridge University Press.

Dean, Jodi. 2010. *Blog theory*. Cambridge: Polity Press.

Dwyer, Tim. 2010. "Net worth: Popular social networks as colossal marketing machines." In *Propaganda society: Promotional culture and politics in global context*, edited by Geralad Sussman, 77–92. New York: Peter Lang.

Feenberg, Andrew, and Norm Freisen, eds. 2012 *(Re)inventing the internet: Critical case studies*. Rotterdam: Sense Publishers.

Fuchs, Christian. 2011. *Foundations of critical media and information studies*. London: Routledge.

Fuchs, Christian, and Vincent Mosco, eds. "Marx is back: The importance of Marixst theory and research for critical communication studies today." *tripleC: Communication, Capitalism & Critique. Open Access Journal for a Global Sustainable Information Society* Special issue, 10 (2).

Gerbaudo, Paolo. 2012. *Tweets and the streets: Social media and contemporary activism*. London: Verso.

Goldberg. Greg. 2010. "Rethinking the public/virtual sphere: The problem with participation." *New Media and Society* 13 (5): 739–754.

Hindman, Mathew. 2009. *The myth of digital democracy*. Oxford: Oxford University Press.

Journal of Communication. 2012. Special Issue: *Social media and political change*. 62 (2).

Laclau, Ernesto, and Chantal Mouffe. 2001. *Hegemony and socialist strategy: Towards a radical democratic politics*. Second edition. London: Verso.

Lievrouw, Leah A. 2011. *Alternative and activist new media*. Cambridge: Polity Press.

Loader, Brian, and Dan Mercea, eds. 2012. *Social media and democracy*. London: Routledge.

MacKinnon, Rebecca. 2012. *Consent of the networked: The worldwide struggle for Internet freedom*. New York: Basic Books.

McChesney, Robert W. 2013. *Digital disconnect*. New York: New Press.

Morozov, Evgeny. 2011. *The net delusion: How not to liberate the world*. London: Allen Lane.

Mouffe, Cantal. 2005. *On the political*. London: Verso.

Papacharissi, Zizi. 2010. *A private sphere: Democracy in a digital age*. Cambridge: Polity Press.

Papacharissi, Zizi and Emily Easton. 2013. "In the habitus of the new. Structure, agency and the social media habitus." In *A companion to new media dynamics*, edited by John Harley, Jean Burgess, and Axel Bruns, 171–184. Hoboken, NJ: Wiley-Blackwell. Accessed February 15, 2013. http://tigger.uic.edu/~zizi/Site/Research_files/HabitusofNewZPEE.pdf.

Pariser, Eli. 2012. *The filter bubble: What the Internet is hiding from you*. London: Penguin.

Schiller, Dan. 2010. *How to think about information*. Champagne, IL: University of Illinois Press.

Straume, Ingrid. 2011. "The political imaginary of global capitalism." In *Depoliticization: The political imaginary of global capitalism*, edited by Ingrid S. Straume and J. F. Humphrey, 27–50. Malmö: NSU Press.
Sunstein, Cass. 2008. *Infotopia: How many minds produce knowledge*. Oxford: Oxford University Press.
Turow, Joseph. 2011. *The daily you: How the new advertising industry is defining your identity and your worth*. New Haven, CT: Yale University Press.
tripleC: Communciation, Capitalism & Critique. Open Access Journal for a Global Sustainable Information Society. Accessed July 23, 2013 http://triplec.at.
Vaidhyanathan, Siva. 2011. *The googlization of everything: And why we should worry*. Berkeley, CA: University of California Press.
van Dijk, José. 2013. *The culture of connectivity: A critical history of social media*. Oxford: Oxford University Press.

12 "The Architecture of Participation"
For Citizens or Consumers?

Tobias Olsson

12.1 INTRODUCTION

During the last couple of years, a lot of discussions concerning the Internet have made use of the concepts "web 2.0" and "social media". What these concepts have in common, is an insistence on the argument that the Internet today is very different from its previous versions. Both "web 2.0" and "social media" point to the fact that the Internet is both updated ("2.0") and more interactive than it used to be and that it also—as a consequence— allows for more lively and varied interaction between users. Hence, it also becomes a more "social" medium.

These new(er) conceptualisations have now made it to the very forefront of contemporary research. For instance, both conceptualisations achieve around 3 million hits on the search engine Google Scholar: the listed works emanate from a wide variety of academic disciplines, ranging from humanistic studies to research in computer science. They have also made their way into policy debates. So for example in the Swedish political debate, the notion of "social media" has been referred to in debates in areas such as foreign policy (with Swedish foreign minister Carl Bildt's notorious blogging at the centre) and governmental efforts to create "sustainable lifestyles". Meanwhile, the public debate has been flooded by media coverage of the ways in which typical "web 2.0"–applications, such as blogs, Facebook and Twitter, have transformed our communicative environment.

Most often these ideas concerning a changing media environment draw—sometimes explicitly, sometimes implicitly—on ideas that have been ascribed to Tim O'Reilly's (2005) effort to catch the transforming web. It was in fact O'Reilly who coined the very term "web 2.0". Even though he was primarily concerned with the new web's technical features—its abilities as a "technological platform" and the ways in which it made "lightweight programming" possible—he also referred to it as an "architecture of participation". When doing so, he also pointed towards possible social and cultural outcomes of the application of the new communication structure. The possible social and cultural outcomes of the "architecture of participation" have also inspired a great deal of theorising, both hopeful, optimistic (cf.

Jenkins 2006; Burgess and Green 2009) and critical (Olsson and Svensson 2012). One specifically central concern within this theoretical discussion has been the "who"-questions: *For whom is this a participatory architecture? And what are the conditions for participation?*

12.2   AN "ARCHITECTURE OF PARTICIPATION": FOR WHOM?

The answers to these questions—"For whom is this a participatory architecture? And what are the conditions for participation?"—vary quite extensively between different parts of the literature on "web 2.0" and "social media". We will briefly look into three different perspectives that are salient within the literature, which provide various answers to these questions, in order to offer an overview of the research field and contextualise the forthcoming analyses of how different web venues appropriate the participatory architecture.

12.2.1   For Corporations (And Capitalism More Generally)

Within critical social science, for instance critical political economy, the "web 2.0" architecture of participation has mainly been interpreted as nothing particularly new. Despite its seemingly novel technological features—such as enhanced opportunities for users to collaborate and to undertake participatory actions—the renewed web is still perceived as a product, or even a manifestation, of social relations of domination within the society that has both invented it and brought it to use. In essence, despite its new technological features, the "web 2.0" becomes an extension of corporate, capitalist logic. This has recently been very clearly pointed out by Des Freedman, who states: "[F]ar from signalling a democratisation of media production and distribution 'prosumption' is all too often incorporated within a system of commodity exchange controlled by existing elites" (Freedman 2012, 88).

As another consequence, "social media"—like all media prior to it—will mainly function according to a commercial, capitalistic logic, despite the fact they are based on a more "participatory architecture". More concretely, this means that they—as platforms for communication and in terms of the content that is produced on them—will be made into sellable products, commodities, in one way or the other. The fact that the media technology per se is somewhat new, does not alter already existing business models for communication in any substantial way. This point has been specifically well-spotted by Christian Fuchs:

> Corporations in the Internet economy make use of gifts, free access, and free distribution in order to achieve high numbers of users, which allows them to charge high advertisement rates and drive up

profits. Especially Web 2.0 platforms make use of this model. (Fuchs 2008, 343)

In general, the dismissive attitude towards the potential for media to create social change, in this case participatory "social media", does not intend to deny their potential for change as such. It is rather a matter of pointing to the fact that real societal and cultural change—for instance a change towards a genuinely more participatory society (Pateman 1970)—cannot start with a reconfigured communication environment alone, but must instead start with changing social and cultural relations of power (Fuchs 2008, 136).

To put it short, from the point of view of critical political economy the answers to the questions ("For whom is this a participatory architecture? And what are the conditions for participation?") are rather clear cut: It is to a very large extent a participatory architecture for already existing (economic, political) elites, and the conditions for participation are mainly decided on by such elites.

12.2.2 For Empowered Consumers

A very different interpretation of "social media" and the "architecture of participation" has been offered by a range of authors that we can refer to as "web 2.0" enthusiasts. This group of authors is very diverse. It includes authors that perceive the new communication environment as an ecology, which fosters new forms of cooperation among people. This group also involves analysts that are inclined to see a great potential for consumer empowerment in the more participatory media environment. What they have in common, though, despite internal differences, is a liberal and celebratory view of the overall potential in new media to transform themselves from mere technological opportunities to actual societal change.

In this context, Clay Shirky has been a prominent figure. The former editor of *Wired* has spent a lot of analytical effort trying to grasp what new and freer organisational forms might emerge out of the widespread application of participatory web technology. His view is that such a development will "increase our ability to share, to cooperate [. . .], and to take collective action" (Shirky 2008, 20–21). This idea has also been effectively captured in the title of his bestselling book: *Here Comes Everybody.* In a very similar vein Yochai Benkler (2006) has noted and commented on this technological transformation. He states that: "[t]hese changes have increased the role of nonmarket and nonproprietary production, both by individuals alone and by cooperative efforts in a wide range of loosely or tightly woven collaborations" (Benkler 2006, 2). Most famous among these authors is probably Chris Anderson, whose book, *The Long Tail,* is read all over at least the Western world as an insightful theory regarding contemporary web developments. Among other things, he foresees "democratized tools of production and distribution" (Anderson 2009, 84) in the "web 2.0".

Another strand in this literature has spotted consumer empowerment in a new and more participatory relationship between brands and their customers. These authors have for instance paid interest to how "[m]arket capital and social capital [converge] more than many recognize" (Hunt 2009, 7). As a consequence, companies would need to build their social capital by allowing customers to participate in efforts to (re)create the brand, which then is interpreted as a form of consumer empowerment (Hunt 2009, 1–33).

Regarding the questions—"For whom is this a participatory architecture? And what are the conditions for participation?"–this part of the literature also offers rather straightforward answers: The "web 2.0" offers new forms of participation for individuals as consumers and as members of self-organised networks. The conditions for participation have also been levelled out by the new web's more interactive features.

12.2.3   For Participating Citizens

Ever since the Internet made its big breakthrough into the Western world in the 1990s, it has been surrounded by both speculations about and analyses of its potential significance for late modern democracy (cf. Chadwick 2006; Loader 2007; Olsson and Dahlgren 2010). One specifically central concern in this context has been citizens' participation. As the Internet evolved during a time in history, when Western democracies experienced an increasing lack of involvement and participation from its citizens, it was rather immediately analysed as a tool holding a potential to create new forms of civic engagement and participation—not least among young people (Bennett 2008; CivicWeb 2009).

The transformation of the Internet into an "architecture of participation" has not made this line of analysis any less prevalent. The supposedly more user friendly and interactive web has for instance been analysed with regards to how it opens up new possibilities for the production of civic online content (Banaji and Buckingham 2013), fosters new and potentially empowering forms of online communities (Bakardjieva 2013) and creates new spaces for young people's civic actions (Lund 2013). Not all such analyses assume that social media result in increased civil participation, but they certainly keep the issue of participation on the agenda.

In this context, Henry Jenkins has presented a specifically salient— and also much debated—set of arguments. In his view, digital media's interactive character helps to promote a new, more participatory culture in which media producers and users no longer occupy separate roles. They are instead perceived as "participants who interact with each other according to a new set of rules [. . .]" (Jenkins 2006, 3). This new relationship between producers and users would constitute a new media ecology, which, in turn, shapes new political subjects, especially among young people. Their experiences from participatory online cultures (see quote 1) would transform into new civic perspectives (quote 2), which will empower citizens in new ways:

[T]he new participatory culture offers many opportunities for youths to engage in civic debates, participate in community life, and even become political leaders, even if sometimes only through the "second lives" offered by massively multiplayer games or online fan communities. (Jenkins et al. 2009, 12)

The step from watching television news to acting politically seems greater than the transition from being a political actor in a game world to acting politically in the real world. (Jenkins et al. 2009, 13)

Also from the point of view of this perspective it is rather easy to answer the two questions: For whom is this a participatory architecture? And what are the conditions for participation? The new media environment, built on the "web 2.0" logic, offers new and hitherto unseen participatory possibilities, and as such it can become a participatory architecture for citizens.

12.2.4 Summing Up: Three Positions and Many Tensions

The interpretations of "social media" and/or "web 2.0" as an "architecture of participation" obviously vary quite extensively. It can on the one hand be interpreted as an extension of corporate interests and the capitalistic logic. On the other hand it can be interpreted as a facilitator of consumer empowerment, which enables new forms of organising and interaction among consumers and in-between consumers and brands. Meanwhile, it can also mainly be looked upon as a resource for civic practices. Obviously, these claims depart from very different points of ontological departure. Despite the differences between them, they nevertheless share the same preference for overarching claims regarding "the architecture of participation". Their ways of looking at it tend to offer an "either/or" view of "web 2.0" and the communication features offered by it.

12.3 THE PRODUCTION OF NET CULTURE: THREE CASE STUDIES

Close to the real, everyday life of contemporary web features and practices, however, things do not appear to be fully as clear cut as some positions suggest. Ethnographic analyses of the production and use of websites and web platforms at the point of everyday connections between producers and users reveal a complicated and diverse view of "the architecture of participation". The remaining parts of this chapter will illustrate and develop this point by analysing three different cases, more specifically three different web venues that are all produced with the ambition to attract attention, activity and participation among young people. The analyses are all parts of an ongoing research project on production of net culture, and they are based on ethnographic studies into the ways in which these web venues are produced, how they are brought to use and (to a lesser extent) how they are perceived by users. The empirical material consists of interviews with website producers, online observations, and to some extent online content analysis.

The three web venues are deliberately very different from one another. We will firstly look into websites produced by two commercial companies, moderskeppet.se and stallet.se. Thereafter we will take a closer look at a website that is produced by a municipal youth community, ungilund.se. The descriptions and analyses will pay specific attention to the ways in which the producers appropriate the participatory possibilities brought about by the "architecture of participation", that is they deal with the question: What becomes of participation in the hands of the different producer organisations?

12.3.1   Moderskeppet.se: Participation as a Positive Connotation

The company behind moderskeppet.se, Pixondu Inc., makes very strategic use of the web (Olsson and Svensson 2012).[1] They run Sweden's leading website for people interested in enhancing their skills in digital photography and editing. On the website, they offer plenty of educational material for free, but also sell instructional DVDs and market their courses in digital photo editing.

Moderskeppet puts a lot of efforts into building and maintaining communication with both existing and possible future customers through their website. These efforts are played out on different venues—on the website, of course, but also on platforms such as company blogs (they have a couple of different blogs) and Facebook pages. Moderskeppet's Internet venues are popular. They have more than 100,000 monthly visitors, as well as thousands of subscribers and "likers" of their Facebook community. These web venues are also platforms for interaction, both between Moderskeppet and their users and between users themselves.

What is most interesting in this case, however, is the fact that these forms of user participation are very strategically brought to use by Moderskeppet. They all emerge on the producers' initiative rather than as a consequence of users' appropriation of a participatory opportunity structure. Interviews with the people involved in Moderskeppet's web production reveal how they very consciously steer participation in certain, preferred directions: "We create all the content and then we offer the users the opportunity to comment or give us feedback on that content. Consequently, they don't actually contribute with anything new. . ."[2]. At another stage during the same interview, the company's CEO insisted: "Consequently, we have declared very clearly: you are included if you contribute to the quality of the content, and will be excluded if you do not!"

In Moderskeppet's case "the architecture of participation" is very much brought to strategic use—to the benefit of the company and the brand. Possibilities for free forms of user participation are actively limited by the web producers, and users are only allowed to participate as long as they conform to their formal and informal norms of online behaviour. Nevertheless, Moderskeppet is a company that is very sensitive towards the participatory spirit of the "web 2.0" and is therefore careful to create a sense of participation among its users. It is also self-reflexive regarding the discrepancy between their aura of being participatory and their actual web practices: "Well, we've got a much better reputation [in this regard] than we deserve".[3]

It is possible to argue in this case that Moderskeppet mainly makes use of participation as a *positive connotation*. The company has a wish to and a strategy for affiliating itself with the popular idea of user participation through the Internet, but works also very carefully in steering such participation. It not keen on actually allowing its users, or rather customers, free forms of participation. They instead make use of various strategies and tactics to shape participation in "useful" directions, directions that help them create and maintain that brand identity. In the hands of Moderskeppet, "the architecture of participation" is being shaped into a space for consumer relations.

12.3.2 Stallet.se: A Commercial Environment for Civic Participation?

Stallet.se (Stallet is Swedish for stables) is a commercial web community aimed mainly at "tweens", that is adolescences aged 10 to 16 years. According to Egmont, the media company that owns the community, Stallet.se is a combination of a "community" and a "game". The backbone of the community is that users create virtual stables, take care of and compete with their horses. Hence, the community relies heavily on content produced by users themselves—it is the interaction and participation between users that creates the community. So far, it has been successful. It was launched in 2002 and in 2010 it was elected "the best Swedish youth site" by the magazine *Internet Worlds*. According to their own statistics—which they present for potential advertisers—the community has 100,000 unique monthly visitors. These visitors also spend a lot of time within the community: the average visit lasts for twenty-seven minutes and the average user visits the website five times a week.

As stallet.se is a community that is built on content produced by users themselves, it can be perceived as a rather typical commercial application of "the architecture of participation". Hence, very basically, its logic works as follows: The content that is produced on the platform (Gillespie 2010; van Dijck 2013) by young people is appropriated by a company, in this case Egmont. The company, in turn, makes use of this content to attract additional users. The participating users can participate "for free", as they are not being charged for it. Meanwhile, if you do pay a fee, you get extra credits that can be used within the game and you are able to enjoy it more fully. Such income from users is not the major source of income for the producers of the community. The fact that the content generated from users attracts attention from additional users also makes it possible for them to sell the community to advertisers (Smythe 1977; Fuchs 2010).

Hence, at first sight it seems obvious enough that stallet.se is a rather evident example of a commercial appropriation of "the architecture of participation". A closer analysis of the actual practices and interactions on the website, however, reveals a less simplistic story of the community (Lund 2013). To the young users—mainly girls—the community is also a place to hang out in. Their participation does not only include individualised gaming, and taking care of horses, but also various forms of interaction between users themselves. In some instances, this interaction even holds what Anna Lund (2013) analyses as civic values and practices (Alexander 2006; Dahlgren 2008). It is mainly within the open forum for discussion and debate that these features emerge. In the forum discussions, all kinds of subjects are debated (see Lund 2013). They involve personal issues concerning relations with parents and boyfriends, as well as teacher and other authority relations at school. When considering the context of this forum it is not very surprising that it also involves discussions about the relationship between human beings and animals. Generally, these discussions are also of good quality in terms of form, as they are open, mutual, and mainly supportive to the young participants. Based on these findings, Anna Lund argues convincingly:

[T]here is interplay between social criticism, democratic integration and entertainment. Production and reception, visual presentations and writing of texts, private and public life are simultaneously present [. . .] The members can switch between different areas of interest at the blink of an eye. They can discuss current personal or political affairs or different horse topics as well as enter the market for digital horses for sale, join in on competitions while continuously working with the design and presentation of their own virtual stable. (2013, 198)

Drawing on this analysis, Anna Lund refers to Liesbet van Zoonen's notion of venues that make "citizenship pleasurable" (van Zoonen 2005, 4). Stallet. se is a commercial web community, but it also offers a space for interaction and participation among (mainly) young girls that sometimes holds civic—or pre-political—dimensions. Despite the fact that the context is commercial, which makes the young participators consumers, the "architecture of participation" is at least partially appropriated by the young users as a space for civic participation.

12.3.3   Young in Lund

The website ungilund.se is the website affiliated with Lund's youth council. Both the youth council and its website were founded in 2002 (see Miegel and Olsson 2012a, 2012b). The youth council receives public funding by Lund municipality, but is entirely managed and run by young people themselves. "Young people" means in this context all people aged 12 to25 years living in Lund.

The backbone of the youth council is its "big meetings"—face-to-face meetings in the town hall. All interested young people living in Lund are invited to join and participate in discussions concerning everything from local issues to global politics. The participants are all also equally invited to contribute to the agenda. In these meeting, usually some hundred young people meet to discuss various issues and—importantly—also to decide how to spend the money that is allocated to the youth council by the municipality. In these discussions and decisions, the young participators are entrusted with total freedom by the municipality.

The work within the youth council is coordinated by two *ombudsmen*. They are hired for the job part-time and are usually between 18 and 22 years old. Apart from coordinating the youth council, they also act as the council's link to local politicians and administrators—they have an overarching responsibility to represent the young generation in local decision making.

The youth council has been successful in creating engagement and participation among young people in Lund. They have even been successful to the point that it has become a role model for similar initiatives in other parts of Sweden, which is not all that surprising as it has managed to uphold and develop its fluid organisational form for more than a decade. Young people in Lund can smoothly both enter and leave the organisation without jeopardising its inclusive and participatory ethos.

The website ungilund.se plays an important part in this process and is also a manifestation of the council's inclusive, participatory ethos. Also the website is produced and maintained entirely by the young people themselves, who are basically amateurs. The website's design is deliberately simple and robust in order to not demand too much expert knowledge from the young people involved in its production.

Hence, the website is anything but spectacular, but works very well as a hub for the youth council. One important task for the website is to inform about and "market" upcoming events. Another important feature is that it offers accounts of past events for those who were unable to attend. The minutes from the big meetings are always very visibly published on the website for anyone to read. The website also has an archive covering minutes from all big meetings since the very start of the youth council. In addition, the website offers tips and tricks of the trade regarding how young people can gain influence in and impact municipal politics. In essence, although it does not have that many fancy, interactive online features, the website does hold a lot of substantial ideas and resources regarding young peoples' civic participation. It is furthermore participatory insofar as any young person in Lund is invited to write for the website. Apart from its website, the youth council's web presence also materialises in the form of a Facebook group, a blog and on Twitter, where the ombudsmen make continuous updates about current events.

Lund's youth council has obviously managed to shape (Woolgar 1996; Miller and Slater 2000) the "architecture of participation" into a resource for actual participation. It offers young people access to and resources for local, civic participation. Still, what is interesting is that this is not mainly a feature that is an inherent part of their web practices per se, but rather a consequence of the ways in which these practices are contextualised in the youth council's overall participatory organisation. The youth council is interactive in itself, but not mainly—and absolutely not solely—on its website.

12.4   CONCLUSION

The three websites that make up the empirical points of departure for this analysis are obviously very different; they appropriate "the architecture of participation" according to various logics. In the first case, Moderskeppet. se, we are dealing with an organisation that is very careful in steering users' participatory opportunities. Users are invited to participate, but in ways that are perceived to be beneficial for the company brand. Moderskeppet is still careful to draw on and affiliate itself with the participatory ethos of "web 2.0" in their self-presentation, but even considers itself to have a better reputation than it deserves in this regard. To simplify, it is possible to say that they manage to produce a seemingly participatory web environment that is perfectly top-down at the same time.

The second case, stallet.se, is essentially a commercial community. It is owned by a commercial media company and works according to commercial principles in that it both sells credits to participants and offers advertising space. Nevertheless, the participatory architecture is still appropriated by users themselves in ways that challenge the overall commercial structure (Lund 2013). Within the discussion forum, they establish lively debates between one-another concerning issues of relevance to them. Several of the discussion threads touch upon personal relations and everyday problems, but some of them also have a political character. More interesting than the actual content of the discussion is perhaps its character. It generally takes on an inviting and inclusive tone, which offers users the possibility to participate. Civic values such as mutuality, critique and deliberation characterise substantial parts of the debates between the young users (Lund 2013). This is the consequence of a bottom up logic, where young users manage to uphold a free, participatory space within a mainly commercial application of the "architecture of participation".

The website affiliated with Lund's youth council, ungilind.se, is based within an already participatory organisation. The organisation itself has the fluid, network like character that Nico Carpentier makes use of when comparing traditional organisations (*arbolic*) to ephemeral, network like ones (*rhizome*) (Carpentier 2013). The fact that the organisation per se has a very obvious bottom up character also influences the ways in which their web venues are produced and maintained. The web venues become hubs (for information, news, updates, etc.) within a flat network of young people wanting to become involved in the youth council's activities. In essence, this is the application of "the architecture of participation" within an already participatory context.

All together, the cases make it obvious that the producers of these websites and/or web venues are informed by different views of what the web should be, and as a consequence they also frame ideas concerning participation very differently. Referring to the overall perspectives presented in the introductory part of this chapter (see Section 12.2.), these are important insights. They make it obvious that at the point of everyday web production, "the architecture of participation" can be shaped to serve very different purposes and practices. What is of further interest in this instance, is that despite producer strategies and tactics, it is also possible for users to decode (Woolgar 1996) and make use of participatory spaces—however defined or encoded by producers—in unpredictable and sometimes even surprising ways (which the analysis of stallet.se makes specifically obvious).

Hence, the three cases certainly point to the need for us, as scholars, to be careful and contextually reflexive regarding what becomes of "web 2.0", "social media" and/or "the architecture of participation" when it is applied by actors in various contexts. It can serve many different purposes and ends, and if we apply too overarching views of it, we might become blind to really see the messy—and intriguing—realities of various configurations of technological opportunities and everyday social and cultural practices.

NOTES

1. This part of the text is a short version of a more extended analysis presented in Olsson and Svensson 2012.
2. Interview with the CEO of Moderskeppet.
3. Ibid.

REFERENCES

Alexander, Jeffrey C. 2006. *The civil sphere.* New York: Oxford University Press.
Anderson, Chris. 2009. *The longer tail. How endless choice is creating unlimited demand.* London: Random House Business Books.
Bakardjieva, Maria. 2013. "Bringing up Bg-mamma. Organized producers between community and commerce." In *Producing the Internet: Critical perspectives of social media*, edited by Tobias Olsson, 145–164. Göteborg: Nordicom.
Banaji, Shakuntala, and David Buckingham. 2013. "Creating the civic web: Exploring the perspectives of web producers in Europe and Turkey." In *Producing the Internet: Critical perspectives of social media*, edited by Tobias Olsson, 221–237. Göteborg: Nordicom.
Benkler, Yochai. 2006. *The wealth of networks.* New Heaven: Yale University Press.
Bennett, Lance W. 2008. *Civic life online: Learning how digital media can engage youth.* Cambridge, MA: MIT Press.

Burgess, Jean, and Joshua Green. 2009. *YouTube: Online video and participatory culture*. Cambridge, MA: Polity.

Carpentier, Nico. 2013. "The participatory organization. Alternative models for organizational structure and leadership." In *Producing the Internet: Critical perspectives of social media*, edited by Tobias Olsson, 63–82. Göteborg: Nordicom.

Chadwick, Andrew. 2006. *State, citizens and new communication technologies*. New York: Oxford University Press.

Christodoulides, George. 2009. "Branding in the post-Internet era." *Marketing Theory* 9 (1): 141–144.

CivicWeb. 2009. *Deliverable 17: Synthesis of results and policy outcomes*. London: Institute of Education. Accessed December 19, 2012. http://www.civicweb.eu/images/stories/reports/civicweb%20wp11%20final.pdf.

Dahlgren, Peter. 2008. "Reconfiguring civic culture in the new media milieu." In *Media and the restyling of Politics*, edited by John Corner and Dick Pels, 151–170. London: Sage.

Freedman, Des. 2012. "Web 2.0 and the death of the blockbuster economy." In *Misunderstanding the Internet*, edited by James Curran, Natalie Fenton, and Des Freedman, 69–94. New York: Routledge.

Fuchs, Christian. 2008. *Internet and society. Social theory in the information age*. New York. Routledge.

———. 2010. "Labour in informational capitalism and on the Internet." *The Information Society* 26 (3): 179–196.

Gillespie, Tarleton. 2010. "The politics of 'platforms'." *New Media & Society* 12 (3): 347–364.

Hunt, Tara. 2009. *The power of social networking*. New York: Three Rivers Press.

Jenkins, Henry. 2006. *Convergence culture: Where old and new media collide*. New York: New York University Press.

Jenkins, Henry, Ravi Purushotma, Margret Weigel, Katie Clinton, and Alice J. Robison. 2009. *Confronting the challenges of participatory culture: Media education for the 21th century*. Cambridge, MA: MIT Press.

Loader, Brian, D. 2007. *Young citizens in the digital age: Political engagement, young people and new media*. London: Routledge.

Lund, Anna. 2013. "The civic potential of the digital horse." In *Producing the Internet: Critical perspectives of social media*, edited by Tobias Olsson, 185–200. Göteborg: Nordicom.

Miegel, Fredrik and Tobias Olsson. 2012a. "A generational thing? The Internet and new forms of social intercourse." *Continuum: Journal of Media and Cultural Studies* 26 (3): 487–499.

———. 2012b. "Civic passion: A cultural approach to the political." *Television and New Media*. First published online May 2, 2012, doi: 10.1177/1527476412442986.

Miller, Daniel, and Don Slater. 2000. *The Internet: An ethnographic approach*. Oxford and New York: Berg.

Olsson, Tobias, and Peter Dahlgren. 2010. *Young people, ICTs and democracy: Theories, policies, websites and users*. Göteborg: Nordicom.

Olsson, Tobias, and Anders Svensson. 2012. "Producing prod-users: Conditional participation in a web 2.0 consumer community." *Javnost—The Public* 19 (3): 41–58.

O'Reilly, Tim. 2005. *What is web 2.0?* Accessed December 19, 2012. http://www.oreillynet.com/pub/a/oreilly/tim/news/2005/09/30/what-is-web-20.html?page=1.

Pateman, Carole. 1970. *Participation and democratic theory*. London: Cambridge University Press.

Shirky, Clay. 2008. *Here comes everybody. The power of organizing without organization.* London: Penguin.

Smythe, Dallas. 1977. "Communications: Blind spot of Western Marxism." *Canadian Journal of Political and Social Theory* 1 (3): 1–27.

van Dijck, José. 2013. "Social media platforms as producers." In *Producing the Internet: Critical perspectives of social media*, edited by Tobias Olsson, 45–62. Göteborg: Nordicom.

van Zoonen, Liesbet. 2005. *Entertaining the citizen: When politics and popular culture converge.* Lanham, MD: Rowman & Littlefield.

Woolgar, Steve. 1996. "Technologies as cultural artefacts." In *Information and communication technologies: Visions and realities*, edited by William H. Dutton, 87–102. New York: Oxford University Press.

Part III

Critical Studies of
Communication Labour

13 Precarious Times, Precarious Work

A Feminist Political Economy of Freelance Journalists in Canada and the United States

Catherine McKercher

13.1 INTRODUCTION

As a career choice, freelance journalism has long had a romantic cachet. It promises no bosses, no shiftwork and no petty office politics. It holds out the possibility of writing about what you want and when you want, the prospect of a front-row seat on history, and the promise of a big payoff when you land the big story. Sure, it lacks security. But who could deny the allure of a job in which, as a UK-based home-study writing program puts it, "if you fancy travelling the world reviewing the latest luxury products, [. . .] you can" (Writers Bureau 2012). Of course in any occupation, there's a gap between the romance and reality. For freelance journalists in Canada and the United States, however, that gap has never been wider than it is today. Incomes are in decline. Layoffs in the mainstream media have thrown more journalists onto the freelance market, which means more competition for work. Tight newsroom budgets mean freelance opportunities are in short supply. The pressure to work for free is growing.

This chapter examines the state of freelance journalism in Canada and the United States. It draws on two sets of ideas to understand how freelancers got to where they are today. The first is Marx's idea on piecework. The second is the question of what happens when an occupation becomes feminised. The chapter concludes by looking at what individuals and groups are doing to try to improve the lot of freelancers. It argues that for these to have most effect, it's critical to recognise a feminist dimension to the issue.

13.2 PIECE WORK AND WOMEN'S WORK

Much of the contemporary scholarship on cultural workers tends to pay relatively little attention to Marx. Marx wrote about the factory system of the nineteenth century, where workers were, in essence, interchangeable cogs in the capitalist machine. A number of scholars see cultural workers as fundamentally different from those who toiled in Marxist alienation (see for example, Florida 2002; Deuze 2007; Banks 2007; Hesmondhalgh 2007). Freelance cultural workers, who control their own labour process, seem the least likely to experience Marxist alienation. Some analysts see cultural workers as constituting their own class, the creative class, existing outside the bounds of the class structure so ably described by Marx. In the creative economy of the knowledge society, the factory system itself seems passé. When it comes to cultural workers, therefore, a traditional Marxist analysis of the relation between capital and labour may be out of date. But is that really the case? As Cohen notes (2012), a central theme in Marx's analysis is exploitation: the relentless attempt by capital to extract as much value as possible from labour, whatever form that labour takes. The relationship between capital and labour is full of tension, contestation and contradiction. It evolves constantly. As labour comes up with new and more creative forms of resistance to exploitation, capital comes up with new and more creative ways to exploit labour, and the struggle continues. Far from being limited to the factory of the nineteenth century, a Marxist analysis can help us understand the fundamentals of capitalist relations, regardless of workplace.

Certainly freelance cultural workers, including creative workers and journalists, have a different degree of autonomy or subjectivity than factory workers. They occupy a somewhat more ambiguous location in the relation between capital and labour (see Mosco and McKercher 2008). A number of scholars have documented the shift to precarious forms of employment—including part-time, temporary or seasonal work, as well as freelance and contract work. This trend is particularly pronounced among women workers (Cranford et al. 2003) and among workers in the cultural industries, where project-based work is common (Brophy and de Peuter 2007; Ross 2009; Murdock 2002). In Canada and the USA, freelance journalists, who tend to be well educated and highly skilled knowledge workers, are legally classified as independent contractors (Cohen 2012). Their apparent subjectivity, autonomy and the creative nature of their work all tend to mask the deeper power relations behind their labour, including the increasingly precarious conditions they face.

One useful way to understand that is to strip away the gloss of subjectivity and look at what freelancers actually *do*: sell the product of their labour, including in many cases their rights as creators, on a one-off basis. Seen this way, their work is closer to piecework. Piecework pays workers a set fee per item produced. The only way for workers to increase their wage is to produce more product—by working a longer day, for example, or by figuring out how to make each piece more quickly. This gives the worker a sense of autonomy and a degree of control over the labour process. But it also allows the purchaser of the piece to get a measure of the intensity of the work that goes into the product, and then pit workers against each other in hopes of driving the price down. As Marx put it,

> [T]he wider scope that piece-wage gives to individuality, tends to develop on the one hand that individuality, and with it the sense of

liberty, independence, and self-control of the labourers, on the other, their competition one with another. Piece-work has, therefore, a tendency, while raising individual wages above the average, to lower this average itself (1867).

Seen from this perspective, the apparent freedom of the freelance journalist is considerably more limited than it might initially appear to be.

As we will see, piecework is a critical idea in understanding the state of the freelancer. Another idea is equally significant: the feminisation of a profession. Women have moved into the workforce in increasingly significant numbers, but they are not distributed evenly across all areas of work. In some professional occupations—pharmacy or teaching, for example—women outnumber men. In others—medicine, dentistry or engineering—women remain in the minority. Sociologists have found that feminisation of a profession is often accompanied by a decline in its social status (for a summary of work in this area, see Adams 2005). There is some murkiness here as to why. In some cases, feminisation is the cause of a decline in social status; in others it's the consequence of such a decline. In addition, some scholars have found evidence of internal segregation within some professions. For example, women doctors practise in disproportionate numbers in the lower-status specialty of general practice, but few women work as surgeons, a high-status specialty (Armstrong and Armstrong 1992). Finally, feminisation is often accompanied by lower wages. Again, the reasons why this happens are complex and murky, although the pattern itself is fairly clear. For example, Jagsi et al. (2012) found that male doctors make about US$12,000 a year more than their female counterparts, even when factoring in medical specialty, title, work hours, productivity and a host of other factors. In occupations where the demand for workers outstrips the supply, feminisation can lead to successful integration and no loss of status. In others, it is linked to ghettoisation and a continuation of gender inequality (Adams 2005). In short, whereas the causes and processes of feminisation are complex and at times contradictory, the consequences are pretty clear: a loss of status and a loss of income.

13.3   THE STATE OF THE FREELANCE WRITER

In Canada and the United States, journalists tend to learn their trade at university or college-level journalism and communication programs. For many years, women students have formed the majority in these programmes, accounting for 73.5 per cent of 2010 US journalism and communication graduates (Yi and Dearfield 2012). The presence of substantial numbers of women is part of a wider trend toward feminisation of higher education. In Canada, for example, the share of women graduates rose from 56 per cent in 1992 to 61 per cent in 2007 (Parsons and McMullen 2009). The distribution varies greatly by field of study, however, with women dominating in the arts, social sciences and education, but making up only a small proportion of graduates in computer science and engineering.

Given that women have constituted the majority of students in journalism and communication studies for decades—since at least 1977, according to Gallagher (2001)—we might expect to see this gender split reflected in the ranks of working journalists. Not so. In all but one area, women continue to be in the minority. They comprised 36.9 per cent of US newspaper reporters, 40 per cent of the US television news force, and 29 per cent of the US radio news force in 2011 (Yi and Dearfield 2012). They are in the minority at US news magazines (43.5 per cent) and US wire services (20.3 per cent) (Media Report to Women 2005). The disparity is even more striking at the management level. For example, less than one-third of TV news directors in the US are women (Yi and Dearfield 2012).

The exception to this pattern is freelance journalism. According to a 2006 report by the Professional Writers Association of Canada (PWAC), the leading professional association in the field, women freelancers outnumber men by almost 2 to 1. The typical Canadian freelancer, the study of members found, is a woman aged thirty-five to fifty-five, who holds a college diploma or university degree and is married to another wage earner. She earned CDN$24,000 before taxes in 2005. Not only is this significantly less than the wage in newsrooms (and especially in unionised newsrooms), it is almost exactly the same income, dollar for dollar, that freelancers earned in 1979. "Factoring in inflation over the past 30 years, independent writers in Canada have watched their standard of living drop by more than 60 per cent in one generation" (Professional Writers Association of Canada (PWAC) 2006, 12). In no other area of journalism have wages been this stagnant. The survey also found a gender gap within freelance wages. Elite women freelancers charged more than top-earning men—92 cents a word compared with 90 cents—but on average, the men earned $3,000 a year more than women.

The survey offered no explanation for this variation in wages, and no explanation of why so many women work freelance in the first place. My experience as a journalist and journalism educator suggests that a number of factors are in play. Some women work as freelancers because they can't find a permanent job. Others want to stay home with young children. Some take on freelance work between jobs, in hopes of keeping their hand in the business—and their name out there for employers to see—until they can land something more permanent. Some end up freelancing after moving for the sake of their partner's career. Others, disillusioned by the state of the news business or the environment of the newsroom, or tired of shift work and unpredictable hours, decide to head out on their own. Some, especially those with a strong resumé and an entrepreneurial streak, decide they can do better financially if they work independently. In their research on full-time Canadian journalists, Robinson and Saint-Jean (cited by Vleig

1999) found that family responsibilities are the biggest determining factor in female participation in newsroom jobs. Full-time women journalists are less likely to be married than man, and more likely to be childless. Many—maybe most—women full-time journalists still have to make the choice between career and family. Men do not.

13.4   PRESSURES ON FREELANCERS INCREASE

Regardless of the reason a woman decides to work as a freelancer, however, it is tougher and tougher to make a living at it. The PWAC study was conducted in 2005, before the recession that followed the 2007 financial collapse. Since then, the difficulties facing freelancers have compounded.

A key source of pressure is the decline in newsroom employment. More and more journalists find themselves thrown out of, or barred entry to, full-time or permanent employment. The size of the decline has been stunning. Data collected by the American Society of Newspaper Editors (1997, 2011, 2012) shows that between 1995 and 2010, newsroom employment in US newspapers dropped by more than 26 per cent, from 55,000 to 41,600. The Paper Cuts blog, launched in 2008 by Erica Smith, the social media editor of the St. Louis Post Dispatch, identified an additional 6,000 layoffs, cuts and buyouts in 2011 and 2012 (Smith, 2008–present). Similar layoffs and buyouts have occurred in Canadian newspapers. Melanie Coulson, a staffer at the *Ottawa Citizen*, the leading daily in the Canadian capital, wrote in her blog in 2012: "I am by nature a positive person. So today, I am working to find a good spin on the fact that our newsroom is nearly 24 per cent smaller than it was yesterday" (Coulson 2012). Broadcasters face similar cuts. At the national public broadcaster, the Canadian Broadcasting Corporation, a three-year, 10–per cent funding cut starting in 2012 has put a number of television and radio jobs on the block (Dixon 2012). The result of these changes is that more journalists are looking for work, including freelance work. In addition, the supply of available journalists vastly outstrips the demand.

Until the last decade or so, most freelance contracts took the form of unwritten agreements between the individual writer and editor. The journalist typically sold first North American rights to a piece, which meant that after a media outlet had published the piece the writer could resell, repurpose or rewrite the piece for a different (typically non-competing) outlet. More recently, major employers have begun demanding that writers sign contracts that give the publisher all rights to a piece, including moral rights, in perpetuity, in the media form for which it was created and in any other media form, including any yet to be devised (see *Ottawa Citizen* 2012). Typically, there is no increase in the fee for the article. Critics say this amounts to a rights grab and tilts the power entirely toward the buyer, in most cases an outlet in a large media company. If the freelancer doesn't sign, the freelancer doesn't get the work.

A less direct but perhaps more insidious source of pressure on freelancers is the rise of "free labour" or unpaid content in the media provided by unpaid or underpaid interns. Historically, journalism and communication students have seen a brief period of precarious work as a way to obtain professional experience and gain an entry into the job market. In journalism as in other fields, unpaid internships have become much more common—in many cases crowding out paid entry-level work. Unpaid internships are legal in Canada and the United States as long as they comply with some rules: for example, the internship should be a learning experience and the beneficiary should be the intern, not the employer.

In the first major study of the internship phenomenon in the United States, Perlin (2011) estimated that the number of internships had doubled since the 1980s, and half of them were unpaid or paid at a level below the minimum wage. If all these unpaid or underpaid interns earned minimum wage, he wrote, the bill would amount to US$2 billion a year (2011, 124). In addition, a significant proportion of internships are illegal—in essence providing employers with US$600 million a year in free labour with no educational value.

Women are far more likely to hold unpaid internships than men. Commenting on a study that found three-quarters of all unpaid internships are held by women, Perlin wrote: "Internship injustice is closely linked to gender issues, both because of the fields women gravitate toward and possibly also because female students have been more accepting of unpaid, unjust situations" (2011, 27). He noted that among communications majors, a group dominated by women, the study found that only 41 per cent of internships are paid. By contrast, 87 per cent of students in the male-dominated fields of engineering and computer science reported having paid positions.

It is impossible to trace a direct line from the rise of legal, unpaid internships to a decline of freelance opportunities. But there is a common thread: the attractive (from the employer's eyes) prospect of free content at a time when the 24-hour news cycle demands a constant stream of new material and when the budget to pay for that content is shrinking.

In some cases, news outlets are trumpeting unpaid work as a democratic virtue, through participatory or so-called citizen journalism initiatives. As Rosen (2006) famously put it: citizen journalists are "the people formerly known as the audience". Thanks to the Internet and cheap digital technology, they are able to report, produce, edit and distribute their own stories, creating a new and more democratic balance of power in the media. Kperogi (2011, 314) finds that citizen journalism initiatives tend to be portrayed as "inherently counter-hegemonic, as the emerging, as yet unformed but nonetheless virile antithesis to the traditional media". Certainly, citizen journalism can take the form of resistance. But it can also be co-opted by the mainstream media. CNN's iReport is a leading example of this. Founded in 2006, iReport claims one million members worldwide, providing five hundred uncensored, unverified and unedited reports a day (CNN, 2012).

Most appear simply on the iReport site. CNN cherry-picks those it wants for the regular network and its websites, and then fact-checks them and taggs them with a red "CNN iReport" bug. "Our producers also give iReport stories extra context, by adding producer notes with further details, CNN reporting, and/or additional quotes from the iReporter" (CNN, 2012). In many ways, it treats iReporters as freelancers, offering "assignments" inviting them to cover specific stories like hurricanes or breaking news and requiring them to comply with lengthy terms of use that license content to the network. There's one big difference between iReporting and freelancing: CNN does not pay iReporters. As Kperogi (2011, 321) writes: "This voluntary cultural labour is exploited by CNN, and other corporate media outlets that have embraced this model, for profit."

The leading example of a media outlet relying on free content is the Huffington Post, which is also the most successful new media launch of the current century. Begun in 2005 as a liberal-leaning aggregator of news, commentary and blogs, the Huffington Post now publishes local, national and international editions in the United States, Canada, Britain and several European countries. AOL bought it from Arianna Huffington and her co-founders for $315 million in 2009. The Huffington Post employs a small, but growing cadre of journalists, but its bloggers—more than nine thousand entertainment figures, journalists, politicians, academics and experts—are at the heart of the enterprise. They earn no pay for their work. As Walker (2011) puts it: "The core of Huffington's justification for not paying is that the Huffington Post is a showcase for writers, and that exposure there leads to paying gigs and greater visibility. Huffington merely—and generously, by her estimation—provides the stage." Walker argues that the Huffington Post's no-pay policy fits with the web's fundamental business philosophy, one that transmutes writing done for pay into content consumed for free.

13.5 EXPLOITATION, ACTIVISM AND RESISTANCE

Capitalist social relations are full of contradictions and unintended consequences, ever-evolving cycles of exploitation and resistance, and struggles for control over labour and the labour process. It's no surprise, therefore, that the exploitation of freelancers and the growing pressure to work for free has been met with a variety of forms of individual and collective resistance.

A number of trade unions and professional organisations representing journalists and creative workers have put new emphasis on organising freelancers. In 2006, a group of Canadian freelancers, mainly magazine writers, joined with trade unionists to form the Canadian Freelance Union. Three years later, it became Local 2040 of the Communications, Energy and Paperworkers (CEP) union, a large converged union that brings together workers across the communications sector (at the time of writing, the CEP was in the process of merging with the Canadian Auto Workers to form the largest private-sector union in Canada). A year later the Canadian Media Guild, the other major union representing Canadian media workers and part of The Newspaper Guild branch of the Communications Workers of America (CWA), signed a unique partnership with a writers' agency, the Canadian Writers Group, automatically giving membership in the union to writers who sign up with the agency (Cohen 2011). In the US, the Pacific Media Workers Guild, which is also part of the CWA's Newspaper Guild branch, has set up a unit for freelancers and has launched a survey of their working conditions. Meanwhile a range of professional groups, including PWAC, the National Writers Union, the Authors Guild and others have become increasingly active in advocacy work on behalf of freelance and creative workers, and in providing concrete member services like health insurance that have typically been hallmarks of trade union contracts.

On the intern front, De Peuter et al. (2012) have tracked what they characterise as a "swell of activism confronting exploitative internships and the cultural conditions that condone them". Groups fighting unpaid and under-paid internships have cropped up in Canada and the US, as well as in Britain, France, Italy, the Netherlands and elsewhere. One of their priorities is to make the unseen exploitation of interns visible, highlighting the use of interns to perform work previously done by entry-level employees and the lack of labour protection for interns. The title of Chapter 4 of Perlin's (2011) book calls internships "a lawsuit waiting to happen". Activists have taken note. De Peuter et al. note a rise in litigation, including class action suits against Fox Entertainment Group and the magazine publisher Hearst Corporation.

Activists have also gone after the Huffington Post over its refusal to pay bloggers. A group led by labour activist Jonathan Tasini, a former president of the National Writers Union, filed a US$105 million class action suit against the Huffington Post in 2011, seeking a share of the US$315 million AOL paid when it bought the Huffington Post (van Voris 2012). The Newspaper Guild, the major journalists' union in the US with a significant Canadian membership, too, called on its twenty-six thousand members to boycott the Huffington Post in support of a "virtual picket line" until a pay schedule for writers was established. Doonesbury cartoonist Garry Trudeau has also gone after the Huffington Post. One of his comic strip's characters, former Washington Post writer Rick Redfern, has been reduced to blogging for the Huffington Post for "exposure" not for pay. In a lovely example of art meeting life, the Pacific Newspaper Guild made Redfern an honorary member of its freelancers unit in 2012.

Some initiatives on behalf of freelancers and unpaid interns have been more successful than others. The Canadian Freelance Union has not grown to the extent its founders hoped, although it has had some success in a class action suit over pay for electronic use of articles. Tasini's suit was unsuccessful, but it managed to draw attention to the issue. A week before the launch of the Huffington Post's Quebec edition in early 2012, at least nine high-profile contributors pulled out over concerns they'd be writing for free (Heinrich 2012). The Newspaper Guild boycott ended after the Guild reported that the Huffington Post had agreed to stop assigning unpaid bloggers to cover news (Bercovici 2011). The lawsuits involving internships have had a similarly modest impact. For example, Condé Nast announced reforms to its internship policy in 2012, including guaranteed (albeit small) stipends for interns, limits on the number of hours an intern can work, and a ban on using interns for personal errands (Greenfield 2012).

None of the interventions to date has resulted in a fundamental change in the relationship between the writers and other creators and the people who buy the products of their labour. Taken together, though, they represent a growing effort to reimagine and renegotiate the role of workers, and especially young workers and women workers, in perilous times. They are drawing attention to issues that, until now, have gone unseen. And they have succeeded in tracing patterns of exploitation that operate across the media landscape in North America.

13.6 CONCLUSION: A FEMINIST POLITICAL ECONOMY OF FREELANCING

This chapter has offered a feminist political economy of freelance writing in Canada and the US, analysing the growing phenomenon of low-paid, underpaid and unpaid labour in the North American media. As the media shed permanent jobs and take advantage of a large pool of freelancers, interns, citizen journalists and aspiring professional journalists, the result is increasing precarity. This is especially the case for women.

Freelance writers tend to see themselves as highly educated (if poorly paid) contractors or small business operators. An alternative way of looking at them—and one that offers deep insights into their life—is to see them as highly educated pieceworkers. Piece work allows owners to assert moral rights to a creator's work, frees owners from any responsibility to the creator beyond a one-off payment for the product, and permits owners to encourage competition among workers over who will accept the lowest rate. It should be no surprise that Marx (1867) saw piecework as "the form of wages most in harmony with the capitalist mode of production." Recognising freelance work, including unpaid internships, as a form of piecework provides a way of reframing the conversation over how to improve wages and working conditions.

At the same time, however, it's essential to recognise the gender dimension of freelancing and the growing split between the full-time journalism workforce and the precariously employed freelancers, interns and would-be journalists. As freelance journalism becomes "women's work", issues surrounding equity, opportunity, discrimination and exploitation take on new significance. For activists and trade unionists who want to address the problem, it's useful to be able to situate freelance journalism within the wider phenomenon of precarious employment, to see it as not simply a journalism problem, but as a problem for knowledge workers of all types. Understanding that freelancing is also a feminist issue enriches the discussion. Just as a study of knowledge workers of all kinds can inform the study of journalists, so can the study of feminisation of other occupations and professions inform the study of journalists too.

REFERENCES

Adams, Tracey L. 2005. "Feminisation of professions: The case of women in dentistry." *The Canadian Journal of Sociology* 30 (1): 71–94.
American Society of Newspaper Editors. 1997. "ASNE Newsroom Census: Minorities hold steady in a shrinking newsroom force, ASNE employment survey shows." Accessed July 23, 2013. http://asne.org/Article_View/ArticleId/1022.
———. 2011. "Newsroom employment up slightly, minority numbers plunge for third year." Accessed July 23, 2013. http://asne.org/content.asp?pl=121&sl=148&contentid=148.
———. 2012. "Total and minority newsroom employment declines in 2011 but loss continues to stabilize" Accessed July 23, 2013. http://asne.org/content.asp?pl=121&sl=122&contentid=122.
Armstrong, Pat, and Hugh Armstrong. 1992. "Sex and professions in Canada." *Journal of Canadian Studies* 27 (1): 118–135.
Banks, Mark. 2007. *The politics of cultural work*. London: Palgrave Macmillan.
Bercovici, Jeff. 2011. "Newspaper guild drops boycott of the Huffington Post." *Forbes* Mixed Media blog, Oct. 21. Accessed July 23, 2013. http://www.forbes.com/sites/jeffbercovici/2011/10/21/newspaper-guild-drops-boycott-of-the-huffington-post/
Brophy, Enda, and Greig de Peuter. 2007. "Immaterial labor, precarity and recomposition." In *Knowledge workers in the information society*, edited by Catherine McKercher and Vincent Mosco, 191–207. Lanham, MD: Lexington.
Cohen, Nicole S. 2011. "Negotiating writers' rights: freelance cultural labour and the challenge of organizing." *Just Labour: A Canadian Journal of Work and Society* 17 and 18: 119–138.
———. 2012. "Cultural labour as a site of struggle: freelancers and exploitation." *tripleC: Communication, Capitalism & Critique. Open Access Journal for a Global Sustainable Information Society* 10 (2): 141–155.
Coulson, Melanie. 2012. "Thoughts from a shrunken newsroom on transitions." Journomel.com blog, Aug. 1. Accessed July 23, 2013. http://journomel.com/2012/08/01/thoughts-from-a-shrunken-newsroom-on-transitions/.
CNN. 2012. "How CNN iReport works." July 2. Accessed July 23, 2013. http://ireport.cnn.com/blogs/ireport-blog/2012/07/02/how-cnn-ireport-works.
Cranford, Cynthia, Leah F. Vosko, and Nancy Zukewich. 2003. "Precarious employment in the Canadian labour market: A statistical portrait." *Just Labour: A Canadian Journal of Work and Society* 3: 6–22.
De Peuter, Greig, Nicole Cohen, and Enda Brophy. 2012. "Interns unite! (You have nothing to lose—literally)." *Briarpatch*, Nov. 9. Accessed July 23, 2013. http://

briarpatchmagazine.com/articles/view/interns-unite-you-have-nothing-to-lose-literally.

Dixon, Guy. 2012. "CBC cuts current affairs shows, 88 news jobs." *The Globe and Mail*, April 10.

Deuze, Mark. 2007. *Media work*. London: Polity.

Florida, Richard L. 2002. *The rise of the creative class: and How it's transforming work, leisure, community and everyday Life*. New York: Basic Books.

Gallagher, Margaret. 2001. *Why do so few women reach the top? Reporting on gender in journalism*. Cambridge, MA: Nieman Reports. Accessed July 23, 2013. http://www.nieman.harvard.edu/reportsitem.aspx?id=101542.

Greenfield, Rebecca. 2102. "Conde Nast's internship reforms show how bad the system really is." *The Atlantic Wire*, March 13. Accessed July 23, 2013. http://www.theatlanticwire.com/national/2012/03/conde-nasts-unpaid-internship-reforms-show-how-bad-system-really/49830/.

Heinrich, Jeff. 2012. "Leaving in a Huff: Huffington Post writers won't work for free." *National Post*, Jan. 31.

Hesmondhalgh, David. 2007. *The cultural industries*. Second edition. London: Sage.

Jagsi, Reshma, Kent A. Griffith, Abigail Stewart, Dana Sambuco, Rochelle DeCastro, and Peter A. Ubel. 2012. "Gender differences in the salaries of physician researchers." *Journal of the American Medical Association* 307 (22): 2410–2417.

Kperogi, Farooq A. 2011. "Cooperation with the corporation? CNN and the hegemonic cooptation of citizen journalism through iReport.com." *New Media & Society* 13 (2): 314–329.

Marx, Karl. 1867. *Capital: A critique of political economy*. vol. 1, pt. 6, chap. 21. Accessed July 23, 2013. http://www.econlib.org/library/YPDBooks/Marx/mrxCpA21.html.

McKercher, Catherine, and Vincent Mosco, eds. 2007. *Knowledge workers in the information society*. Lanham, MD: Lexington.

Media Report to Women. 2005. "Industry statistics." Accessed July 23, 2013. http://www.mediareporttowomen.com/statistics.htm.

Mosco, Vincent, and Catherine McKercher. 2008. *The laboring of communication*. Lanham, MD: Lexington.

Murdock, Graham. 2002. "Back to work: cultural labour in altered times." In *Cultural work: understanding the cultural industries*, edited by Andrew Beck, 15–35. London: Routledge.

Ottawa Citizen. 2012. "Freelance writer agreement."

Parsons, Greg, and Kathryn McMullen. 2009. "Trends in university graduation 1992 to 2007." Statistics Canada. Accessed July 23, 2013. http://www.statcan.gc.ca/pub/81-004-x/2009005/article/11050-eng.htm.

Perlin, Ross. 2011. *Intern Nation: How to earn nothing and learn little in the brave new economy*. London: Verso.

Professional Writers Association of Canada (PWAC). 2006. *Professional writers survey: a profile of the freelance writing sector in Canada*. Toronto: Professional Writers Association of Canada.

Rosen, Jay. 2006. "The people formerly known as the audience." *Pressthink* blog, June 27. Accessed July 23, 2013. http://archive.pressthink.org/2006/06/27/ppl_frmr.html.

Ross, Andrew. 2009. *Nice work if you can get it: life and labor in precarious times*. New York: New York University Press.

Smith, Erica. 2008–present. *Paper Cuts* blog. http://newspaperlayoffs.com.

van Voris, Bob. 2012. "Huffington Post bloggers' suit against AOL is dismissed." *Bloomberg News*, March 30.

Vlieg, Janet. 1999. "How far have Women come in journalism?" *Media Magazine*, Spring.
Walker, Michael. 2011. "Why should writers work for no pay?" *Los Angeles Times*, April 1.
Writers Bureau. 2012. "Writing careers." Accessed July 23, 2013. http://www.writersbureau.com/writing/writing-careers.htm.
Yi, Robin H. P., and Craig T. Dearfield. 2012. *The status of women in the US media 2012*. New York: Women's Media Center.

14 Flight as Fight
Re-Negotiating the Work of Journalism

Margareta Melin

I'm just too critical to stay in the newsroom. And I'm fed up with [Kevin] taking all the good stories. (Frances, radio journalist, 1992)

I didn't like the politics of the newsroom. That's why I left. It's a male dominated area. It's a middle-class, bright grammar school boys-culture, and if you're not into sexist and racist jokes, and don't like cricket, you've had it. Then you're isolated. (Ruth, TV-reporter, 1992)

14.1 INTRODUCTION

Research about journalism and media workers usually focuses on those that work in newsrooms. If the focus is on media/news institutions or organisations, or newsrooms, it is those working within these that receive attention. Equally natural, if the focus is on the sociology of journalists, it seems reasonable to use media organisations as sample-frames to find journalists for a study.

In this chapter I want to focus on those journalists that leave the newsroom, and in some instances leave journalism, in order to cope, whether it is to cope with life in general or to cope with journalism itself. I will address issues of how women (and others) use the tactic of flight to re-negotiate their professional conditions in the field of journalism.

14.2 SITUATING MY KNOWLEDGE

Before discussing the analysis of my results, I first need to briefly say something about my methods and the theoretical framework within which I analyse my results. The citations starting off this chapter are voices from two of the thirty-three journalists I interviewed and observed in 1992, 1998 and 2002. They were women and men, Scots and English, working in different media and covering different beats. The interviews were informal and discussions ranged across a number of themes, although each interview started off with the question "Tell me the story of why you became a journalist". Observations were made in the journalists' newsrooms or workplaces. The aim was to study the UK journalism culture, with its doxa and everyday practices, and the changing nature of British journalism. These interviews gave me an opportunity to see the changes in the news-production process, the media industry, and in journalism culture, from the professional—and personal—lives and career turns of some journalists. Now, ten years later, I interviewed the same journalists again. In this chapter I will show some first findings. Obviously, I cannot generalize based on interviews of thirty-three journalists, albeit made over a long period. I can, however, substantiate my findings with research results from other studies.

Having studied journalism for over twenty years means that not only journalism, but also the theoretical world of media studies, and indeed myself, have changed. I have walked several theoretical paths the past couple of decades and brought with me different ways to see and to question journalism. These led me to the crossroad between political economy, feminism and cultural study, where I have found a way to study journalism. Seeing journalism as culture signifies a theoretical standpoint (cf. Deuze 2005; Allan 2010). In order to find easier ways for studying journalism and news production, I have found the conceptual worlds of Pierre Bourdieu and Michel de Certeau useful.

14.3 WAR-LIKE PRACTICES OF EVERYDAY LIFE IN JOURNALISM

Both Bourdieu and de Certeau use the metaphor of war to describe the struggle between the dominating and the dominated. De Certeau (1984) distinguishes two ways of acting in war (like the fight for journalism). Strategy, he argues, is for the powerful, the dominating, those that have a place as a base for their power. Their place of power could be a physical property or theoretical places. Tactics, on the other hand, are the art of the dominated others. They have no place on which to rely so they need to rest on a clever utilisation of time. Just as a strategy is organised by the holders of power, a tactic is determined by the absence of power and limited by the possibilities of the moment. Open warfare against the powerful would only lead to defeat, so the weak seek out the weaknesses of the powerful and use deception, trickery and guerrilla warfare as tactics.

Central to Pierre Bourdieu's field theory is that players on the social field are positioned hierarchically. Their continuous permanent relations of inequality result in a struggle to master the game (of journalism). When entering into the field, journalists put on professional spectacles. These are perception-categories, or invisible structures that organise perceptions (Bourdieu 1998). What Bourdieu (2005) refers to are journalists' ways of seeing the world, thinking about reality, and thinking news. He terms this doxa: what we believe about the world and ourselves. It is thought patterns, language patterns, dress patterns, ways of acting, being, i.e. the way journalists talk, dress, interview, value news, organise news production. No one questions the doxa, as no one would even think of questioning it. Doxa is a kind of common sense. Doxa is, however, not unitary. Indeed, elite groups (of journalists) use strategies in their fight to define doxa, to define journalism. That is what opposition-groups challenge. They have what Bourdieu terms an allodoxa, a different, opposing way of seeing reality, which they try to augment. Thus, doxa is what is at stake in the fight in the field of journalism.

Unlike de Certeau, Bourdieu (2001) sees the gendered nature in this power struggle. The male-dominating fractions, that defend their status and doxa and places of power in the social field, do indeed use various strategies in their defence. One strategy is symbolic violence, which is used by men to keep women in place, and which results in sexual oppression and the legitimisation of domination.

14.3.1 Strategies

Bourdieu (1998) argues that journalism is doxic, that there are no struggles over what is journalism. I disagree. I found strong oppositional groups amongst the UK journalists I interviewed, particularly women journalists. The so-called "female turn" during the 1990s meant that the number of women journalists rose dramatically, in Britain from 15 per cent to around 30 per cent—and it is continuously increasing, although not yet reaching the magic number 33 per cent which supposedly brings feminine change about (Allan 2010). This increase of other groups created a response, and I found a number of strategies being used.

These strategies include screening who will become a journalist, being gatekeepers (social bankers in Bourdieu's terms), for example by employing the "right" kind of journalist or by setting up and deciding the curriculum of journalism courses. If new journalists from unwanted groups (like women or people of colour) entered, the infamous glass ceiling would put a stop to too powerful positions, guarded by the all-important social old-boys-network. Other strategies had more to do with the news organisation: the strict hierarchy and routinization allows for conflict ridden morning meetings, dispersion of (hard) status jobs to the dominant group (men) and low status "soft news" to women on the grounds that they are better at it because they are women. I found very much what I expected to find, given the plethora of other research within the area.[1]

These were, however, not strategies that the women journalists I interviewed found the most suppressive or problematic. To them it was the everyday work in the newsroom, where open symbolic violence was used to suppress and belittle female colleagues. Every woman I interviewed on all occasions gave witness to the sexist, racist and homophobic nature of the newsroom culture. Sports-talk, sexual jokes and innuendoes were used to keep women out of the core group of journalists, or to make them feel uncomfortable. A we–them culture was established in the newsroom, where "we" were the tough, professional guys that created a comradeship through their patter, banter and pints, and "them" were the women journalists that were told their place. The guys' banter worked as clear keep out signs. And this continued after hours in the pub (Melin-Higgins 2004, Melin 2008).

Table 14.1   The Dichotomised Gender Logic of Journalism

Masculine Journalism	Feminine Journalism
Public sphere/elites	Private/intimate sphere/everyday life
Male sources and perspectives	Female sources and perspectives
Distance/neutrality/objectivity	Intimacy/empathy/subjectivity
Autonomy ("professional criteria")	Audience orientation (the audience's needs/interests)

Source: Based on Djerf Pierre 2007b, 97.

Another strategy is the socially constructed black-and-whiteness of journalism. I argue that essentialism is not just a cultural feature, but is used as a strategy to put oppositional groups in positions of otherness. By creating a dichotomy, distinctions between those in power and other groups are upheld, like making women into women and men into journalists. Djerf Pierre (2007b) discusses this dichotomised gender logic of journalism (see Table 14.1). She points out that these perceptions exist in different places and at different times.

14.3.2   Tactics

In order to survive this strategic symbolic violence, and in order to actually remain in journalism, women (and other dominated groups) use a series of tactics. In fact, every single strategy is met resiliently by a tactic, as is graphically shown in Figure 14.1.

Many are the female journalists who did not get a job or promotion because of the old-boy's-network (Chambers et al. 2004). In my study I found that that creating a social network of one's own that served to give support was utterly necessary to survive the field if choosing a tactic that openly challenged the doxa (cf. Djerf Pierre 2007a; Delano 2003). So, Women in Journalism becomes a way to fight off the old-boy's-network.

Another strategy that had been turned on its head and used as tactics was the essentialist gender dichotomy. As I have shown, there are those who rejected being cast as a "female journalist", and avoided the entire essentialist dichotomy by stepping over the gendered barrier and entering into the domain of masculine journalism. Denying one's femininity, aggregating male capital and hexis, learning the rules of the game and playing it well, means securing a good position in the field (Chambers et al. 2004). The other tactic to meet the essentialist strategy was to play on femininity, play on acting or being the "sweetie-pie". The tactic was successful in that the women that played along with the gendered rules of the field managed to create a career for themselves often by choosing a niche that was part of the "pink/velvet ghetto" (Lachover 2005). Another response to the essentialist dichotomy-strategy was to fight for femininity. Women who chose this tactic wanted to create a revolution within

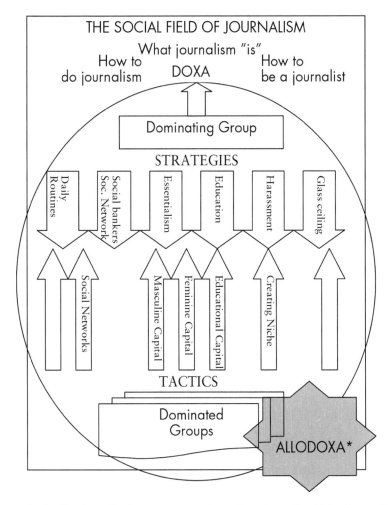

Figure 14.1 The interplay between strategies and tactics in the field of journalism. *Source*: Melin 2008, 221.

the field of journalism. Whilst in many cases agreeing with the essentialism of the gendered dichotomy, they tried to overturn it, and raise the status for feminine journalism. They tried to change the doxa.

14.4 FLIGHT

The tactic I am particularly interested in is the tactic of flight, of fleeing the newsroom in order to avoid the supressing strategies and patriarchal symbolic violence. Having heard the stories of sexism, racism and homophobia in the newsroom, I am not surprised that journalists want to leave. But there were other reasons. The stressfulness of the constant struggle to make deadlines was for some hard to take. Being a journalist and a mother is almost impossible in Britain. Other women left because they were harassed for their looks and considered too old for the TV screen. All these were reasons given to me, during the twenty years of interviews, for leaving the hub of the newsroom and seeking refuge in other parts of the media. There were those that chose to be a part-time producer rather than a hotshot foreign correspondent. Going freelance or working with web news were other options. This might today seem like a good deal, but in the 1990s and early 2000s these were low-status positions and very poorly paid. Five of the journalists I interviewed quit journalism altogether and went into PR or journalism education by 2002. The flight tactic could thus be seen as a tragic victimisation, of people having to leave the newsroom.

I do, however, argue that flight must not be seen as tragic. Fleeing the newsroom is tragic in the sense that the women who have opted for this often are forced by patriarchal structures, strategies and symbolic violence to do so. And indeed, for those two interviewees who became long-term ill and the two that died "on the job" from stress-related reasons, the structure and strategies of journalism caused personal tragedies. But one can also see the tactic of flight as survival instinct. It is a way of finding new usages of one's aggregated capital. Djerf Pierre (2007b) names this the "Strategy of Expansion". They seek out the empty spaces, the weaknesses of normal journalism, and use those to their advantage and create new genres and styles in un-gendered territory. They expand journalism. In de Certeau's (1994) eyes this is a truly creative guerrilla tactic. Not tragic at all, but rather very strong and creative.

14.4.1   Using Journalistic Capital

Leaving the newsroom, but still staying in journalism, was a solution for many, and a way of overcoming the dichotomised positioning of journalist on the one hand and woman/mother/person of colour/disabled on the other. Taking part-time low status jobs, or going freelance, were thus ways of beating both essentialist and newsroom strategies and managing to combine both professional and personal spheres, albeit with the cost of missing the newsroom buzz and the security and better pay of a regular journalism job. Rose, who worked as a foreign correspondent in 1992, as a journalist trainer in 2002, and as BBC manager in 2012, gives a voice to this:

> There's been time in my career when I think: "God, I've done this long enough". I left /the TV-news/ after the election in 1997 because I wanted to spend more time with my kids. And that's another issue.

Journalism and family life can be tricky, particularly hard for women. [...] Now I'm back working in journalism but in a different way. (Rose, interview in 2002)

Another way to see the flight-tactic of the men and women, who chose to work in PR or in journalism education, is that they might leave journalism, but still use their journalistic capital. Journalism courses are, thus, not only a new way (at least they were in 2002) of getting on in journalism for many women, but also a space to flee to the newsroom. Polly, who worked as a newspaper reporter in 1992 and as a journalism-lecturer in 1998 explains this:

I started at BBC radio as a trainee and a researcher. My contract wasn't renewed, though I know some funny things went on behind my back. Definitely sexist—all my fellow trainees, they were guys, stayed. [...] Also I was pregnant. [...] Now all I want is to go into academia and do a PhD. (Polly 1992)

I argue this makes journalism education into a very successful tactic for those that want to change journalism, as some of those that "flee" into education bring with them an allodoxic view of what journalism is, which in turn means the curriculum is discussed, fought over and changed. Thus, the increasing number of journalism students will be taught different ways of doing journalism (Melin 2008).

14.4.2   Finding Spaces to Do One's Job

If the tough culture of newsroom is a problem, some of the journalists I interviewed fought, or negotiated, for new spaces; new programmes, pages, sections, columns, beats, and even new media, like starting a magazine, a newspaper.

14.4.2.1   Finding a Niche

Above I discussed women using feminine hexis and capital to get a career in journalism, often by making do with working low status soft news. On the other hand, designated female spaces, like British Women's Page and Women's Hour, are examples where women have created their own niche inside existing news-media. These "pink/velvet ghetto" are often belittled, but as such are removed from the scrutinous eyes of the field-elite as they are deemed unimportant. Thus, they become spaces where these journalists are left in peace to get on with the job and their career. This tactic has not only been used by women journalists. There are examples amongst my interviewees of choosing to work with indie-music, the chemical industry or Scottish issues in England—all deemed low status, but of high interest to the journalists that chose them. The men and women that chose this tactic were all aware of the low status, but at the same time proud of their area. As Amanda puts it:

> Women's section has though changed [. . .] the most of all kinds of news the past fifteen years/she sounded apologetic/. Now it's exciting. [. . .] Women's journalism is to inform and be polemical. To give controversial news. Equality wouldn't have a chance if not some serious women journalists had discussed it. (Amanda, interviewed in 1992)

They did not raise conflicts or fight loudly for other beats, or for higher status. They got on unobtrusively. Thus they managed to create space and power over their own professional lives. Ailsa was quite aware of her choices and situation:

> Those aggressive feminists [never marry] get lonely and bitter, and they still won't get their copies in. I enjoy my job and my lifestyle, and don't care if some see me as a wee lassie. I still always get my copies accepted. [. . .] The Women's Own did focus-groups and that, and they found people want fashion, slimming and that. I mean, it still means an awful lot in journalism, despite people looking down their noses at it. And I actually don't care, after having worked as a news-journalist when I started in a weekly paper, and you know, it's not my scene. I was never going to be Scoop McGee. I think the thing about journalism, you know, it's for everyone, there are all aspects of journalism. (Ailsa, interviewed in 2002)

What I found over the ten years that lapsed between the interviews was that the choice of tactic seemed to be successful for these women who chose it. They had all advanced their careers—none of which ended up in mainstream journalism—and were very happy with them and with their private lives. The frustration and inner conflicts I met when speaking to other female journalists was absent in this group.

14.4.2.2   New Newsroom

There are also examples of the creation of alternative media. Two of my interviewees, Lilidh and Frances, were part of a co-operative women's group with negative experiences in traditional newsrooms. They started a feminist magazine *Harpies & Quinnes* (1992), with the specific aim to create a friendly and effective newsroom and a platform from which to spread news from a feminist perspective.

> *Harpies & Quinnes* is spare time and not paid. My task there is more managerial. I love it! Working with other women! We get things done

[. . .] there's not so much politics and playing with egos going on. It's more co-operative. (Lilidh, interviewed in 1992)

Another interviewee, Charles, set up a co-operative writers group supplying research and manuscripts for the radio and producing radio programmes, which they found were lacking in the BBC. One of the advantages of getting one's own space was the control over areas of interests—important content—and indeed the structures of the space. But these, more historic examples, are old news. They were resource-wise limited as it was and is expensive to print magazines, or make radio or television programmes. In 1994 *Harpies & Quinnes* went bankrupt and by 2002 Charles and Frances were back working in newsrooms and Lilidh was long-term ill.

14.5   FLEEING TO A NEW WORLD OF NEWS

When I started with my journalism studies in 1992 the World Wide Web (WWW) was to me the popular culture imperialism of Spiderman. The world of news media consisted of newspapers, television and radio. Every morning I read my regional morning paper and watched the news on TV at night. Today, I read news on the TV and watch TV on my mobile. Radio producers write news, newspapers broadcast news, and news is twittered and blogged by journalists, their sources and audience alike. The number of women in journalism exceeds the "magic number" 33 per cent. Even in Britain. How has this new world of news affected the thirty-three journalists I interviewed in 1992 and 2002?

The career-shifts of the interviewed journalists over the twenty-year span is shown in Table 14.2. Several things strike out while reading the table. Two-third of the journalists are still in work, all use their journalism capital in some form, and for all, the technological changes have had a large impact on their everyday work. Brian summarises these changes:

I think really the big change was the advent of building 24-hour news. When I first started, journalism was relatively easy. We had two or three deadlines a day. Then, first came late news, then breakfast news, then luchtime news, with several more deadlines during the day. Then along came 24-hour news and there is no such thing as a deadline. (Brian, interviewed in 2012)

Ten journalists work in traditional media newsrooms (including freelancers), eleven work in-house in newsrooms, management or other positions. Nine of the journalists work mainly with web-based news-tools, and fourteen work with journalism in traditional or new medium.

Table 14.2   The Career of 33 UK Journalists from 1992 to 2012

Journalist	Work in 1992	Work in 2002	Work in 2012
Ailsa	Tabloid paper, fashion editor	Freelance, feature and fashion	Director of a PR firm for fashion and lifestyle companies
Alsdair	Tabloid paper, crime reporter	Off work because of illness	Deceased?
Amanda	Broadsheet, editor of Women's Page	Freelance, long-term ill	Broadsheet, columnist
Bob	Broadsheet, general reporter	Broadsheet, political reporter	Broadsheet, chief Scottish political reporter
Brian	TV, editor home news	TV, administrator, assistant editor news gathering	Retired
Billy	Tabloid, crime reporter	Medically retired, heart problem and depression	Deceased?
Charles	Broadsheet, popular culture reporter	Broadsheet, arts columnist, radio presenter	Redundancy 2009, Internet radio DJ, sitcom writer
Dave	Tabloid, assistant editor	Tabloid, editor	Fired, on trial
Diana	Broadsheet, home affairs correspondent	Political magazine, senior reporter, home with child	Political magazine, senior reporter
Edward	TV, Scotland correspondent	TV, Scotland correspondent	Web production company, director
Elisabeth	Broadsheet, chief feature writer and radio presenter	Broadsheet, chief feature writer and radio presenter	Retired, broadsheet columnist, part-time
Flora	Radio, editor of Woman's Hour	Radio, management and production trainer	Broadcast, head of training and web management trainer, freelance
Frances	Radio, presenter, and feminist magazine reporter	Broadsheet, home correspondent, made redundant, then radio presenter	Freelance, podcaster, blogger, web journalist, broadsheet columnist, PhD student
Frank	ITV Scotland correspondent	Political party work	Broadcast chief economics correspondent

(continued)

Table 14.2 (continued)

Journalist	Work in 1992	Work in 2002	Work in 2012
Georgina	Radio, news reporter	Housewife with children, web reporter	Journalism lecturer
Henry	Tabloid editor	Retired, freelance	Not found
Iona	Freelance court correspondent	Housewife, home with child	Not found
Jack	Tabloid, general reporter	Broadsheet, editor	Web media company, executive director
Jenny	Broadsheet, social affairs Correspondent	Housewife, home with children	Internet magazine and communications company, executive editor
Kevin	BBC radio, political and industrial correspondent	BBC radio, chief political reporter, later deceased	Deceased
Liam	ITV Scotland reporter	Not found	Freelancer, politics
Lilidh	Tabloid, general news reporter, and feminist magazine reporter	Long term-ill	Trade union, communications officer, social welfare issues
Magnus	Broadsheet, chemistry correspondent	Broadsheet, foreign correspondent 1998, PR communication officer 2002	Financial web news, vice president
Martin	Broadsheet, Scotland correspondent	Tabloid, political correspondent	Tabloid, political editor
Mary	Retired, broadsheet, editor of Women's page	Deceased	Deceased
Mary-Anne	Broadsheet, department editor of Women's Page	Writer	Published author, university lecturer in creative writing, USA
Maureen	TV, news correspondent	TV, news correspondent, retiring	Retired, media trainer for politicians
Nicholas	TV, news presenter	TV, presenter, current affairs programme	Retired, part-time TV presenter of popular shows
Polly	Broadsheet, feature writer and women's columnist	Journalism lecturer, PhD student	Deceased

(continued)

Table 14.2 (continued)

Journalist	Work in 1992	Work in 2002	Work in 2012
Ray	ITV Scotland, camera man	Freelance news photographer	News agency, photographer
Rose	TV, editor of foreign news	TV, foreign correspondent, webnews and home with child	TV, senior manager
Ruth	Radio, producer	TV, senior producer	TV Journalism college, trainer
Steve	TV, general reporter	TV, general news reporter	TV, manager

Note: All journalists have been anonymised and given fictional names. Deceased? means that I have found an obituary with the journalist's name, but not found verifying evidence.

14.5.1 Space Control

Numbers only say so much. Of the ten journalists still working in newsrooms, five are women. Of the eleven working in traditional news medium, four are women. The reality behind these figures is that the women working within newsrooms are either freelance columnists or have found an in-house niche to work from. The other two women working in-house in traditional news medium are in management. The women journalists I interviewed say that working in a traditional newsroom is almost impossible for women in the long run, unless you find a niche in a medium or a perceived non-important part of a medium. The strategic symbolic violence used by (male) colleagues wears you down over time.

As I argued earlier, this must not be seen as victimisation. The journalists I interviewed are indeed resourceful, and use their capitals cleverly to their advantage and use a wide variety of tactics, which can be changed depending on what their particular situation demands at a particular time. Of the nineteen journalists I interviewed that de Certeau would have termed powerless, only three kept the same tactic over the first ten-year period of my study and only one (retired but still active) in the 2012 study. Furthermore, women have the most widespread careers. They have all changed directions in their careers over the course of the two decades I have followed them, but not in the straight line of their male colleagues. New technology has made it easier to find tactics which suit journalists' personal life as well as creating possibilities to stay in the field of journalism (if not necessarily in the newsroom) and to fight for their convictions, whether it is through management, journalism education, novel writing, blogging or PR.

Some of the journalists were quite aware of these changes and the choices they had made. Amanda and Diana, the two women that had chosen to still work in newsrooms, had made this choice based on the opportunities new technology created, which made it possible for them to work full time, but half of that time from their homes, quite some distance away from their newsroom. This, and choosing what medium (political magazine) and what beat (women's issues) to work with, have been necessary conditions for their choice of still working in traditional news media.

Others left news journalism. Lilidh, for example, who was long-term ill in 2002, after having been harassed by colleagues when working as a tabloid-news reporter, found her way back to the field of journalism in a broader sense. She now works as a communication officer, writing for a trade union web-magazine. Ruth left a radio news programme to avoid the sexism and racism she experienced, and for nearly twenty years worked as a television producer. She found, however, the constant reorganising and redirection tiresome and now works as a journalism college trainer.

Another example is Frances. Over the years she has cleverly used different tactics, according to what best suited her different life-situation. She started off as a tough radio reporter, trying her best to be Scoop McGhee and downing pints with the rest of the guys. Whilst feeling that she was been held back because she was a woman, she decided to start a feminist magazine with some female colleagues. This lasted two years, after which the production costs became too high. Frances became a broadsheet journalist, trying her best to increase space and status for the subjects she believed important. Eventually, the fight for space became too much, so she chose to find her own spaces. She is thus a good example of one of my main findings, namely that with today's new technology, a number of new tools and new alternative spaces have turned up on the media landscape, making it cheaper and easier than ever before to produce media. It is possible for those with an allodoxic approach to journalism, like Frances, to create their own news, set their own agenda and their own version of reality through their own medium.

New technology opens up new opportunities, but also create new demands. An individual journalist can no longer rely on doing one type of journalism (like writing), but must use a multitude of tools. Frances discusses this:

> New media have transformed the way I work as a journalist. I use Twitter and Facebook to proof ideas before writing columns and ask for examples if there's something specific. I search blogs to see what's rumbling on subjects as one part of research. I often tweet up to 20–30 times during important events and conferences instead of saving up the comment till later. And we use the interest generated by a regular online presence to distribute a weekly podcast—bypassing the vetting procedures (and income) of working through a conventional broadcaster. I suppose new media has encouraged me to develop a distinct identity larger than the sum of my journalistic parts. (Frances, interviewed in 2012)

Frances now runs a feminist web-magazine, a feminist blog, a pod radio and a web magazine for women journalists in Africa. By tactical career choices, she and other journalists I interviewed who were suffering from the strategies to do with the newsroom like routines and harassment, have managed to create better working conditions. They have, however, faced other strategies.

14.5.2   Controlled Space

All strategic actions get a tactical response, and all guerrilla warfare and tactics get strategic response (de Certeau 1984). Although I see the opportunities new technology brings to those searching for tactics to stay or advance in the field of journalism, I am in no way blind to a strategic political, economic and cultural backlash.

As the journalists I interviewed now are in their 50s to 70s, they have managed to make very successful careers. Indeed, several are amongst the most noted journalists in Britain. They have followed the traditional career ladder—starting off as a reporter, becoming correspondent and then ending up either as a columnist or a manager/editor. With new technology, there seems now to be a new path, that of starting up or heading production companies or web-based companies. And this reveals new strategies, or rather old strategies using new technology. Looking again at the careers of the remaining twenty-five active journalists (Table 14.2) the following is evident:

- Women have made the most widespread career-choices.
- Women work in the most widespread beats.
- Only women work as journalist educators.
- Only men still work with traditional political or economic news.
- Five men and four women work as media managers.
- Only men work with the economic side of media organisations.
- In 2002 only women worked with web news, in 2012 five out of nine journalists working mainly web-based news are men.

In the analysis of my 1992 to 2002 studies (Melin 2008) I found social bankers using symbolic violence and essentialism to put a stop to others' unwanted careers. In my 2012 study this is more evident than ever, although all the remaining thirteen female journalists have reached far in their career. To explain this apparent discrepancy, I need to apply Djerf Pierre's (2007b, see Table 14.1) gendered dichotomy and look at its political-economic consequences. She argues that the essentialist journalism dichotomy remains, although what is on either side of the gender demarcation line changes.

From the interviews I have learnt that traditional hard news still has the highest status, thus only men still work with traditional news and women try to find other paths to remain in the field. There are, however, other areas that have crossed the line. Ten to fifteen years ago, working with web news had fairly low status in the UK. Web newspapers or webcast were in budding forms. Blogs were static, non-interactive websites. Producers of web content were still only producers, and women worked the web from home as a way to have a family or to avoid the newsroom (Melin 2008). With the technological upsurge, web news production today has completely different political and economical conditions. That also means that the cultural positioning of web-news has changed, as well as its status on the field. It is no longer a low-status, part time job that you can do from home. It thus attracts other kinds of journalists. Men have entered the field and amongst my interviewees dominate the dominant web positions.

There are also economic sides to this status equation. Despite the infamous glass ceiling, women have increased in media management positions, and amongst the journalists I interviewed there are just about as many women as men in leading positions. As Djerf Pierre (2007a) shows, however, women tend to take the lower status management positions, whereas men take those that give most power, ergo controlling economy. This is also true amongst my interviewees: men working mainly with web news do so as executive directors, whereas women produce web news.

Money comes into digital media in many ways. Several of my interviewees, who talked about leaving the newsroom, said that working digitally enabled them to work with what they found interesting and important. Feminist issues were mentioned by most of the women doing this. To work as a journalist, however, one has to make a living. Whilst Lilidh has to work as a communication officer and Frances has to lecture to make a living, despite being famous journalists, Ailsa manages to live very well off her web company with her fashion blog. She does web PR for lifestyle companies (like bridal shops and up-market hairdressers) and provides wedding advice. In 1992 she was aware that she got her copies in, and today she gets the money.

14.6 FIGHT AS FLIGHT

In this chapter I have discussed the tactics of those journalists who have left the newsroom in order to re-negotiate their careers in the British field of journalism. As base for this discussion I have interviews conducted with thirty-three UK journalists in 1992, 1998, 2002 and 2012 and I have used concepts from Pierre Bourdieu and Michel de Certeau to analyse them.

My main arguments are, first, that there is a discernible power-struggle in British journalism and that this is permeated by a gender logic. The field of journalism is defended and challenged through an interplay between strategies used by dominant media players and tactics used by those fighting for a place in journalism. Thus, these vary over time. This means that in order to stay in the field of journalism, individual journalists choose different ways of fighting back symbolic violence dependent on what best suits their private and professional situations.

My second argument is that the tactic of flight has been very successful. Feeling that one has to leave the newsroom to manage privately or professionally should not necessarily be regarded in terms of victimisation. Finding new means to do journalism and new paths to a career in the field can be strong and creative tactics of finding new usages of one's aggregated (journalism) capital. Working with journalism in new ways can thus be means of creating your own space and your own newsroom. It means fighting through flight.

Fighting is a hard burden to carry alone, and my interviews show that those most successful with their flight tactic have fought together with colleagues. Setting up a political web-magazine with political interested colleagues like Jenny, or starting an indie-pop pod-radio station with like-minded friends like Charles, or creating an African web-paper as a platform for African female colleagues like Frances, are successful stories. These have been made possible through the persistent use of networking, and fighting together through flight.

A fourth argument is that new technology has increased the number of possibilities flight has to offer. Working from home, setting up a blog, web newspaper, podcast, or production company have been made easier—and possible—through new digital technology.

In order to avoid conspiracy theories involving a patriarchal, capitalist media elite, it is easy to over-emphasise positive sides of new developments, like the increase in number of women, or the opportunities of new technologies. One must not forget that the field of journalism is not an insulated island, but exists in the larger (British) social space, which means that journalism doxa and strategies used are reflections of the more general (British) political, economical and cultural values (Bourdieu 1993, 1998).

And one pertinent question remains: Where is the money in it? Ailsa, the fashion reporter, who deliberately used her blond looks as career leverage, now a lifestyle blogger, has become the financially most successful journalist of all those I interviewed.

NOTES

1. Some references are Chambers et al. 2004; de Bruin and Ross 2003, Hesmondhalgh 2006, Allan 2010.

REFERENCES

Allan, Stuart. 2010. *News culture*. Maidenhead: Open University Press.
Bourdieu, Pierre. 1993. *The field of cultural production*. Cambridge: Polity Press.
———. 1998. *On television*. New York: New Press.

———. 2001. *Masculine domination*. Cambridge: Polity.

———. 2005. "The political field, the social science field and the journalistic field." In *Bourdieu and the journalistic field*, edited by Rodney Benson and Erik Neveu, 29–47 Cambridge: Polity.

de Bruin, Marjan, and Karen Ross, eds. 2004. *Gender and newsroom culture. Identities at work*. Cresskill, NJ: Hamtpon Press.

de Certeau, Michel. 1984. *The practice of everyday life*. Berkeley, CA: University of California press.

Chambers, Deborah, Linda Steiner, and Carole Fleming. 2004. *Women and journalism*. London: Routledge.

Delano, Anthony. 2003. "Women journalists: What's the difference?" *Journalism Studies* 4 (2): 273–286.

Deuze, Mark. 2005. "What is journalism? Professional identity and ideology of journalists redonsidered." *Journalism* 6 (4): 442–464.

Djerf Pierre, Monika. 2007a. "Medieeliten (Media-elite)." In *Maktens kön (Gendered power)*, edited by Anita Göransson, 301–324. Falun: Nya Doxa.

———. 2007b. "The gender of journalism. The structure and logic of the field in the twentieth century." *Nordicom Review*, Jubilee Issue: 81–104.

Hesmondhalgh, David. 2006. *Media production*. Maidenhead: Open University Press.

Lachover, Einat. 2005. "The gendered and sexualized relationship between Israeli women journalists and their male news sources." *Journalism* 6 (3): 291–311.

Melin-Higgins, Margareta. 2004. "Coping with journalism. Gendered newsroom culture." In *Gender and newsroom culture*, edited by Marjan De Bruin and Karen Ross, 197–222. Cresskill, NJ: Hamtpon Press.

Melin, Margareta. 2008. *Gendered journalism cultures. Strategies and tactics in the fields of journalism in Britain and Sweden*. Göteborg: JMG, Göteborgs universitet.

15 Marx is Back, but Will Knowledge Workers of the World Unite?
On the Critical Study of Labour, Media and Communication Today

Vincent Mosco

15.1 INTRODUCTION: MARX RETURNS

The Bearded One has rarely looked better. Businessweek (September 14, 2011)

The global economic crisis that filled the headlines beginning at the end of 2008 led to an immediate resurgence of popular interest in the works of Karl Marx. Those who had made use of his contribution questioned whether Marx had ever left, but that was beside the point, as the media were filled with anecdotal accounts of strange sightings and even stranger sound bites. The *Times* of London led the charge on October 21, 2008, when, as capitalism appeared to be crumbling, the normally stodgy newspaper declared in a headline: "Marx is Back". The *Times* of India wrote about "Marx in the time of pink slips" (Saxena 2008). *Das Kapital* rose up the bestseller list in Germany and, across the border, Nicholas Sarkozy, never one to miss a photo opportunity, was snapped leafing through a copy. Even Pope Benedict was quoted as praising Marx's "great analytical skill" (Hunt 2011). Not to be outdone, the Archbishop of Canterbury praised Marx for demonstrating that "capitalism became a kind of mythology", and went on to assert that its boosters were engaging in nothing short of "idolatry" (Gledhill 2008). This strange dalliance with the theorist of revolution continued well into 2011 as evidenced by a story in *Bloomsberg Businessweek*, which declared in "Marx to Market" that "The Bearded One has rarely looked better" (September 14, 2011). Indeed a headline in Canada's leading national newspaper declared that it was "Springtime for Marx" (Renzetti 2011). Two years later, a full five years after the economic cataclysm, the *Guardian* newspaper restated the theme in an article whose title says it all: "Why the ideas of Karl Marx are more relevant than ever in the 21st century" (Sunkara 2013).

Marxist scholars, accustomed to toiling in relative obscurity, found themselves courted by mainstream media to explain these developments. The cover of *Foreign Policy* magazine featured an article by the editor of the annual *Socialist Register* called "Thoroughly Modern Marx" (Panitch 2009). Invited to lunch with George Soros, the now deceased Marxist historian Eric Hobsbawn worried about whether he would have to tiptoe around radical talk, only to have one of the world's leading capitalists admit that Marx "discovered something about capitalism 150 years ago that we must take notice of" (Renzetti 2011).

One can certainly make too much of all this Marx talk. As government bailouts calmed the markets, the homage to Marx has diminished a bit. But it still resonates enough to turn attention to the relevance of Marx's thought for communication studies.

15.2 BUT WHICH ONE?

No thinker in the nineteenth century has had so direct, deliberate, and powerful an influence on mankind as Karl Marx (Berlin 1970, 1)

The world would not be in such a snarl, had Marx been Groucho instead of Karl (Berlin 2005, 489)

One of the first thoughts on facing the prospect of writing about Marx is to wonder about which of the many persona of Marx one should emphasise. It is clear that today's media care about Marx the political economist and revolutionary because he provided at least some food for thought about what was for many the shocking meltdown of financial markets and the deepening fears for the future of capitalism. It is certainly understandable that one would document the importance of *this* Marx, the Marx of *Capital* and of political economy, for understanding global communication. Yet there is another Marx not unrelated to the first whose writing about culture and ideology featured in *The German Ideology*, *The Economic and Philosophical Manuscripts*, and other works of the younger Marx have inspired analysis and critique in cultural studies. It is not an exaggeration to conclude that the Marx of political economy and of cultural studies form pillars of critical communication study.

Nevertheless, an exclusive emphasis on this bifurcated "young Marx/culture-old Marx/political economy" risks missing at least two other key elements of Marx that are vital to contemporary communication studies. Indeed, although there are many ways to divide Marx, one particularly useful one is to see him in four parts—and no, this does not mean Groucho, Harpo, Chico and Zeppo. In addition to the Marx of political economy and the Marx of cultural studies, there is the Marx of his notebooks the *Grundrisse* and the work of Marx the professional journalist. Indeed although Marx practiced journalism throughout his life, both the *Grundrisse* and the best of Marx's journalism bridged the critical period in time between the earlier and later years of his career.

15.3   THE *GRUNDRISSE*

What has come to be called the *Grundrisse* is actually a collection of seven notebooks written over the period 1857 to 1858, midway between the *Manifesto* and the first volume of *Capital*. They were produced in the midst of one of capitalism's first great economic crises, certainly its first crisis of overproduction. The notebooks have been depicted conventionally, by Martin Nicolaus (1973), as the precursor to *Capital*. They also have been described less conventionally by Nick Dyer-Witheford as "the delirious notebooks" that "Marx used to prophesy a moment when capital's development would depend not on the direct expenditure of labour power in production but rather on the mobilization of social and scientific knowledge".[1]

There are good reasons to see the *Grundrisse* as anticipating key arguments in *Capital* and in other later works. But it also explores themes that Marx never had the time to develop in a sustained fashion and some of these have been taken up in contemporary Marxist scholarship. As he would come to argue in *Capital*, Marx acknowledges the contribution of technology and especially that of new communication media like the telegraph for the expansion of global capitalism. For Marx,

> Capital by its nature drives beyond every spatial barrier. Thus the creation of the physical conditions of exchange—of the means of communication and transport the annihilation of space by time—becomes an extraordinary necessity for it. Only in so far as the direct product can be realized in distant markets in mass quantities in proportion to reductions in the transport costs, and only in so far as at the same time the means of communication and transport themselves can yield spheres of realization for labour, driven by capital; only in so far as commercial traffic takes place in massive volume—in which more than necessary labour is replaced—only to that extent is the production of cheap means of communication and transport a condition for production based on capital, and promoted by it *for that reason*. (1973, 524)

This passage captures the duality of communication in capitalism. Communication contributes to the commodification of all productive forces and also becomes a commodity in its own right. In the process, communication technology is used as a key tool, alongside the means of transportation, in the spatial expansion of capitalism, what we now euphemistically call globalization. At another point in this work, Marx makes clear that commodification and spatialisation are intimately connected to the process of structuration and the development of social relations, including new forms of communication:

> Not only do the objective conditions change in the act of reproduction, e.g., the village becomes a town, [. . .], but the producers change too, in that they bring out new qualities in themselves, develop themselves in production, transform themselves, develop new powers and ideas, new modes of intercourse, new needs and new language. (1973, 494)

These ideas are central to developing a Marxist theory of communication. They both build upon the early work and prepare the way for *Capital*. But the *Grundrisse* is much more than a way station on the long march to *Capital*, a point missed by one of the first scholars to bring the *Grundrisse* to an English-speaking world. The critical difference between this work and *Capital* is not the difference between the creative display of a work in progress and a fully formed creation, as Nicolaus maintains. Rather, the *Grundrisse* is, however dishevelled or even delirious, a substantive creation in its own right and a touchstone for vital developments in critical communication research. It contains ideas that *Capital* never got around to addressing but which matter considerably to scholarship and politics today.

As Marx describes it, the process of ever more deeply commodifying labour, including both intelligence and affect, demonstrates the need to expand these very human capacities. Capital no longer needed just the labourer as an appendage to a machine; it needed then and more than ever needs now the full "social body" of the individual. This passage and others like it acknowledge, at a remarkably early stage in capitalist development, the requirement for knowledge and affective labour. Capital needs to create the worker in its fullest subjectivity and then make it part of a process that channels that subjectivity into productivity. On the one hand such a process holds great potential for expanding capitalism into what we now call the knowledge, culture and information industries. On the other hand, controlling such labour is far more challenging than it is to control and channel manual labour, whose knowledge and affects were less consequential to meet the needs of industrial capitalism. In essence, the *Grundrisse* suggests that understanding the labour of knowledge, cultural and creative workers is vital to understanding the future of capitalism. What is capital's capacity to control these workers? What are their capacities for resistance? What is capital's ability to control their labour process and what is their ability to give it new direction? It is the very utopian quality of many of the notebooks' passages, ("the absolute working-out of his creative potentialities"), that makes it so powerful because it acknowledges just how important the stakes are in this struggle. It is not only a matter of understanding or even of dismantling capitalism, themes that fill the pages of *Capital*; it is also a matter of appreciating what is to be won, i.e., full control over one's humanity, including the creative potential of both intellect and affect.

15.4   MARX THE JOURNALIST

Scholars who teach about Marx in communication programmes focus exclusively on his theoretical writings and tend not to have much to say about Marx as a journalist. There are exceptions, particularly in the work of the critical journalism scholar Hanno Hardt (2001). On the other hand, professors who teach journalism practice exclude Marx completely. When academic journalism instructors do teach Marx, it is typically by equating his views with the totalitarian Marxism of Soviet and Chinese communism. This is unfortunate because there is a great deal to learn about journalism from an analysis of Marx's career as a professional communicator. A genuine appreciation of Marx the theorist is significantly diminished without consideration of his journalism because it was his concrete analysis of companies, governments and worker organisations that helped propel Marx to the analysis of capitalism. Indeed the eminent political philosopher Isaiah Berlin maintains that it was in the course of putting together a story in 1843 that Marx came to recognise "his almost total ignorance of history and principles of economic development" and leapt into the formal study of political economy (Berlin 1970, 12), Moreover, there is a close connection between Marx's *Grundrisse* and his journalism. Although he practiced journalism throughout his life, arguably Marx's best journalism came in the "middle" period of his life, as he was producing the notebooks. In essence, Marx's most interesting theoretical reflections on what we have come to call knowledge and immaterial labour were penned at about the same time that Marx engaged in his most mature work of knowledge labour as a practicing journalist.

It is a remarkable fact, one passed over all too casually, that one of the most profound social theorists of the nineteenth century, someone whose work continues to resonate powerfully today, also practiced the craft of journalism throughout his life. It is all the more stunning that his journalism takes up a full seven volumes of the fifty that comprise his collective works. Marx's journalism was most intensive in two periods, in the early years when, starting in his twenties he wrote for and soon thereafter took on the job of editor in chief of the *Rheinische Zeitung* and then again as writer and editor for the *Neue Rheinische Zeitung* in Prussia. He decided to pursue journalism because, like so many new PhDs then and today, he could not find an academic job, particularly under the stifling controls over the university that the Prussian government fiercely enforced. So he turned to journalism and used it to shine a light on the authoritarian political establishment of Prussia with courageous articles on censorship and freedom of the press. This landed Marx in constant difficulty with the authorities, ultimately leading to his banishment from Prussia. Marx produced his most mature journalism in the period of 1852 to 1862 when he became a foreign correspondent for the *New York Tribune*, a newspaper founded by Horace Greeley, a leader in the American anti-slavery movement. Greeley's goal was to counter the dominant sensationalist press with in-depth coverage of news and public affairs and he turned to Marx who wrote from his London home for the last half of his life.

Marx's journalism consistently follows principles that provide valuable lessons for any journalist, but especially for those learning about what it means to practice journalism. Moreover, they are principles that also began to emerge in the *Grundrisse* and which therefore might apply in varying degrees to all knowledge workers. Throughout his career in journalism Marx was consistently opposed to all forms of censorship and regularly made the case for free expression. Consider this assessment of a proposed new censorship law in Prussia:

> Censorship brings us all into subjection, just as in a despotism everybody is equal, if not in worth, then in unworthy; it's a kind of press freedom that wants to introduce oligarchy into the mind. At best, censorship declares a writer to be inconvenient, unsuitable within the boundaries of its domain. Freedom of the press proceeds on the presumption of anticipating world history, sensing in advance the voice of the people which alone has hitherto judged which writer was "competent" which "incompetent". (Marx 1974, 43)

When Americans like Thomas Jefferson wrote lines like this, they were venerated as champions of freedom. Marx typically does not enjoy the same response, not when he wrote them and not now. Harassed by the censor and ultimately the police and government officials, he was made to resign from the newspaper, which itself was disbanded by the authorities.

In addition to holding fast to the principles of free expression and of journalism as a political calling, Marx used his reporting to address critical issues facing the world. His was certainly not the journalism of on-scene reporting nor that of interviews with official and unofficial sources. On the latter, the well-known journalist Murray Kempton wrote of Marx: "Of all the illusions one brought to journalism, the one most useful to lose is the illusion of access to sources. [. . .] Persons privy to events either do not know what is important about them or, when they do, generally lie. . . . Marx had neither the temptation nor the opportunity of access" (cited in Ledbetter 2007, xix). Rather, his approach was to take an event in the news such as the second Opium War in China or the American Civil War and, using the most up-to-date material, address its political economic significance. In this respect he did not disappoint. His writing for the *Tribune* covered imperialism, including groundbreaking work on China and India, free trade, war and revolution in Europe, British politics and society, the changing world of economics and finance, and the slave question in America.

Marx's journalism provides vital evidence of his praxis and the unity of theoretical knowledge and practical experience that animated his life. It is also primed with examples of what journalism can be when it rises above the stifling conventions that capitalism requires in order to deliver audiences to advertisers. These include his complete commitment, whatever the cost, to freedom of expression and opposition to censorship, an unwavering belief in journalism as a political calling, and an unrelenting focus on the major issues facing the world. He has earned the assessment of one current biographer who observed that "[e]ven if he had done nothing else, Marx would deserve to be remembered as one of the great nineteenth-century journalists" (Wheen 2007, xiii).

15.5   WILL KNOWLEDGE WORKERS OF THE WORLD UNITE?

In his theoretical work and in his professional practice, Marx pointed to the importance of knowledge labour. The remainder of this chapter identifies current research and social struggle around this concept today. First, it takes up issues on the border of labour and language by examining the importance of viewing communication as mutually constituted out of these two components. Second, it addresses the boundary between workers and users by explaining the need to incorporate workers more directly into communication studies research. Third, it aims to integrate information labour with communication and cultural work. Finally, it points to the importance of bridging the divide that separates knowledge labour in rich countries from labour in poorer regions of the world. In doing so, it sheds light on why communication studies scholars and practitioners need to spend more time on the study of labour.

There are important conceptual grounds to pay more attention to labour. Communication can be defined as mutually constituted out of language and labour. That is, communication is not just the arrangement of symbols into an understandable form. It is also the result of work, specifically the intellective labour that conceives of the form that a particular arrangement of symbols should take and then carries out the operations that formally construct meaning. The phrase "mutual constitution" is used to assert that neither language nor labour has priority in the constitution of communication and to indicate that language and labour work on one another to create communication. It is important to emphasise this conceptual move because, particularly because the development of computers and the Internet, the focus has been on the linguistic side of the definition: language, discourse, meaning, content and the technological means of producing, distributing and consuming information. Hence, a "labouring of communication" is required to shift the definition's centre of gravity.

This shift does not require a radical rupture in theorising information because there is a subterranean stream of thought, a heterodox challenge to the dominant view of communication as discourse, that for nearly three hundred years has occupied social philosophy. Major figures include Henri

Saint-Simon (1952), who in the seventeenth and eighteenth centuries explored the expansion of practical knowledge that the new empirical sciences were yielding and the new class of technicians who were shaping it. In the nineteenth century, Karl Marx (1973) produced a vision of the General Intellect that documented how the expansion of knowledge worldwide, along with the rise of capitalism and of the working class, would propel social transformation. Later, the political economist Thorstein Veblen (1934) documented the enormous impact of professions like engineering and economics for the expansion of wealth and for the growth of a "leisure class" of mainly knowledge workers. Still later Daniel Bell (1973) documented the acceleration of informational and cultural labour, which would create the economic growth and cultural disjunctions that would challenge the capacity for political management. Alongside Bell, John Kenneth Galbraith (1985) spent part of his career as an economist and social critic examining the informational technostructure whose concentrated power and bureaucratic operation severely challenged the capacity for democracy and freedom. Finally, Harry Braverman (1974) renewed the spirit of labour studies by examining the new working class of clerical, informational and marketing labour that, in the 1960s was transforming not only the nature of work but also of wage-labour in general with important political consequences.

There are other works that fill this subterranean stream. It is hard to leave out C. Wright Mills (1959), who trained his sharp-eyed "sociological imagination" on the growth of a white-collar workforce and those who spearheaded the statistical analysis of informational labour (Fourastié 1954, Machlup 1962, Porat 1977). But the most important point to keep in mind here is that their work, although read, constituted a heterodox vision for communication studies. It suggested, sometimes forcefully, sometimes gently, that dominant models of communication needed to take into account labour and the workers whose jobs were increasingly made up of the production, distribution and exchange of information.

My research on labour (Mosco and McKercher 2008) joins a contemporary stream of thought led by the work of Ursula Huws (2003), whose research on the growth of a gendered "cybertariat" brought attention to the factory-like qualities of the contemporary digital workplace. This also includes works by Andrew Ross (2009) on the rise of informational "permatemps", the regimented hourly workers in today's knowledge-creation centres; Dan Schiller (2000) on digital capitalism; Nick Dyer-Witheford (1999) whose conception of "cyber-Marx" updated class struggle for a world of computers; Michael Denning (1996) who writes on the "labouring of culture"; and those international scholars like Carol Upadyha and A. R. Vasavi (2009), Jack Linchuan Qui (2009) and Yu Hong (2011), whose work illuminates how knowledge works in the networked worlds of India and China.

It is important for information scholars to travel down this subterranean stream, but not just for the intellectual satisfaction of uncovering the labouring of the field's history. This has important practical significance as well, particularly in this time of economic upheaval. If the dot.com and banking bubbles taught us anything, it is that the key question facing us today is not: What will be the next new thing?—as in the smartphone, social networking software or some other version of the digital sublime (Mosco 2004). Rather, it is more likely: Will information or knowledge workers of the world unite?

There are three cogent reasons for concentrating on knowledge workers. First, as nations become more reliant on the wealth produced by informational as opposed to agricultural and industrial work, the labour of knowledge workers takes on greater economic significance. Second, as some knowledge worker struggles have already demonstrated, knowledge workers are better equipped with the communication skills to carry out labour struggles (Mosco and McKercher 2006). Finally, the study of knowledge workers is especially important for the praxis of scholars who all too often view themselves as separate from the labouring classes, including fellow knowledge workers. As a result, opposite conventional research that tends to view workers as a dependent variable whose fate is determined by business, technology and government, research should concentrate on worker agency or what workers are doing about the many challenges they face.

Knowledge workers have certainly begun to explore new ways to increase labour's power. This is especially the case in the information technology and knowledge sectors, which provide the equipment that makes globalization possible, and the production and distribution of the ideas that make it work (Mosco and McKercher 2008). One approach is to pursue trade union convergence or mergers, designed strategically to restructure labour unions along much the same lines as the corporations that employ their members. There is considerable research on the value of merger or convergence among trade unions, including in the communication and information industries (Batstone 1984; Katz 1997; Mosco and McKercher 2008; Mosco et al. 2010). Convergent unions like the Communications Workers of America (CWA) or the Communications, Energy and Paperworkers Union of Canada (CEP) bring together workers in what were once independent industries—newspapers, telecommunications, sound recording, broadcasting—but are now part of cross-media conglomerates. In 2012 the unions representing workers in the entertainment industries, the Screen Actors Guild and the American Federation of Television and Radio Artists, agreed after decades of conflict, to unite and thereby better defend their interests against media conglomerates in Hollywood. These unions also recognise that it is not just the boundaries between employers that have become blurred; the boundaries between what were once distinct forms of work have also been obscured through the spread of digital technology. Labour convergence, therefore, is seen as an appropriate response to technological and corporate convergence (McKercher 2002; Swift 2003; Bahr 1998).

A second approach is to create non-traditional worker organisations, which draw into the labour movement people who cannot or will not join a traditional trade union. Such groups provide a range of services and support for workers, their families and their communities but do not engage in collective bargaining. In North America, they are particularly prominent in the information arena (Mosco and McKercher 2008).

It is understandably difficult to take seriously these suggestions that we should focus on new forms of labour organising, especially in North America, because these are not the best of times for organised labour. However, the growth of trade union convergence that, for example, has brought together unions from across the communication sectors in North America, is creating some grounds for optimism. To a degree, the unions see these actions as defensive, or as ways of protecting their members. But, significantly, they also see labour convergence as an attempt to take advantage of synergies brought about by growing convergence in the nature of their work (Bahr 1998). Because these unions represent workers who are increasingly involved in producing for a converging electronic information services arena, they see improved opportunities for organising and bargaining. In essence, converging technologies and converging companies have led workers to come together across the knowledge industry (Mosco and McKercher 2008) and across national borders in the form of global trade union federations such as the Union Network International which represents knowledge worker unions that are breaking down divides between workers in rich and poor nations (Mosco and Lavin 2009). The global expansion of knowledge worker unions has certainly come at the right time, because worker exploitation has grown in Asia, including in the sprawling call centre business of India where workers have built ties to tech workers (Stevens and Mosco 2010) and in the hardware fabrication plants of China where workers who produce products for Apple and other tech firms have demonstrated great courage and resolve.

It is uncertain just how far the urge to merge or the convergence movement will take trade unions in the communication, knowledge and cultural industries. Will it bring back the idea of One Big Union, once popular a century ago with the Knights of Labour and Industrial Workers of the World? Can it expand democracy and citizen engagement by empowering a segment of society that has declined over the past three decades? Is it a genuine new start for labour or a last gasp?

A second response to the crisis in organised labour is the formation of worker associations or worker movements that provide benefits to workers without formally negotiating collective agreements. These have been especially visible in the high tech sector, where union organising has been especially difficult. Worker associations are particularly prominent among part-time permanent workers who are difficult to organise by traditional unions because they typically work for an employment agency, not the high tech company itself. Such is the case in California's Silicon Valley, where fully 40 per cent of workers are employed in non-standard ways and in Microsoft's territory in the Pacific Northwest, which gave rise to the term "Permatemp" or permanent temporary worker, so named because they work full time, but on hourly contracts that contain practically no benefits or overtime pay. Among the goals of these associations are portable benefits for a highly mobile workforce, lifelong

training, job placement, providing assistance to individual workers, dissemi-
nation of information to workers and offering health care plans to workers
who are not eligible for employer-paid benefits.

Two types of such associations feature significantly in the knowledge
sector, those that represent technology-intensive workers and those that
primarily produce content, including cultural workers. Perhaps the leading
example and model of the former is WashTech, an offshoot of the CWA in
the Seattle high-tech industry formed by disgruntled Microsoft permatemps
who were successful in a legal action against the company for salary and
benefits denied them because they were placed in the temporary worker
category (Brophy 2006; Rodino-Colocino, 2007).

Worker associations are also increasingly prominent among content or
cultural producers, such as The Freelancers Union, a national non-profit
organisation that was founded in 1995 to provide benefits to people working in the New York City electronics district known as Silicon Alley. It now
counts over 170,000 members in all fifty US states. The Graphic Artists
Guild–representing people who work in illustration, graphic design, photography, cartooning, web design, multimedia, and other forms of design—
combines elements of a professional association with trade unionism. The
National Writers Union that participated in the early meetings that founded
WashTech, gives members advice on freelance contracts and on asserting
or protecting copyright. It also runs a job hotline and a campaign to get
employers to hire union writers. In Canada, the Communications, Energy
and Paperworkers union has organised a freelance writers' union, working
in co-operation with the Professional Writers Association of Canada.

Finally, building on the freelance writers' movement and demonstrating
that practically every form of new media, from the telegraph to the Internet,
has given rise to labour agitation, bloggers are beginning to join forces against
exploitive employers like the Huffington Post and in support of providing
material benefits often denied to bloggers. It is difficult to say whether these
social movement worker organisations will be able to sustain their ability to
help communication workers in the long run. This will depend on the ability of technology and content workers to join together across the hardware-
software divide. It will also depend on the ability of the digital workforce to
build ties to social media consumers who increasingly give away their labour
and information on their identities and choices to companies like Facebook
(Scholz 2012). Finally, it will also depend on the extent to which knowledge
workers can join forces with other global movements such Occupy to turn a
global labour movement into a global political movement.

NOTES

1. "Faculty Member Profile: Nick Dyer-Witheford," Western University, accessed
   July 23, 2013, http://www.fims.uwo.ca/peopleDirectory/faculty/fulltimefaculty/
   full_time_faculty_profile.htm?PeopleId=3667; see also Piccone 1975.

REFERENCES

Bahr, Morton. 1998. *From the telegraph to the internet.* Washington, DC: National Press Books.
Batstone, Eric. 1984. *Working order.* Oxford: Basic Blackwell.
Bell, Daniel. 1973. *The coming of post-industrial society.* New York: Basic Books.
Berlin, Irving. 2005. *The complete lyrics of Irving Berlin.* New York: Hal Leonard Corporation.
Berlin, Isaiah. 1970. *Karl Marx: His life and environment.* Oxford: Oxford University.
Braverman, Harry. 1974. *Labour and monopoly capital.* New York: Monthly Review.
Brophy, Enda. 2006. "System error: Labour precarity and collective organizing at Microsoft." *Canadian Journal of Communication* 31 (3): 619–638.
Denning, Michael. 1996. *The cultural front.* London: Verso.
Dyer-Witheford, Nick. 1999. *Cyber-Marx.* Chicago and Urbana: University of Illinois Press.
Fourastié, Jean. 1954. "Predicting economic changes in our time." *Diogenes* 2 (5): 14–38.
Galbraith, John Kenneth. 1985. *The new industrial state.* Fourth edition. Boston: Houghton Mifflin.
Gledhill, Ruth. 2008. "The archbishop of Canterbury speaks in support of Karl Marx." *Times Online*, September 24. Accessed July 23, 2013. http://www.the-times.co.uk/tto/faith/article2099665.ece
Hardt, Hanno. 2001. *Social theories of the press.* Lanham, MD: Rowman and Littlefield.
Hong, Yu. 2011. *Labor, class formation, and China's informationalized policy of economic development.* Lanham, MD: Lexington Books.
Hunt, Tristram. 2011. Why Marx was right by Terry Eagleton—review. The Guardian Online, http://www.guardian.co.uk/books/2011/may/29/why-marx-was-right-eagleton-review Accessed July 23, 2013.
Huws, Ursula. 2003. *The making of a cybertariat.* New York: Monthly Review.
Kapital Gains. 2008. *Times Online*, October 20. http://www.timesonline.co.uk/tol/comment/leading_article/article/4974195.ece
Katz, Harry C. 1997. "Introduction and comparative overview." In *Telecommunications: Restructuring work and employment relations worldwide*, edited by Harry C. Katz, 2–28. Ithaca: Cornell University Press.
Ledbetter, James, ed. 2007. *Karl Marx: Dispatches for the New York Tribune.* London: Penguin.
Machlup, Fritz. 1962. *The production and distribution of knowledge in the United States.* Princeton, NJ: Princeton University Press.
Marx, Karl. 1973. *The Grundrisse.* Translated by Martin Nicolaus. London: Penguin.
———. 1974. "Debates on freedom of the press and publication." In *Karl Marx on freedom of the press and censorship*, edited by Saul K. Padover, 3–47. New York: McGraw Hill.
McKercher, Catherine. 2002. *Newsworkers unite: Labor, convergence and North American newspapers.* Lanham, MD: Rowman & Littlefield.
Mills, C. Wright. 1959. *The sociological imagination.* New York: Oxford.
Mosco, Vincent. 2004. *The digital sublime.* Cambridge, MA: MIT Press.
———. 2009. *The political economy of communication.* Second edition. London: Sage.
Mosco, Vincent, and McKercher, Catherine. 2008. *The laboring of communication.* Lanham, MD: Lexington Books.

———. 2006. "Convergence bites back: Labour struggles in the Canadian communication industry." *Canadian Journal of Communication* 31 (3): 733–752.

Mosco, Vincent, Catherine McKercher, and Ursula Huws, eds. 2010. *Getting the message: Communications workers and global value chains.* London: Merlin Press.

Mosco, Vincent, and David Lavin. 2009. "The labouring of international communication." In *Internationalizing Media Studies*, edited by Daya Thussu, 147–162. London: Routledge.

Nicolaus, Martin. 1973. "Foreword." In *Grundrisse*, 5–66. London: Penguin.

Panitch, Leo. 2009. "Thoroughly modern Marx." *Foreign Policy*, April 15. Accessed July 23, 2013. http://www.foreignpolicy.com/articles/2009/04/15/thoroughly_modern_marx.

Piccone, Paul. 1975. "Reading the *Grundrisse*: Beyond orthodoxy." *Theory and Society* 2 (2): 235–255.

Porat, Marc Uri. 1977. *The information economy: Definition and measurement.* Office of Telecommunications Special Publication 77–12, May. Washington, DC: U.S. Department of Commerce.

Qui, Jack Linchuan. 2009. *Working-class network society.* Cambridge, MA: MIT Press.

Renzetti, Elizabeth. 2011. "Springtime for Marx." *The Globe and Mail*, March 26: F5.

Rodino-Colocino, Michelle. 2007. "High-tech workers of the world, unionize! A case study of WashTech's new model of unionism." In *Knowledge workers in the information society*, edited by Catherine McKercher and Vincent Mosco, 209–227. Lanham, MD: Lexington Books.

Ross, Andrew. 2009. *Nice work if you can get it.* New York: New York University Press.

Saint-Simon, Henri Comte de. 1952. *Selected writings.* Edited and translated by F. M. H. Markham. Oxford: Basil Blackwell.

Saxena, Shobhan. 2008. "Marx in the time of pink slips." *Times of India*, November 2.

Schiller, Dan. 2007. *How to think about information.* Urbana: University of Illinois Press.

———. 2000. *Digital capitalism.* Cambridge, MA: MIT Press.

Scholz, Trebor, ed. 2012. *Digital labor. The internet as playground and factory.* New York: Routledge.

Stevens, Andrew, and Vincent Mosco. 2010. "Prospects for trade unions and labour organisations in India's IT and ITES industries." *Work Organisation Labour and Globalisation* 4 (2): 42–62.

Sunkara, Bhaskar. 2013. "Why the ideas of Karl Marx are more relevant than ever in the 21st Century." *The Guardian.* January 25. Accessed July 23, 2013. http://www.guardian.co.uk/commentisfree/2013/jan/25/karl-marx-relevant-21st-century.

Swift, Jamie. 2003. *Walking the union walk.* Ottawa: Communications, Energy and Paperworkers Union of Canada.

Upadhya, Carol and A. R. Vasavi, eds. 2009. *In an outpost of the global economy: Work and workers in India's high technology industry.* New Delhi: Routledge.

Veblen, Thorstein. 1934. *The theory of the leisure class.* New York: Modern Library.

Wheen, Francis. 2007. "Foreword." In *Karl Marx: Dispatches for the New York Tribune*, edited by James Ledbetter, ix–xiii. London: Penguin.

Contributors

Thomas Allmer studied media and communications at the University of Salzburg (Austria) and the Victoria University of Melbourne (Australia). He is a PhD candidate at the University of Salzburg and research associate in the project "Social Networking Sites in the Surveillance Society", funded by the Austrian Science Fund (FWF). In addition, Thomas is a member of the Unified Theory of Information Research Group and of the editorial board of *tripleC: Communication, Capitalism & Critique. Journal for a Global Sustainable Information Society*. He is author of the book *Towards a Critical Theory of Surveillance in Informational Capitalism* (Peter Lang, 2012). Further information can be found at http://allmer.uti.at. Email: thomas.allmer@uti.at

Mark Andrejevic is an ARC QE II Research Fellow and Deputy Director of the Centre for Critical and Cultural Studies at the University of Queensland. He is the author of *Reality TV: The Work of Being Watched*, *iSpy: Surveillance and Power in the Interactive Era*, and *Infoglut* as well as numerous articles and book chapters on surveillance, popular culture, and digital media. Thanks to the support of the Australian Research Council's *Discovery Projects* funding scheme (project number DP1092606), he is currently studying public attitudes toward the commercial collection and use of personal information online and over mobile phones. Email: m.andrejevic@uq.edu.au

Gunilla Bradley (GB) is Professor Emerita in Informatics at Royal Institute of Technology (KTH)—School of ICT in Stockholm. GB is originally a psychologist and has a broad background in the social and behavioural sciences. Her research concerns the interplay between Information and Communication Technology (ICT), Human Beings, and Society—Social Informatics. Her cross-disciplinary research groups were first hosted by Stockholm University for twenty years. She was then a visiting professor at Stanford University for two years and Professor of Technology and Social Change at the Royal Institute of Technology. From 1997 to 2001 she served as professor in Informatics at Umeå University and Mid Sweden University. In 1997 GB received the prestigious Namur Award from IFIP for her pioneering research to increase the social awareness of the impact of ICT. GB has authored thirteen books and contributed extensively in international scientific journals and the popular science press. Her latest book *Social and Community Informatics—Humans on the Net* (Routledge 2006) is widely used in both ICT-related disciplines and in the social sciences. In 2008 GB was invited to be a guest professor in Salzburg. She initiated and chaired the annual IADIS (International Association for Developing the Information Society, NGO) conference on "ICT, Society and Humans", which took place in 2011 in Rome and in 2012 in Lisbon. In 2010 she was honoured by a "Fest Symposium" at the newly inaugurated Linnaeus University in Sweden and a "Festschrift" (eds. Haftor and Mirijamdotter, 2011). More than forty distinguished researchers from all continents of the world contributed with chapters. For more information visit http://gunillabradley.se. Email: gbradley@kth.se

Peter Dahlgren is Professor Emeritus at the Department of Communication and Media, Lund University, Sweden. His work focuses on media and democracy, using the horizons of late modern social and cultural theory. Most recently he has focused on the Internet and political participation, looking at how the net, combined with other factors, can promote or hinder civic identities and engagement, especially among young people. He is active in European academic networks and has also been a visiting scholar at several universities in Paris, Grenoble, Stirling, and Rhodes, South Africa, as well as at the Annenberg School for Communication at the University of Pennsylvania. Along with journal articles and book chapters, his recent publications include *The Political Web* (Palgrave, forthcoming 2013), *Media and Political Engagement* (Cambridge University Press, 2009), the co-edited volume *Young People, ICTs and Democracy* (Nordicom, 2010), as well as the collection *Young Citizens and New Media* (Routledge, 2007). Email: peter.dahlgren@kom.lu.se

Nick Dyer-Witheford is Associate Professor and Associate Dean of the Faculty of Information and Media Studies at University of Western Ontario. He is author of *Cyber-Marx: Cycles and Circuits of Struggle in High-Technology Capitalism* (University of Illinois, 1999), and co-author, with Stephen Kline and Greig de Peuter, of *Digital Play: The Interaction of Technology, Culture, and Marketing* (McGill-Queen's, 2003), and with Greig de Peuter of *Games of Empire: Global Capitalism and Video Games* (Minneapolis: University of Minnesota Press, 2009). He is currently working on a manuscript provisionally titled *The Global Worker and the Digital Front.* Email: ncdyerwi@uwo.ca

Andrew Feenberg is Canada Research Chair in Philosophy of Technology in the School of Communication, Simon Fraser University, where he directs the Applied Communication and Technology Lab. His books include *Heidegger and Marcuse: The Catastrophe and Redemption of History* which appeared in 2005 with Routledge Press, *Between Reason and Experience: Essays in Technology and Modernity* published by MIT Press in 2010, a co-edited collection entitled *Community in the Digital Age* published by Rowman and Littlefield in 2004, and a co-edited collection entitled *The Essential Marcuse* published by Beacon Press in 2007. A book on Feenberg's philosophy of technology entitled *Democratizing Technology*, appeared in 2006 with the State University of New York Press. His most recent book is the co-edited collection *(Re)Inventing the Internet* (Sense Publishers, 2012). His forthcoming book *Realizing Philosophy: Marx, Lukács and the Frankfurt School* will be published by Verso Press in 2014. Dr. Feenberg is recognized as an early innovator in the field of online education. For more information visit www.sfu.ca/~andrewf. Email: feenberg@sfu.ca

Christian Fuchs is Professor of Social Media Research at the University of Westminster's Communication and Media Research Institute. He is Chair of the European Sociological Association's Research Network 18—Sociology of Communications and Media Research, co-founder of the ICTs and Society Network (http://www.icts-and-society.net), editor of *tripleC: Communication, Capitalism & Critique. Journal for a Global Sustainable Information Society* (http://www.triple-c.at) and vice-chair of the EU COST Action "The Dynamics of Virtual Work". His fields of research are critical theory; Internet, social media and society; media and society; and critical information society studies. Among his publications are the books *Internet and Society* (Routledge 2008), *Foundations of Critical Media and Information Studies* (Routledge 2011), *Occupy-Media! The Occupy Movement and Social Media in Crisis Capitalism* (Zero Books 2013), *Karl Marx and Digital Labour* (Routledge 2014), *Social Media. A Critical Introduction* (Sage 2014). For more information visit http://fuchs.uti.at. Email: c.fuchs@westminster.ac.uk

Wolfgang Hofkirchner was educated as political scientist and psychologist. He acquired the venia docendi in Technology Assessment. His fields of expertise comprise ICTs and Society, science of information, and complex thinking. He did research and teaching at the Austrian Academy of Sciences; the Vienna University of Technology; the Federal University of Bahía, Salvador, Brazil; the Paris-Lodron University of Salzburg, Austria; the University of León, Spain; the Open University of Catalonia, Barcelona, and he was University Professor for Internet and Society 2004 to 2010. He co-founded the ICTs and Society Network, the Unified Theory of Information Research Group, the International Society for Information Studies, the Bertalanffy Center for the Study of Systems Science, the open-access online journal *tripleC: Communication,*

Capitalism & Critique. Journal for a Global Sustainable Information Society, the open access online journal Systems. Connecting Matter, Life, Culture and Technology", and the book series Exploring Unity through Diversity. He has been appointed an academician of the Leibniz-Sozietät der Wissenschaften zu Berlin and of the International Academy for Systems and Cybernetic Sciences. He counts more than 180 publications, among them the monograph Emergent Information—A Unified Theory of Information Framework. For more information visit http://www.hofkirchner.uti.at. Email: wolfgang.hofkirchner@tuwien.ac.at

Verena Kreilinger is a postgraduate student at the University of Salzburg, majoring in communication studies. She currently is a research associate in the project "Social Networking Sites in the Surveillance Society". Verena graduated from the University of Applied Sciences Salzburg with a master's degree in Digital Media Studies in 2007. Prior to joining the Unified Theory of Information Research Group, she worked in advertising and production. Verena is member of the editorial team of *triplec: Communication, Capitalism & Critique. Journal for a Global Sustainable Information Society* and participant in the European Cooperation in Science and Technology Action "Living in Surveillance Societies". Email: verena.kreilinger@gmail.com

Catherine McKercher is Professor of Journalism and Communication at Carleton University in Ottawa, Canada. A former newspaper and wire service journalist in Canada and the United States, she holds a Bachelor of Arts in Political Science from Carleton, a Master of Journalism from Temple University in Philadelphia, Pennsylvania, and a PhD in the Humanities from Concordia University in Montreal, Quebec. She is the author, co-author and co-editor of a number of books and articles on knowledge and communications workers and the labour organizations that represent them. Her most recent books are *Getting the Message: Communications Workers and Global Value Chains*, co-edited with Vincent Mosco and Ursula Huws (London: Merlin, 2010; simultaneously published as vol. 4, no. 1, of the journal *Work Organisation, Labour and Globalisation*) and *The Canadian Reporter: News Writing and Reporting*, third edition, co-authored with Allan Thompson and Carman Cumming (Toronto: Nelson, 2010). Email: catherine_mckercher@carleton.ca

Margareta Melin, PhD, is a Senior Lecturer in Media and Cultural Studies at the School of Arts and Communication (K3) at Malmö University. She has previously worked at Queen Margaret University in Edinburgh, and at Gothenburg University. Her research area lies in the crossroad of feminism, political economy, sociology of journalism and creative industries, and she has conducted (Bourdieuan) field-studies over twenty years on British and Swedish journalism. She has been involved in research projects relating to visual methodology and media didactics, as well as a collaborative project on new media economy. Presently she is involved in two research projects: "The in-between spaces of knowledge", a project on how knowledge is created using both theory and *gestaltung* (praxis) in art-based research and education. This project is based on field studies in Sweden, Germany, and Tanzania. Her second project is "New Media Professionals", a project (together with Dr. Pernilla Severson, K3) about the logic of the new media professional field, and the professionalization processes between new media professionals and new media education. For more information visit http://forskning.mah.se/en/id/k3mame. Email: margareta.melin@mah.se

Vincent Mosco is Professor Emeritus, Queen's University, Canada, where he was Canada Research Chair in Communication and Society and Professor of Sociology. He received his PhD in Sociology from Harvard University where he subsequently was a longtime research associate in the Program on Information Resources Policy. Mosco's most recent publications include *Marx is Back—The Importance of Marxist Theory and Research for Critical Communication Studies Today*, edited with Christian Fuchs; Special issue of *tripleC: Communication, Capitalism & Critique. Journal for a Global Sustainable Information Society* (http://www.triple-c.at) 2012; *Getting the Message: Communications Workers and Global Value Chains* (co-edited with Catherine McKercher and Ursula Huws, Merlin, 2010); *The Political Economy of Communication*, second edition (Sage, 2009); *The Laboring of Communication* (co-authored with Catherine McKercher, Lexington Books, 2008); *Knowledge Workers in the Information Society* (co-edited with Catherine McKercher, Lexington Books, 2007); and *The Digital Sublime* (MIT Press, 2004). *The Digital Sublime* won the 2005 Olson Award for outstanding book in the field of rhetoric and cultural studies. He is currently working on two projects, an edited collection entitled *Critical Studies in Communication and Society*, with Cao Jin and Leslie Reagan Shade to be published by the Shanghai Translation Publishing House, and a book on the political, economic, and cultural significance of cloud computing. For more information visit http://www.queensu.ca/sociology/people/emeritusfaculty/mosco.html. Email: moscov@mac.com

Graham Murdock is Professor of Culture and Economy at Loughborough University and Professor of Sociology at Auckland University. His recent and current research examines the relations between communications, power and change through a distinctive critical political economy. His writings have been translated into nineteen languages. He has held the Leerstoel (Teaching Chair) at the Free University of Brussels, the Bonnier Chair at Stockholm University, served as Professor II at the University of Bergen, and held visiting professorships at a number of other universities including California at San Diego and Mexico City, and taught at a number of universities in China. His recent publications include, as co-editor *Digital Dynamics: Engagements and Discontinuities* (Hampton Press, 2010), *The Handbook of Political Economy of Communication* (Wiley-Blackwell, 2011), and *The Idea of the Public Sphere* (Lexington, 2011). Email: g.murdock@lboro.ac.uk

Tobias Olsson, PhD, is Professor of Media and Communication Studies at Lund University, Sweden. He is head of the Department of Communication and Media. He has extensive research experience within the areas of media and citizenship, Internet culture and mediated participation. Between 2009 and 2013 he coordinated the research project "Organized Producers of Young Net Cultures" (funded by the Swedish Knowledge Foundation) and he has recently initialized a research project on user generated content within newspaper companies (Hamrin foundation, 2012–2017). His most recent publications include the edited volume *Producing the Internet: Critical Perspectives of Social Media* (Nordicom, 2013). Email: tobias.olsson@kom.lu.se

Robert Prey is completing his doctorate in the School of Communication, Simon Fraser University, in Canada. Prior to beginning his PhD, Robert worked with Migrant World Television in Seoul, South Korea, and was a Visiting Researcher in the Department of Sociology at Sungkonghoe University (South Korea). His research interests include the political economy of communication, global communication, social/cultural theory and migration. His peer-reviewed articles have appeared in journals such as *tripleC: Communication, Capitalism & Critique. Journal for a Global Sustainable Information Society, Global Media Journal*, and *The Asia-Pacific Journal*. Email: robp@sfu.ca

Jernej A. Prodnik is a researcher at the Social Communication Research Centre and a teaching assistant at the Media Studies Department, Faculty of Social Sciences, University of Ljubljana, Slovenia. He is a PhD candidate at the University of Ljubljana's Faculty of Social Sciences, where he studied political theory. His principal research interests include political economy of communication, structural transformations of post-Fordist capitalist societies, and the wider social context of technological changes and democratic potentials brought about by new technologies. He has published articles in both national and international journals and books, including the journals *Javnost—The Public* and *tripleC: Communication, Capitalism & Critique. Journal for a Global Sustainable Information Society*. For further information visit http://www.komunikologija-mks.si/predavatelji/jernej-prodnik/. Email: jernej.prodnik@gmail.com

Marisol Sandoval is a Lecturer in Culture, Policy and Management at City University, London. In her dissertation entitled "Monster Media? Critical Perspectives on Corporate Social Responsibility in Media and Communication Industries" Marisol contributed to the development of a critical political economy perspective on CSR. Her doctoral research was funded with a DOC scholarship from the Austrian Academy of Sciences and published as the book *From Corporate to Social Media. Critical Perspectives on Corporate Social Responsibility in Media and Communication Industries* (Routledge 2014). Marisol's main research interests include alternative media, critical political economy of media and communication, the global division of labour in the culture industry, and Corporate Social (Ir)Responsibility. Marisol is managing editor as well as editorial board member of the open access journal *tripleC: Communication, Capitalism & Critique. Journal for a Global Sustainable Information Society.* Email: marisol.sandoval.1@city.ac.uk

Sebastian Sevignani studied media and communication, philosophy, and theology at the University of Salzburg, Austria. After receiving his master's degree, he worked as research associate at University of Sazburgs's Department of Communication Studies and in the project "Social Networking Sites in the Surveillance Society" financed by the Austrian Science Fund (FWF). His doctoral thesis focuses on the political economy of privacy in informational capitalism. Sebastian's further research interests encompass critical social theory, ideology, (digital) labour, social media, and alternative modes of (media) production. He is a member of the Unified Theory of Information Research Group (UTI) and a member of the editorial board of the journal *tripleC: Communication, Capitalism & Critique. Journal for a Global Sustainable Information Society.* Further information can be found at http://sevignani.uti.at. Email: sebastian.sevignani@uti.at